THE SPIRIT OF
NOTRE DAME

THE SPIRIT OF
NOTRE DAME

LEGENDS, TRADITIONS, AND INSPIRATION FROM ONE OF AMERICA'S MOST BELOVED UNIVERSITIES

EDITED, COMPILED, AND WRITTEN BY
Jim Langford and
Jeremy Langford

FOREWORD BY
Regis Philbin

INTRODUCTION BY
Rev. Edward A. Malloy, C.S.C.

AFTERWORDS BY
Rev. John I. Jenkins, C.S.C.
Rev. Theodore M. Hesburgh, C.S.C.

DOUBLEDAY
New York London Toronto Sydney Auckland

PUBLISHED BY DOUBLEDAY
a division of Random House, Inc.

DOUBLEDAY and the portrayal of an anchor with a dolphin are registered
trademarks of Random House, Inc.

Book design by Richard Oriolo

Library of Congress Cataloging-in-Publication Data
Langford, Jim, 1937–
The spirit of Notre Dame : legends, traditions, and inspiration from one of America's most
beloved universities / foreword by Regis Philbin ; introduction by Edward A. Malloy ;
afterwords by John I. Jenkins, Theodore M. Hesburgh ; edited, compiled, and written by
Jim Langford, Jeremy Langford.—1st ed.
p. cm.
Includes bibliographical references.
ISBN 0-385-51081-0 (alk. paper)
1. University of Notre Dame—History. I. Langford, Jeremy. II. Title.
LD4113.L36 2005
378.772'89—dc22   2005045448

September 2005
First Edition

1 3 5 7 9 10 8 6 4 2

THIS BOOK IS DEDICATED TO the priests, brothers, and nuns; the unsung and famous heroes; and the administrators, faculty, staff, and students who built Notre Dame and all those who sustain her spirit. We also offer a special dedication to Walter Langford, who first stepped foot on campus as a student in 1926 and went on to serve Notre Dame as professor, chairman of the Foreign Languages Department, coach of men's fencing and tennis, and director of the ND Peace Corps program in Chile until his retirement in 1973. Until his death in 2001 at the age of ninety-two, Walter remained active by directing a foundation that made grants to educational and humanitarian efforts in the Dominican Republic, traveling, and writing. His dear friend, Father Theodore Hesburgh, celebrated Walter's funeral Mass at Sacred Heart Basilica before family, friends, and former students.

If you want to belong, you have to learn the myth. You have to wrap your heart and mind in it. You have to believe that the merest rocks of the place tell a story. . . . Behind the myths is a cast of hundreds working in loyalty for the Notre Dame of their dreams, in a love affair that lasts a lifetime.

—REV. ROBERT GRIFFIN, C.S.C.

CONTENTS

WHAT IS THE SPIRIT OF NOTRE DAME?

BY REGIS PHILBIN

WHAT IS THE spirit of Notre Dame? That's a tough one. It's so difficult to explain. You really have to be there to walk the campus to feel it, to understand it, to be influenced by it.

There were nights when I first arrived there—and incidentally, it was my first stop ever west of the Hudson River—when I actually thought I felt the spirits of those who had preceded me. Those nights when I walked the campus in my freshman year were mesmerizing. I never got over it. There was something there, something in the air, something that made you feel better, something that made you want to be better.

And through the years it has never changed for me. Every time I go back to Notre Dame, it's there. And I'm not ashamed to tell you I get quite emotional, even teary-eyed. I stand on the main quad and look in every direction and I am filled with awe. I have brought New York City cops back as my guests, show business personalities,

Catholic priests, people of every religion, and they feel it too. They understand. There is a difference.

This book hopefully will define the spirit of Notre Dame better for you. But if you ever have the chance to go to Notre Dame, walk the campus. You'll feel it. You'll get it. And maybe someday you'll even be able to explain it to me.

—REGIS PHILBIN '53[1]

LOVE THEE, NOTRE DAME

*To have a history is to have a name, and
the richer the history the more glorious the name.*

—REV. THOMAS MCAVOY, C.S.C.,
FORMER UNIVERSITY ARCHIVIST AND HISTORIAN

WHEN TRACE MURPHY—Doubleday's religion editor and a Notre Dame graduate from the class of 1991—invited us to do this book, we were honored. "While there are a lot of Notre Dame books out there," he said, "nearly all of them are about football; what we need is a book that captures Notre Dame's spirit on *and off* the field." Because our family has been part of Notre Dame for three generations, we agreed wholeheartedly and began conjuring our own memories, combing through archives, researching the relevant literature, inviting key people to tell their stories, interviewing the famous and not-so-famous, and making decisions about what to include and how to present it.

From the outset, creating this book has been a daunting task. As anyone who loves Notre Dame knows, the soul of the place defies definition. And any attempt to explain or summarize it is sure to fall short of its mark and therefore risk disappointing. Yet the same indescribable spirit calls all who are touched by it to name what they so love. This book is our response to that call. While we make no claim to being comprehensive, we have tried to include here seminal stories that exemplify the spirit of Notre Dame.

Our greatest hope is that this book captures enough glimpses of Notre Dame's spirit to honor the founders; the dedicated women and men who have poured their blood into the bricks as administrators, professors, rectors, coaches, ministers, and staff; the students and alumni/ae who still get chills walking the campus; and all who have allowed their lives to be touched by the school. Together, the voices from the past and present gathered here sing in unison about the mystique that is Notre Dame.

Our own family has had a deep relationship with this mystique as students and faculty for several generations, beginning in 1926 when Walter Langford first stepped foot on campus as a student and went on to serve the school for forty-two years as a professor, chairman of the Modern Languages Department, coach of men's tennis and fencing, and director of the Notre Dame chapter of the Peace Corps. Walter and his second-generation French-American wife, Alice "Dit" Joubert Langford, embodied the Notre Dame spirit by attending to the minds, bodies, and souls of Notre Dame students. They opened their hearts and home to students and members of the Notre Dame family for over four decades. Their four children all attended the schools Father Edward Sorin founded—Walter, Jr., and Jim went to Notre Dame, while Lois and Liz went to St. Mary's. On the day Walter retired, his son Jim—who as a teenager delivered campus mail; gave campus tours; and remembers when his father was given Knute Rockne's former office, which still housed personal papers and first-edition copies of the legendary coach's novel *The Four Winners* in a vault sunk into one of the office walls—began his job as director of the University of Notre Dame Press. He held that post in conjunction with teaching in the Core program until 1999 and continued teaching until 2002, marking an unbroken string of seventy-one years that a Langford was on faculty at Notre Dame. As did many of Walter's grandchildren and members of the extended family, Jim's sons, Jeremy and Josh, not only grew up in the shadow of the Dome but graduated from Notre Dame in 1992 and 1994, respectively. As with so many families who have been affiliated with the school since 1842, Notre Dame is a part of our family's fabric. Quite simply, we love Notre Dame.

NOTRE DAME HAS a mystique grounded in both concrete qualities and transcendental truths that extend far beyond its campus or any one person, sports team, or accomplishment. Many who have never attended a single class as a student or set foot on the campus feel a close connection to the institution itself and to the people who have shaped and been shaped by it.

As Father Edward "Monk" Malloy has said, "For those nurtured on its campus and proud of its tradition and spirit, Notre Dame evokes a sense of family. Whatever one's origins or time of matriculation or employment, there is a bond that links the generations and makes them comfortable with the symbols, sites, and songs of the place."[1] The very soul of Notre Dame—Our Mother—is rooted in the most sacred of families: Mary, Jesus, and Joseph. Two hundred years before Father Edward Frederick Sorin stepped foot on what would become Notre Dame's campus, French missionaries settled the land and invited any and all into the family of God. When Sorin left his close-knit French Catholic family to join the priesthood, he eventually joined the newly formed family of the Congregation of Holy Cross in 1840 because he was impressed with their dedication to education and to helping those in need. Two years later and thousands of miles from his homeland, he created a new home in northern Indiana where his fellow religious, students, and townspeople formed a family that miraculously survived tremendous hardship in the hope that Notre Dame would be a home to many for generations to come.

The familiar sights, symbols, and songs we know today call us to connect with the stories behind them and the families forged on campus that have given them meaning. The log chapel and Old College remind us of Notre Dame's humble beginnings, yes, but more important, they tell a story of brothers banded together under simple shelter in faith and in manual labor as they made bricks out of the marl from the lakes and built the school piece by piece. Mary atop the Golden Dome shines proudly as one of the most recognizable icons in America, but to those who look deeper, she tells the story of how, after the fire of 1879 that destroyed the original domed main building and most of the campus, Father Sorin joined together with his faculty and students to build an even better school than the original to honor her. The Grotto, built in 1896, is a remarkable replica of the Grotto of Massabielle near the French town of Lourdes, but more than that it is a testimony to Father Sorin's profound devotion to Mary and a sacred place where students have paused to pray and connect with the holy family, their own families, and their Notre Dame family for more than one hundred years. From the South Dining Hall to the House that Rockne built; Touchdown Jesus to the Basilica of the Sacred Heart; Sorin Hall to the Stepan Center; the "Victory March to Notre Dame, Our Mother," the sights, symbols, and songs of Notre Dame bespeak a commitment to tradition and excellence, to faith, hope, and love.

Notre Dame is one of the most visible and well-known universities in the nation, if not the world. As Damaine Vonada explains in her official campus guide, "Pope Paul VI said that Notre Dame was his favorite university, and yet it is also a place that captures the intense devotion of thousands of 'subway alumni.' . . . Notre Dame lays claim to what are arguably the nation's most famous college coach (Knute Rockne), most often heard fight song (the Victory March), most recognizable nickname (Fighting Irish), and most legendary players (the Four Horsemen). One survey even discovered that more people wear clothing with the Notre Dame logo than that of any other college or university in the nation."[2] Notre Dame's unique combination of religious values, athletic tradition, academic achievement, and loyalty among students and alumni/ae makes the University a symbol of optimism and possibility.

WHILE NOTRE DAME is known for its storied football program, it is the legends of the classrooms, chapels, dining halls, labs, theaters, social justice centers, and hallowed halls that make the place so special. For every Knute Rockne or Ara Parseghian, there are people like Father Theodore Hesburgh, Sister M. Aloysius, Frank O'Malley; for every George Gipp or Daniel "Rudy" Ruettiger, there are the likes of Regis Philbin, Anne Thompson, or Judge Ann Williams; for every Joe Montana or Raghib "The Rocket" Ismail, there are those like Father Don McNeill, Judge Alan Page, or Al Sondej; for every win or National Championship, there are countless eureka moments in classrooms, prayers sent aloft, or research advances in the arts and sciences.

Quarterback Joe Theismann once said that if you could find a way to bottle the Notre Dame spirit, you could light up the world. While no bottle, or book for that matter, is big enough to do the job, we have organized the stories in this volume around key virtues that both form and flow from the spirit of Notre Dame. Every brick, every statue and piece of stained glass, every professor and student give testimony to virtues like faith, hope, love, community, humor, mind, body, and spirit. Our hope is that by sharing legends, traditions, and inspirational stories around these basic virtues, this book captures enough of the Notre Dame spirit to ignite a flame in the hearts of all who read it.

—JIM LANGFORD '59 AND JEREMY LANGFORD '92,
NOVEMBER 26, 2004, THE 162ND ANNIVERSARY OF
THE FOUNDING OF NOTRE DAME

THE SPIRIT OF
NOTRE DAME

THE SPIRIT OF NOTRE DAME

BY REV. EDWARD A. MALLOY, C.S.C.

I HAVE SPENT a good part of my adult ministerial and professional life trying to convey and to define the spirit of Notre Dame. The closest I have come to an adequate answer is to suggest that it is best experienced rather than talked about, that it is constituted by no one aspect of the institution in isolation, but by a whole range of values, traditions, and practices seen in concert. The University itself is a physical campus located in northern Indiana, a complex modern university, a center of residential life, a focal point of prayer and devotion, a hub of extracurricular activities (especially athletics and the arts), and a site of pilgrimage. Most especially, it is a place of pilgrimage.

During the course of a given year, the University welcomes back to the campus thousands of its graduates and friends; they come for alumni reunions, for home football weekends, for retreats, and as part of vacation journeys. And while they are with us, they savor the beauty and the peacefulness of the natural environment, they

respond to the stimulation of concerts and lectures, and they cultivate the sense of personal renewal that is fostered by being in this
sacred space. In this regard, Sacred Heart Basilica and Sacred Heart
Parish, and the adjacent Grotto, all serve as Catholic Christian gathering points for the Eucharist, for public and private prayer, and for
the celebration of the sacraments, from weddings and funerals to
ordinations and baptisms. Here and in the hall chapels (and elsewhere for large-scale liturgical moments), Notre Dame gets in touch
with its spiritual sense of community.

In the same way that the Gospel pushes us to test the quality of
our faith commitments by the integrity of our personal and communal lives and by the service that we render to others, especially those
with the greatest manifest needs, so the spirit of Notre Dame plays
itself out in our classrooms and other learning environments, in the
vitality and inclusiveness of our residential communities, and in the
thoughtful and properly motivated service that we direct to the poor
and homeless, to young children and senior citizens, to neighborhood organizations and those with specialized needs.

The faculty are charged with special responsibility for the intellectual and moral growth of the students entrusted to their care.
Above all, they model the excitement and privilege that is pursuit of
the truth in all of its disciplinary subdivisions, but always with a keen
eye for connections among the partial truths discerned in a given discipline and with fitting openness of mind, both to the intellectual
grounding in perennial wisdom and to the excitement of the new and
the previously undiscovered. The professors among us must treat
their students and colleagues with respect even in the midst of dis-
agreement and controversy. Most of all, they must pass on the habits
of mind and heart that encourage their students to become lifelong
learners.

As an intellectual community (where the Church does its thinking), Notre Dame must take on the great issues of the day in both
Church and society—through the excellence of the research and

scholarship that take place here, we must describe accurately, engage in value-based analysis, weigh alternative proposals for action, and empower those who can be agents of amelioration and commitment. In our centers and institutions, in the conferences and symposiums that we sponsor, and in the focused conversation that spontaneously calls us to question and to probe, we assure ourselves a distinctive role in higher education and in the broader society around us.

One of the results of active engagement with the world is the need to grapple with the full mystery of the human condition—to account for both sins and grace. This requires a kind of self-awareness by each member of our university community (about his or her potential for good or evil) and a regular assessment of the structures of the common life to determine whether they foster or deter our common life and our mutual obligation to one another. Thus, Notre Dame is replete with representative bodies of students, faculty, and administrators, as well as organizations with responsibility for either part of the outreach to our graduates and friends (like the Alumni Association), or some section of our academic mission (like the various advisory councils), or for the University as a whole (the Board of Trustees and the Board of Fellows). The Indiana Province of the Congregation of Holy Cross has long-standing and frequently affirmed commitments to the University that flow from its status as founding religious community and from its involvement in every dimension of the present realities of the school.

But the realities of sin and grace are not simply pertinent to the internal life of the institution; they also help us to ponder how to keep hope alive in a world too often inclined to despair and cynicism. It is one of the great temptations of the modern academy to stand on the sidelines of history satisfied with occasional ironic utterances or glib put-downs directed at the power brokers of the political, economic, and social spheres. A much better alternative is to try to produce thoughtful leaders, informed prophetic voices, and people of integrity and good sense. Not everyone can develop a cure for the common cold or design an architectural wonder or write the next great novel. Many of our graduates will spend the majority of their time in ordinary tasks of the workplace and the household and in service rendered in their local churches and not-for-profit organizations. They will vote in an informed fashion and respond to the life-cycle needs of their own children and their own parents.

In the same way that the Church inspires us to lives of holiness and generosity by recounting the stories of the holy men and women who have gone before us in the community of faith, the Notre Dame family has its own heroes and heroines, some well known outside the campus, others simply renowned for their persistent deeds of love. Some of the legendary figures are rectors or other hall staff who accompanied the students entrusted to their care through the grief of death in the family or the first academic failure or the news of a lost relationship. Others might be faculty who cultivated in a student some special gift or shared a personal excitement about the life of learning. Still others might have preached a pivotal homily or organized the response to a dramatic need. Or, from the testimony of many graduates, it could be a staff member in the dining hall or in one of the offices or in the Health Center who manifests such a spirit of acceptance of others despite the problems of the day that everyone around him has their spirits uplifted and their hearts made right.

One of the reasons that Notre Dame is filled with such stories is that most of us are not smart enough at the time to speak words of gratitude and appreciation. However, the spirit of Notre Dame is built upon countless gestures of sincere thankfulness. It includes letters from parents to administrators about their sadness that the four (expensive) years are over, about how much they will miss the visits to the campus and the meeting of their own offspring's roommates and friends and parents. But most of all, it is about the passage of time and how Notre Dame's version of *in loco parentis* has worked and how proud they are to have shared in this journey into maturity. It also includes the gift-giving of the Christmas season and the recognition of birthdays and anniversaries—maybe most of all, it is the presence of the prized other in moments least expected.

Life under the Dome usually has the seriousness of purpose that it deserves. Yet any good community can laugh at its foibles and appreciate the occasional creative antic. Students, in particular, are always ready to maximize the fun that the common life allows for. It can be anything from the phantom phone call, to the dunk in the lake, to the generous use of shaving cream or hot sauce. Students pull pranks on one another, their rectors, and on their teachers (if they are really brave). Still, not all the laughs are at someone's expense. Sometimes just youthful exuberance is enough to carry the day. And then there are all the organized (sometimes loosely) shows, satires, and entertainments that offer commentary on campus life, on youth culture or the media, and on the political scene. Some among us have an innate gift for imitation, and there is always plenty of material for the astute observer.

From the grist of all these elements is forged the intense loyalty to Notre Dame that is so characteristic of its graduates and friends. They proudly wear the colors, sing the songs, and recognize one another's presence near and far. In my own travels, I have met Notre Dame people in every corner of the globe. They are our best emissaries in recruiting new students and in representing the University in their home communities. The loyalty of our supporters is not mindless or whimsical. They are proud to be related to Notre Dame for what it represents. They cherish the friends that they made, the formative experiences that they enjoyed, and the values that they tested out. Indeed, a tear comes to the eyes when the Alma Mater is sung (often swaying arm-in-arm). When the athletic teams compete, they root with great intensity. When the various choral groups or the bands travel, they seem always to be there as though they had nothing else to do.

One of the most startling dimensions of the common life at Notre Dame from the days of yore is how the presence of women, of students, and of faculty from underrepresented groups and of international students and faculty have transformed our notions of ourselves and our visibility and presence to the multiple worlds within which we interact. As we have come close to resembling the demographics of the United States, a richer and more intriguing set of possibilities opens up for all who join our community. The social interactions are more realistic and the questions that get raised in the classroom are more invasive. Notre Dame can no longer be defined by gender, color, or religious or ethnic heritage. As creatures of a loving Creator, we are more aware of our commonalities in the midst of the exploration of our differences. And the same is true of those who join us from the other continents of the earth. They can now share their customs, their music, and their cuisine.

Let me conclude these brief reflections about the spirit of Notre Dame by returning to the foundational image that we have become a place of pilgrimage. Like the Holy Land, and Rome, Canterbury, and Santiago de Compostela, we welcome visitors from afar. They come to pray with us, they come to experience the serenity of the two lakes, the Grotto, and the well-trod pathways that link us together. They come for enlightenment and wisdom from a storehouse of reflection and debate. They come to reminisce about the past or ponder the future. They come to celebrate life commitments. They come to seek forgiveness for paths wrongly taken or dreams only partially realized.

But for those of us who carry the torch in the present tour, we are the spirit of Notre Dame. We are the privileged few who are charged with a grand and glorious responsibility. As we continue on our way, may we continue to invoke the patronage of Notre Dame, Our Mother, and of her Son, Jesus the Lord.

—REV. EDWARD A. MALLOY, C.S.C., EARNED THREE DEGREES FROM NOTRE DAME: A BACHELOR OF ARTS DEGREE IN ENGLISH IN 1963 AND TWO MASTER'S DEGREES, THE FIRST IN ENGLISH IN 1967 AND THE SECOND IN THEOLOGY IN 1969. HE SERVED AS PRESIDENT OF THE UNIVERSITY FROM 1986 UNTIL 2005.[1]

FAITH OF OUR FOUNDER:
REV. EDWARD FREDERICK
SORIN, C.S.C.

When this school, Our Lady's school, grows a bit more, I shall
raise her aloft so that, without asking, all men shall know why we
have succeeded here. To that lovely Lady, raised high on a dome, a
Golden Dome, [all] may look and find the answer.

—REV. EDWARD FREDERICK SORIN, C.S.C.

WHEN FATHER EDWARD Frederick Sorin and seven fellow brothers reached the land that would become Notre Dame's campus, they
literally jumped for joy. On that freezing, snowy day on November
26, 1842, Sorin knew he had found the sacred spot he could finally
call home, where he would fulfill his destiny. A large man with dark
skin and brooding eyes, Sorin was an imposing figure with an equally
imposing faith and sense of divine mission. At just twenty-eight, he
was a new priest in a fledgling religious order who embraced the
New World as his path to salvation. By all accounts he was ahead of
his years: bold, confident, shrewd, practical, and on fire with faith in
God and in his fellow human beings. Father Edward Sorin was a man
of destiny whose vision for the University of Notre Dame became a
reality during his lifetime and has grown in size and shape through
extraordinary leadership and the loyal participation of those who
have let the spirit of the place light the spirit in them.

FROM PAPER VESTMENTS TO PARISH PRIEST
AND BEYOND

EDWARD SORIN WAS born in the wake of the French Revolution on February 6, 1814, in La Roche, France. The seventh of nine children of Julien Sorin and Marie-Anne Louise Gresland, he could easily have been lost in the hustle and bustle of his home life and turned off by faith in a world that was highly secularized. Instead, he stood out and embraced the faith of his family, a faith that led his parents to offer their nine-acre farm as a station on the underground network for priests during the French Revolution. With his mother's encouragement, by age twelve Sorin was already studying Latin and, as many children in pious French Catholic families did, role-playing the part of a priest by "saying Mass."

To the delight of his devout parents, Edward traded his homemade paper vestments for real ones by entering the Little Seminary at Precinge and working his way through the Major Seminary in Le Mans. Throughout his studies he often dreamed of missionary work in China, but in 1836 he heard a moving talk by a fellow Frenchman, Bishop Simon Bruté de Rémur, who had returned to Brittany from the United States to plead for vocations to his Diocese of Vincennes, which encompassed Indiana and Illinois. The seed of going to the New World as a missionary had been planted, but it almost did not take root. Following his ordination on May 27, 1838, the young Father Sorin was assigned as an assistant pastor in the small village of Parcé, where his creative energies were stifled. After fifteen months in Parcé, however, Sorin decided to join a small but very impressive band of priests and brothers (the Brothers of St. Joseph founded by Canon Jacques François Dujarié) brought together by Father Basil Antoine Moreau, a professor he knew from Le Mans. On August 15, 1840, Father Sorin took the vows of poverty, chastity, and obedience with what came to be known as the Congregation of

Holy Cross, named for the suburb of Le Mans, Sainte-Croix, where Moreau was given a piece of property referred to as Notre-Dame from an old priest friend. As a man of vision and impatience, the vow of obedience would prove to be one of the hardest for Sorin to follow.

A year before Sorin became a Holy Cross priest, Moreau had received another appeal from Bruté in Vincennes for brothers who could teach and work and a priest who could direct them. When Bruté died his successor, Célestin Guynemer de la Hailandière, continued the appeal. Two years later, Moreau decided to make a sacrifice and send six brothers to the United States. He chose Father Edward Sorin, then just twenty-eight years old, to go with them as their religious superior and advisor. Filled with enthusiasm and hope, Sorin wrote to Bishop de la Hailandière, "The road to America seems clearly to me the road to heaven. . . . I expect all kinds of suffering, and providing the Good Master continues to protect me, it is all I wish for I have need of suffering. . . . How long these six months will be! My body will be in France, but my heart and mind will be with you, Monseigneur! I can only live for my dear American brethren. There is my country, the center of all my affections, the object of all my pious thoughts."[1]

As if Sorin were able to see into his future, two things proved to be very true for him: He would embrace the American way of life, and he would suffer.

GOD, THE NEW WORLD, AND NOTRE DAME DU LAC

ON AUGUST 8, 1841, Sorin and the brothers, none of whom spoke English, left port from Le Havre aboard an overcrowded passenger ship named the *Iowa*. When they reached New York harbor thirty-five days later, Father Sorin knelt down and kissed the ground. From the moment he rose to his feet until he died at Notre Dame on October 31, 1893, Sorin never stopped moving in service of God, country, and Notre Dame. Upon arriving in New York, he and the brothers made the difficult trek to Indiana by steamboats, horse-drawn canal boats, stagecoaches, and foot. At the end of the twenty-seven-day excursion—which included a side trip to Niagara Falls, fighting off would-be robbers, and bad weather—the men reached Vincennes one morning in time for Mass and breakfast with Bishop Hailandière.

Once they settled in, the bishop offered Sorin and the brothers one hundred acres in St. Francisville, ten miles to the west in Illinois, to teach and work with people in the area. Immediately, Sorin exerted his strong will and declined the assignment. Hailandière then offered the men the assignment of establishing a school and novitiate in the well-established mission station called St. Peter's, which was twenty-seven miles to the east in Indiana and consisted of 160 acres. After praying over it, Sorin and the brothers accepted and went to work. When one of the brothers successfully raised money for their efforts, Sorin replaced the existing log school with a brick building. Not content to stop there, he then decided to build a college. Without consulting Moreau or Hailandière, Sorin and his brothers gathered building materials, borrowed money from the Bank of Vincennes, and began building. When Hailandière learned of the plans, he ordered Sorin to stop because the diocese already had a small college, St. Gabriel's, only thirty miles away. But after further consideration, Hailandière decided instead to offer Sorin a plot of land he owned in northern Indiana for Sorin's plan. Sorin was so excited by the offer that he and his brothers ignored the bishop's caution to wait until spring and made the 250-mile journey through the November ice and snow. Several days after their arrival, Father Sorin wrote the following letter to Father Moreau:

December 5, 1842
Beloved Father,
When we least dreamed of it, we were offered an excellent piece of property, about 640 acres in extent. This land is located in the county of St. Joseph on the banks of the St.

Joseph River, not far from the city of St. Joseph (Michigan). It is a delightfully quiet place, about twenty minutes from South Bend. This attractive spot has taken from the lake which surrounds it the beautiful name of Notre Dame du Lac. . . . It is from here that I write you now.

Everything was frozen over. Yet it all seemed so beautiful. The lake, especially, with its broad carpet of dazzling white snow, quite naturally reminded us of the spotless purity of our August Lady whose name it bears, and also of the purity of soul that should mark the new inhabitants of this chosen spot. . . . We were in a hurry to enjoy all the scenery along the lakeshore of which we had heard so much. Though it was quite cold, we went to the very end of the lake, and like children, came back fascinated with the marvelous beauties of our new home. . . . Once more, we felt that Providence had been good to us and we blessed God from the depths of our soul.

Will you permit me, dear Father, to share with you a preoccupation which gives me no rest? Briefly, it is this: Notre Dame du Lac was given to us by the bishop only on condition that we establish here a college at the earliest opportunity. As there is no other school within more than a hundred miles, this college cannot fail to succeed. . . . Before long, it will develop on a large scale. . . . It will be one of the most powerful means for good in this country.

Finally, dear Father, you cannot help see that this new branch of your family is destined to grow under the protection of Our Lady of the Lake and of St. Joseph. At least, this is my deep conviction. Time will tell if I am wrong.

—E. Sorin[2]

But "the spot was already a holy place," writes university historian Arthur Hope, C.S.C., in his 1948 book *Notre Dame: One Hun-*

dred Years. The first white explorers to set foot on this land were likely the Jesuit Jacques Marquette, in 1675, and Robert Sieur de La Salle in 1679. In 1686, the French Jesuit Claude Allouez established a couple of missionary stations near the river his fellow missionaries had christened the Saint Joseph. One of these he named Ste.-Marie-des-lacs (Saint Mary of the Lakes), because it stood on a hill overlooking a pair of small lakes. One hundred and fifty years later, Father Stephen Badin, the first priest ordained in the United States, set up a mission in this area and built a log cabin chapel, which later served as the first home of Sorin and his brothers. Badin originally bought the land from the U.S. government and two private individuals and eventually gave it to the Bishop of Vincennes, who in turn gave it to the spirited Sorin. Father Sorin, not yet able to see the second lake on the property under the snow and ice, named his school l'Université de Notre Dame du Lac, Our Lady of the Lake. While the roots of Notre Dame are French, explains historian Robert Burns, in the first group traveling with Sorin from Vincennes, only two were among his original companions from Le Mans, and four of the five others who had joined the society in Vincennes were recent immigrants from Ireland, a land whose inhabitants have played a major role in the life of the school from the start.

THE SPIRIT OF NOTRE DAME IS BORN

FROM ITS BEGINNING and many times throughout its early life, the University of Notre Dame would have closed down had it not been for Father Sorin and the dedicated women and men who believed in his vision and mission. In the pre–Civil War era, some 700 colleges were established, mainly under religious auspices, and most of them failed. But not Notre Dame. Without the luxuries of many Eastern schools, which enjoyed dense populations, a more cultured applicant pool, and a higher income base, Sorin began modestly while dreaming big. The first of the thirty-four buildings he constructed was a log cabin much like Badin's. Next, in lieu of a main building, he built the "Old College" with bricks donated by Benjamin Coquillard, the brother of Alexis Coquillard, founder of South Bend, Indiana. Amazingly, this squat building housed classrooms, a student dormitory, a dining hall, a dormitory for the brothers serving on the faculty, a clothes room, and a kitchen. The building, still in use today, is the only remaining building of the first decade. As early as 1843, Sorin realized that the lakes on campus were rich in marl deposits that yielded raw materials for bricks. By 1844, kilns were producing marl bricks as well as lime plaster and mortar. Until the 1880s, the University kilns created the distinctive "Notre Dame brick" that characterized the look of the buildings and, through commercial sales, helped pay the bills to keep the University running. Since then, most of the University has used Belden brick to maintain continuity with the look and feel of the early buildings.

Sorin's enthusiasm was so infectious that only a year after he began building his school, local resident and state senator John B. Defrees, a Methodist, paid Sorin a visit and offered to procure from the legislature a charter establishing Notre Dame as a university with the legal right to exist and grant degrees. After quickly mobilizing his faculty to establish the necessary curriculum, on January 15, 1844, Father Sorin's school became a university by legislative act. In addition to establishing a modest collegiate program, Sorin opened a grade school, a prep school, and a vocational institute known as the Manual Labor Training School, the first Catholic trade school in the United States. Other Notre Dame firsts soon followed: *Scholastic* magazine began publication in 1867, what has become one of the most active alumni/ae associations in the country was founded in 1868, the law school opened in 1869, the first Catholic engineering program in America opened in 1873, and in 1889 Notre Dame became the first American college to have electric lights and Sorin Hall the first Catholic dormitory to have private rooms.

"Then and for decades thereafter," writes Kerry Temple, "Notre Dame was a frontier school, with wood-burning stoves, outhouses, and mandatory weekly baths in the lake. Staffed almost entirely by the Holy Cross religious—priests, brothers, and sisters—the school soon had bakers, carpenters, a locksmith, and a shoemaker. Benches and desks were homemade; buildings were constructed with bricks made from the marl of Saint Mary's Lake. Fish and ice were harvested from the lakes, and a farm provided meat and milk, corn, wheat, eggs, and vegetables for a growing student population of grade-schoolers, high-schoolers, and collegians."[3] Always hard up for money, Notre Dame worked diligently not to turn students away—allowing some to pay their way through manual labor, livestock, or long-term loans. In the meantime, Father Sorin found resources wherever he could—turning over his own inheritance while encouraging other priests to do the same, convincing the Brothers to work for next to nothing, soliciting funds from the Societies for the Propagation of the Faith in Lyon and Paris, begging throughout the East and Northeast and other areas around the country where Catholics congregated, and signing prom-issory notes on his own authority and then mailing the bills back to France for his order to pay. He even sent a band of Brothers out west during the gold rush of 1849–50. Not only did the Brothers return empty-handed, one of their own died on the trip.

Despite his own issues with authority and reputation as a maverick, Father Sorin relied on the respect of his students, faculty, and staff for his authority and the rules and regulations he had estab-lished. From the "minims" in the grade school to the oldest colle-giate, Sorin ran a tight ship with the belief that a regimented day filled with classes and activities would keep students, and faculty, out of trouble. "When he was seen about the campus, his mighty frame moving with measured countenance, his gigantic head and flashing black eyes on the alert for some irregularity," writes Hope, "both students and faculty straightened up." Sorin never used corpo-ral punishment and only in extreme cases gave a student his "trunk" and sent him home; he believed strongly that part of his duty was to work with even the worst of students to help build moral character.

At the same time, Sorin was beloved as one who knew how to enjoy life and, even when there was no money, throw a party. His celebrations for commencement, Founder's Day, Washington's Birthday, the Fourth of July, and many other holidays showed his love for his adopted country while allowing him to enjoy the fruit of his labor with the Notre Dame community. His love of fine food and wine, art, and architecture brought attention to his school and instilled a sense of pride in those fortunate enough to attend it. In 1845, the school barely alive, he swapped some property in Detroit for a museum collection of "beasts, birds, fishes, reptiles, and antiquities from the various parts of the world," explains Hope. Four years later, he opted not to buy insurance for his new Church in lieu of using what little budget he had to throw a party for the visiting Bishop who consecrated it. He built grandiose buildings—most notably Washington Hall, Sacred Heart Church, and the Main Building—and brought back from his travels enormous bells and fancy altars. All the while, he let the students and staff know how much he loved them—from playing marbles and sharing baskets of peaches with the minims (his "little princes" for whom he also wrote plays), to hosting dinner parties, singing songs, and playing the clarinet for all who would join.

"TO THAT LOVELY LADY, RAISED HIGH ON A DOME,
A GOLDEN DOME, [ALL] MAY LOOK AND
FIND THE ANSWER"

IN 1855, SORIN took drastic measures to control an outbreak of cholera and malaria that had killed twenty-three priests, brothers, sisters, and students between 1847 and 1855. Convinced that a marsh created by a dam on an adjoining plot of land owned by a Mr. Rush was responsible for the outbreak, Sorin badgered Rush to sell the land so that he could drain the marsh, which would also allow him access to more marl for brick production. When Mr. Rush finally agreed to sell, he skipped town before the deal was done. Not a man to wait around, Sorin sent six men to destroy Rush's dam anyway. Once the marsh was drained, the cholera vanished. Rush eventually returned, found his dam destroyed, and closed the sale for $8,000 as originally agreed, giving the University an additional 185 acres.

But Sorin's greatest show of love for the University and witness of faith came in 1879, when he was called back from Montreal (where he was on his way to Europe for the thirty-sixth of fifty-two transatlantic trips he made since settling in America) because his university had burned to the ground except for the church and a few buildings. Arthur Hope recounts the devastating affair:

> The morning of April 23, 1879, was refreshing. There was sun enough to be pleasantly warm. And from the lake to the west, a slight breeze was blowing. And it was Wednesday, a free day for the students. . . . On this lazy April day, so dangerously close to spring fever epidemic, the air was unexpectedly rent with the sudden, shrill cry that rose from voices of the Minims—they were the first to see it—"Fire, fire! The college is on fire!" It was eleven o'clock.
>
> The flames were low on the college roof, close to the little railing that ran around the dome. Workmen had been on the roof as late as ten o'clock making some repairs. At that hour they had descended, locking the door behind them. If, when the fire was first detected, water in any quantity could have been brought to the roof, it would have been easily extinguished. But the building was six stories high; the buckets placed for just such an emergency were empty; and in the confusion that ensued precious time was lost. In ten or fifteen minutes the pitch roof began to blaze, sending forth clouds of dense smoke.

Water, by steam pressure, was finally forced into the great tanks on the roof. Everyone who could help rushed to form the lines of a bucket-brigade, but soon the water in the tanks was exhausted. Some heroic souls, panting and shouting, stayed on the roof, hoping against hope that the fire might be crushed out. But when the supports of the dome burned away, and the statue went crashing below in a billow of sparks and flame, even the most courageous thought only of saving whatever effects might be carried out of the burning building.

. . . In the midst of disaster, a good-natured sense of humor expressed itself when the students, looking about at their unaccustomed plight, began singing, "The old home ain't what it used to be!" Of course, it was a heavy night for Father Corby. His most anxious thought was: "How will this affect Father Sorin?" And it was a matter of no small concern. Father Sorin was no longer a young man. It was feared that news of Notre Dame's disaster would be too great a shock for him. They determined, therefore, to notify the superior at St. Laurent College, Montreal, asking him to keep the news from Father General until a messenger could arrive from Notre Dame. That night, at nine o'clock, trusty Jimmy Edwards took the train to Montreal to break the sad news to Father Sorin personally.

The loss was estimated at $200,000. Only $45,000 was forthcoming in insurance. It was a terrible blow, for in three hours was wiped out the result of thirty-five years of hard, grueling sacrifice. It took something more than courage to face the future. Father Corby had promised the students a new Notre Dame by September. But as the ashes began to cool, he himself wondered if he had not been too optimistic. How would Father Sorin feel about it?

A few days later, April 27th, he found out. The sixty-five-year-old man walked around the ruins, and those who followed him were confounded by his attitude. Instead of bending, he stiffened. There was on his face a look of grim determination. He signaled all of them to go into the church with him.

One of Sorin's faculty members, Professor Timothy Howard, describes the moment as Father Sorin stood in Sacred Heart:

> I was then present when Father Sorin, after looking over the destruction of his life-work, stood at the altar steps of the only building left and spoke to the community what I have always felt to be the most sublime words I ever listened to. There was absolute faith, confidence, resolution in his very look and pose. "If it were ALL gone, I should not give up!" were his words in closing. The effect was electric. It was the crowning moment of his life. A sad company had gone into the church that day. They were all simple Christian heroes as they came out. There was never more a shadow of a doubt as to the future of Notre Dame.[4]

Sorin went even further: "The fire was my fault. I came here as a young man and founded a university which I named after the Mother of God. Now she had to burn it to the ground to show me that I dreamed too small a dream. Tomorrow we will begin again and build it bigger, and when it is built, we will put a gold dome on top with a golden statue of the Mother of God so that everyone who comes this way will know to whom we owe whatever great future this place has."[5] Incredibly, in less than four months some 300 laborers working from dawn till dark built the new Administration Building in time for the fall semester. At the age of sixty-five, Father Sorin had rebuilt nearly from scratch the university he had founded thirty-five years earlier.

In the course of those thirty-five years and until his death, Father Sorin not only built and rebuilt Notre Dame as part of his vision for the work of the Congregation of Holy Cross, but he also founded or administered nine other institutions, including Saint Mary's College near South Bend; Saint Edward's University in Austin, Texas; and other colleges and universities in Chicago, Cincinnati, and Wisconsin. He also founded untold numbers of missions, schools, orphanages, parishes, academies, farms, and manual labor schools in America and abroad.[6]

In 1865, his community compelled Sorin to pass the presidential reins. He chose a native of Galway and Chicago's South Side, Father Patrick Dillon, as his successor and took on the role of Superior General of the Congregation of Holy Cross. With an increasingly Irish and German immigrant student body, Dillon was a good choice for the job of president.

Though he was no scholar himself and could barely call his school a university until the end of his life, Father Edward Sorin was greatly revered as a man of faith and vision. In August 1888, the leadership of the American Church honored him on the golden jubilee of his priesthood. Archbishops, bishops, heads of religious orders, and priests and nuns from all over the world gathered on Notre Dame's campus to honor him. Throughout that summer, the Notre Dame community honored their leader by naming a hall after him, completing Sacred Heart Church after seventeen years of construction, and completing the Administration Building with the Golden Dome.

As he lay dying in the house behind Sacred Heart Church on a cold day in mid-October 1893, Father Edward Sorin heard a commotion on the walk outside his door. "What is it?" he asked the sisters tending to him. After peeking out the window, they told him that the student body and the faculty were assembled outside to wish him a happy feast day, the Feast of St. Edward. With the little energy he had left, he put on his cassock and his cord, his crucifix, and his biretta and opened the front door. After a weak wave to his greeters, he said in a voice only those at his side could hear, "I bless you in her name!" and pointed to the Lady on the Dome.[7] Nearly fifty years earlier, Sorin had proclaimed, "When this school, Our Lady's school, grows a bit more, I shall raise her aloft so that, without asking, all men shall know why we have succeeded here. To that lovely Lady, raised high on a dome, a Golden Dome, [all] may look and find the answer."

—JEREMY LANGFORD

THE VIRTUES OF
NOTRE DAME

THE SPIRIT OF Notre Dame is rooted in virtue, a basic commit-ment to excellence and moral goodness. As a Catholic institution, the University's understanding of virtue is shaped by faith, revelation, and tradition. Each of these sources affirms the sacredness of every life and calls people to come together for the common good of all.

Notre Dame has always worked hard to be a vehicle of virtue in its own right. For this reason, the school's legends, traditions, and inspiring stories collected and retold here naturally gather around three groupings of virtues: faith, hope, and love; community and humor; and mind, body, and spirit. These virtues are taught in the classrooms, prayed over in dorm chapels, and experienced in the very grounds of Notre Dame. They are what attract students and families in the first place, and what travel from campus into the world with graduates and all who love the place. They are the virtues of Notre Dame.

FAITH

Reverence for God is the main reason for Notre Dame's existence.

—EDWARD FISCHER '37, LONGTIME PROFESSOR,
JOURNALIST, AND FILMMAKER

THE UNIVERSITY OF Notre Dame was founded on faith. Faith in God compelled Father Sorin and his small band of Holy Cross brothers to journey to America; faith in one another led these men and others from their order not only to survive the rigors of life in the mid–nineteenth century but also to be creative and to take risks; and faith in the power of education led them to stake their claim on what was already holy ground and to build—and rebuild, with the help of the women religious working alongside them—Notre Dame in the improbable location of northern Indiana.

From the log cabin chapel to Sacred Heart Church, from dorm services to the annual commencement Mass, the heartbeat of Notre Dame is faith. Faith permeates the place. You can feel it when you tour the campus or look up and see Mary peering down from the Golden Dome. You can hear it as professors of theology explore the mystery of God with their classes or as students share their deepest hungers on walks around the lakes. You can see it in the stories stained into glass, in the art and architecture, and in the flickering flames of individual intentions that merge into one bright blaze in the cave of candles that is the Grotto. Notre Dame is a place where faith in God, self, and neighbor abounds.

Throughout its many years on campus, Notre Dame's Log Chapel has been the site of countless University-related religious services: Weddings, anniversaries, baptisms, and prayer services have been held within its four walls. The present Log Chapel is a historical replica of the original log cabin chapel Father Stephen Badin built in 1831 when he established his mission at Lake St. Mary and named it Ste.-Marie-des-Lacs. Father Sorin and his seven Brothers resided in Badin's Log Chapel at the mission site when they arrived in 1842 while they were establishing the University of Notre Dame. Father Badin's chapel fell into disuse in 1848. Known as the "Indian Chapel," it was destroyed by fire in 1856.

The present replica of Badin's Log Chapel was constructed in 1906. Hand-hewn with a broadaxe by William Arnett, an ex-slave from Kentucky, it is an authentic reconstruction. A strong supporter of the Log Chapel as a place that honors the past, Father Hesburgh made it a point before he retired to move the bodies of three priests who were instrumental in the early life of Notre Dame—Fathers Louis DeSeille, Benjamin Petit, and François Cointet—from the basement crypt of the Basilica to the Log Chapel.

—DOROTHY V. CORSON[1]

THE STATUE IN front of Corby Hall, a residence for priests on campus, has been nicknamed "Fair Catch Corby." It is a man, a priest, with one arm raised and poised to give a blessing. His name was William J. Corby, C.S.C., and his story is one of heroism and gentleness.

Chaplain of the famed Irish Brigade in the Union Army, Corby put priestly care ahead of personal safety. A statue of him also stands at Gettysburg, a memorial of his conviction and courage. When the Brigade was summoned to lead the charge on the morning of July 2, 1863, Corby galloped to the front of the line, told his men to make an act of contrition, gave them absolution, and then rode with General Meagher into the battle. Within half an hour, 506 of the men he had absolved lay on the ground, either dead or wounded. He recalled:

"I shall never forget how wicked the whiz of the enemy's bullets seemed as we advanced into that battle. As soon as my men began to fall, I dismounted and began to hear their confessions on the spot. . . . Every instant bullets whizzed past my head."

The following afternoon, with the Irish Brigade posted on Cemetery Ridge, the Confederates attacked, and it became clear that the Brigade had to enter the battle. Corby told the officer in charge: "My men have not had a chance to get to confession. I must give them one last bit of spiritual comfort. Let me stand up on this rock, where they all may see me. Let me speak to them."[2] He urged the men to have a contrite heart, then he raised his hand in a blessing of absolution. As he finished, they were ordered into battle, many never to return.

This same Father Corby was president of Notre Dame when the great fire destroyed much of the campus in 1879. His thoughts were not about himself. His anguish came from how he would tell an aging Father Sorin, then in Montreal, the catastrophic news. How do you tell someone that his vision, his life's work, has crumbled to the ground? Corby would probably have been more willing to face the perils of battle again than to do that.

But he did what duty obliged him to do. And when Sorin returned and gave his inspired talk to the small community, saying that they would have to build it bigger this time, Corby saw the same kind of courage he had seen . . . and exhibited at Gettysburg. No absolution was needed this time!

—JIM AND JEREMY LANGFORD

THE REVEREND CHARLES L. O'Donnell, C.S.C., president of the University of Notre Dame, has announced the adoption of official armorial bearings for the University. Father O'Donnell some time ago commissioned M. Pierre de Chaignon la Rose, of Harvard University, perhaps the foremost authority on heraldry in the United States, to design a coat-of-arms for Notre Dame. . . .

The colors blue and gold [or gold and blue] are the colors of the Virgin to whom Notre Dame (her very name) is dedicated. There are various heraldic emblems symbolic of the Virgin Mother of God in addition to the colors blue and gold (or as heraldry has it, azure and gules). Since the official title of the University is "Universitas Dominae Nostrae a Lacu" (by the lake), the star, reminiscent of the beautiful epithet Star of the Sea, was chosen as Mary's symbol in the new shield of arms. At the Base of the shield are two wavy broad lines of silver, always used in heraldry to represent water, here used to express "a Lacu" of Notre Dame's name. Thus the star and the waves of silver become poetically expressive of the dedication of the University to the Star of the Sea.

The Cross represents the Congregation of Holy Cross, whose members founded and still administer the University. The open book is always emblematic of an institution of learning. The phrase "Vita, Dulcedo, Spes," taken from the ancient prayer to the Virgin, the "Salve Regina," means "our life, our sweetness, our hope"; the combination of these phrases with the symbol for the university indicates the dedication of all Notre Dame's activities, intellectual, spiritual, athletic, and so on, to Our Lady.

The heraldic shield, bound with a circular device in which is inscribed "Sigillum Universitatis Dominae Nostrae a Lacu," becomes the seal of the University, used on all official documents including degrees . . . [as] the authoritative symbol of what Notre Dame is, was and ever hopes to be.

—FROM A FEBRUARY 1931 ARTICLE IN *THE NOTRE DAME ALUMNUS*
DESCRIBING THE SPIRITUAL SIGNIFICANCE OF NOTRE DAME'S NEWLY
CREATED COAT OF ARMS

FROM THE TIME I was old enough to think about the future, I wanted to be a priest. And that is all I ever thought about doing. As I grew older, I learned about other careers, but I only wanted to be a priest. And that's all I want to be today.

When you're a priest, you belong to everybody. You do what you can to help everybody. I didn't aspire to be the university president, but that role allowed me to get jobs in the government, which in turn allowed me to help even more people. But the thing I'm most proud of in my life is simply being a priest.

—REV. THEODORE M. HESBURGH, C.S.C.[3]

LOOMING OVER THE north end zone of the stadium is the famous "Word of Life" mural—commonly known as "Touchdown Jesus"—on the Hesburgh Library. Unveiled May 7, 1964, at the library's formal dedication, the mural is one of the nation's most recognizable collegiate monuments and a main attraction for visitors to campus. Designed by artist Millard Sheets, the mural measures 134 feet high and 68 feet wide, and is composed of some 6,700 individual pieces of granite that form 324 panels. Highlighting the university's goals as a first-rate academic institution, the mural's theme incorporates saints and scholars throughout the ages and emphasizes the pride of place that the library's collection holds.

Inspired by a passage from the first chapter of John's Gospel, the mural depicts Christ the Teacher amid images of prophets and historical figures in Christianity in ascending order, with classical and Old Testament scholars at the base and Byzantine, Medieval, and Renaissance figures at the top. A team of workers constructed Sheets's creation, under the direction of the artist, using granite in more than 140 colors from 16 foreign countries and 11 states. Addressing the fact that the mural has become a popular icon seen across the world on television during home football games, Father Hesburgh has said, "Thinking of this as Touchdown Jesus was just not in my mind, or anybody else's for that matter, but it's become a kind of nice, friendly familiar name for this beautiful piece of art."[4]

BETWEEN FEBRUARY THE 11th and August the 16th of 1858, Bernadette Soubirous experienced eighteen separate visions of a "Lady" in the Grotto of Massabielle near the French town of

Lourdes. This humble and guileless young woman, who did not know her catechism and could only recite the "Our Father" and the "Hail Mary," nonetheless stoutly withstood both the religious and the civil authorities of her day who challenged her account of the apparitions. "The Lady" requested prayers and religious processions, penance and deeper conversion, and the construction of a chapel at the Grotto. On March the 25th, Bernadette, at the insistence of her parish priest, asked "the Lady" who she was. The woman smiled and answered in the local dialect of that region: "Que soy Immaculada Councepiou" or "I am the Immaculate Conception." Bernadette said of herself: "I served the Blessed Virgin as a simple broom. When she no longer had any use for me, she put me back behind the door."

Father Basil Moreau, the founder of the Congregation of the Holy Cross, and Father Edward Sorin, the founder of the University of Notre Dame, both visited Lourdes on several occasions and both firmly believed in the miraculous nature of Bernadette's visions. In fact, the first organized pilgrimage to Lourdes from outside of France was led by Holy Cross priests from the University of Notre Dame. The earliest known representation of Our Lady of Lourdes in the United States can be seen in a stained glass window in the west transept of Notre Dame's Basilica of the Sacred Heart. It was always Father Sorin's fond desire to build a replica of the Lourdes Grotto at Our Lady's School. His dream was accomplished three years after his death when in 1896, Father Corby constructed and dedicated Notre Dame's Grotto.

Loving devotion of Mary is, of course, an ancient component of Catholic faith. Long before the writings of the New Testament were ever gathered into a single volume, Christians of both the East and the West honored Mary not only as the Mother of the Redeemer but also as the first and greatest of the Lord's disciples. In Catholic tradition, Mary is a symbol of the fidelity of ancient Israel and of the faith of the Church, the new "Israel of God." Mary was the first to receive Jesus Christ into her life. At her request, Jesus worked his first miracle in Cana of Galilee. Mary remained faithful, even at the foot of the cross. At the very birth of the Church on Pentecost Sunday, Mary was praying in the midst of the Apostles when they received the Holy Spirit. Now clothed in glory with the great Communion of Saints, Mary continues to pray with and for God's Church on earth.

Almost everyone who visits Notre Dame spends at least some time at the Grotto of Our Lady of Lourdes. For the last hundred years, nearly every student who has ever studied here has found the Grotto to be a place of welcome and prayer. Countless candles testify to the devotion of generations, all inspired by the loving witness of Mary. Here the Mother of Christ is deeply revered as the Blessed Mother of all those who believe in his Gospel and trust in the power of his grace. Hearts are comforted, lives are changed, and real miracles continue to happen. Faith is at the very heart of this University's life and mission, and the Grotto is at the very heart of Notre Dame.

—REV. DANIEL R. JENKY, C.S.C., '70, BISHOP OF PEORIA, IL, AND
FORMER RECTOR OF THE BASILICA OF THE SACRED HEART[5]

I REALLY BELIEVE that Our Lady watches over this place. I feel I ought to stop and say thanks, and also pray that she keeps watching over it. I usually get down to the Grotto in the wee hours of the morning when I leave the office. There is almost always someone down there . . . rain, sleet, or snow. Every university has a place where students hang out for their social life, libraries where they study, and fields where they play sports. But how many have a praying place?

—REV. THEODORE M. HESBURGH, C.S.C.,
QUOTED IN THE OBSERVER, FEBRUARY 13, 1986

FROM THE GREAT Golden Dome of her University, Our Lady reigns as our Queen. Yet at the Grotto, she seems to have stepped down a little closer to us that she might emphasize the other side of her personal relationship with us—that of Our Mother.

—REV. JOHN E. FITZGERALD, C.S.C.[6]

THE GROTTO IS a place of faith. How wonderful that Father Sorin and his successors brought the spirit of Lourdes, the spirit of Mary, to the heartland, to inspire the prayers of young people for generations to come.

—REV. EDWARD A. MALLOY, C.S.C., AT THE GROTTO'S
CENTENNIAL COMMEMORATION

THERE ARE MANY memories of that special place on the Notre Dame campus called the Grotto:

Where we students in the '40s marched from the South Dining Hall for devotions each evening in May.

Where we burned many a candle prior to examinations.

Where I asked that most important question of my wife to be.

Where through the years visits were mandatory upon occasions we returned to campus—like football weekends.

Where I said "Good-bye" and asked Our Lady's protection upon leaving for service in February 1943.

And a memory that will always remain special:

As a B-24 pilot I flew missions into enemy territory from southern Italy. On one mission, enemy flak wiped out one engine and pierced our fuel tank. The crash landing was the best landing I ever made— the crew and I survived and most were awarded the Purple Heart.

In April of 1945 the 376th Bomb Group, to which I was attached, was ordered back to the States for B-29 training prior to assignment to the Pacific Theater. (Subsequent events canceled that assignment.)

We landed at Newport News on April 30th, went through the necessary processing, and were given 30 days leave. I'm sure Mom and Dad, sister and aunt, relatives and friends, were as pleased to see me as I was to see them, but when these pleasantries were taken care of, there was something else I had to do. From Rochester I took a train west.

Where were you on V/J Day? On V/J Day, May 8, 1945, I was at the Grotto at Notre Dame saying "Thank You." Our Lady heard my prayer asking her protection back in February 1943.

—JOHN R. KLEE '44

CREATED BY SCULPTOR William Schickel, the three-sided drinking fountain at the Grotto depicts Jesus at the well, preaching from the boat, and washing the feet of his disciples. It stands at the spot where builders struck a natural spring during construction of the Grotto. The water emerged in the same location relative to the Grotto as it had at Lourdes.

. . . THE GROTTO AT Notre Dame is not internationally known. It has never shared even a fraction of the publicity afforded to this University's football team. But, to the students, to the alumni, to the priests and sisters of the Holy Cross, to many of the visitors to this campus, and to friends of Notre Dame, it has a quiet fame and is a place of high importance in their hearts. For it is the first place to visit when they come to campus and the last place to visit when they leave.

If one would take some time to observe the Grotto, it would seem that there is always somebody there. A student in his sweatshirt, a priest in his black robe, a young couple, an old man, an important visitor, a curious tourist . . . Why the attraction? Why the attention? To those of us who have visited the Grotto many times, these questions are easy to answer. But it is hard to explain certain things in words that must be felt by the heart and accepted by one's faith.

Somehow, there a cold day does not seem so cold; a hot day, not so hot; and a rainy day, not as damp as other places on the campus. The pleasant sunny days are even more beautiful at the Grotto. The Grotto itself is a shallow cave, built with common Indiana granite

rocks and reinforced with cement. Its back is against a small hill, which is behind Sacred Heart Church on the campus. Above, behind, around, and in front of the shrine, tall pines, stately oaks and maples, and leafy shrubbery lend their green beauty to the scene. While standing before the Grotto, one can see the brilliant gold of the dome of the Administration Building glistening in the sun. An iron railing and kneeler encloses the entrance to the cave, and within the cave itself are several candle stands. The walls of the cave are blackened with the carbon of the continually burning candles. To the right, and slightly above the larger cave, in a small nook or crevice, rests the statue of the Blessed Virgin Mary as she appeared to Bernadette. She is dressed in white, holding a rosary, golden roses at her feet, and a halo with the words "Oh, Mary, Conceived Without Sin, Pray For Us" surrounds her. Before her, on the ground, kneels a small whitewashed statue of Bernadette. A park-like area stretches in front of the shrine, with green grass and benches, to the shores of St. Mary's Lake. Still and placid, its surface rippled only by a slight breeze, and its clear color contrasted by the billowy white of a few swimming swans.

. . . Could not a miracle be a relative thing? Is this day of reason, science, and society so far advanced that it is no longer fashionable that God helps us if we pray to His Mother and ask for help? To be a miracle, does the happening have to be publicized and acclaimed by the Church? Could there not be little personal miracles, important, oh so very important, to those to whom they happened?

In May, the month dedicated to the Blessed Virgin Mary, the night shadows of the Grotto are dispelled by five thousand pinpoints of light, as the students of the University pay homage to the Mother of God. The termination of a procession, which winds its way across the campus, is Her shrine. From every dormitory, the students come, a candle carried by each one, a rosary in their hands. The rosary is completed en route, and Benediction of the Blessed Sacrament is offered on the small altar at the right of the Grotto. A few words are said about the Virgin, and hymns of praise are offered to her. Those who take part in this simple ceremony leave with a clean peaceful feeling. There is the birth of new hope and nourishment for the soul and the mind.

Once on the night of this May procession, the air was hot and sultry, the night sky split and illuminated with ragged streaks of lightning. The prayers of the students were drowned out by the rumbling of heavy thunder, and the whistling fury of the wind. The rest of the campus received a drenching downpour. There was no rain at the Grotto and the candles of faith remained burning. There are many scientific explanations possible for this phenomenon, but those there at the time were sure that the Blessed Mother smiled down at her sons that night in their efforts to please her.

Many people come to the Grotto. Their reasons and their prayers are greatly diversified. For many months an older couple brought their son to the Grotto. The three of them would sit there for an hour or so, on one of the benches. The man and woman looked at Mary. The son, crippled and deformed, was unable to focus his eyes. Not a word did they utter, but each day would wait in silent vigil. One day, the son was not with them, and never was he seen again. But daily, they returned. Perhaps now they prayed to the Heavenly Mother to care for their child and somehow they knew he would never suffer again in her loving care.

Many different requests, thanksgivings, and sorrowful stories must have been heard by Mary at the Grotto. A plea to win a game, a request for a passing mark, a petition to find the right girl for a wife and mother of a good Catholic family, a prayer for peace, and so many others have had their turn here. And then there are the thanksgivings for a wonderful vacation, a passing exam, a football victory, and for being alive in a world blessed by a loving God. So very many have experienced a feeling of pride, of special honor, and of such sweet love, when they brought that special person to Mary and presented her to his Heavenly Mother.

Formal prayers, deep meditation, and long sermons would not be out of place here. But, it seems more natural to feel that this is a favorite spot of Mary, who is the Mother of us all. Therefore, I don't think she minds at all when one of her visitors just says, "Hello, Mary." And stops to talk to her. It seems so easy to talk to her as a mother there.

It will remain forever, a hallowed spot on the University of Notre Dame campus. It will be remembered by those who have been there, and the countless number to follow, as the Grotto continues to bring hope, help, and understanding into a troubled world.

—JOHN J. GAIDO, JR., WROTE THIS TRIBUTE TO THE GROTTO, TITLED "THOUGHTS ON A SUNDAY AFTERNOON," IN 1954, AS A SOPHOMORE AT NOTRE DAME. THE ESSAY WAS DISCOVERED BY HIS DAUGHTER, MARY KATHRYN GAIDO WERNER, IN 1995, TWO YEARS AFTER HIS DEATH.[7]

BEING A RECTOR is a function of my priesthood, which itself is a special, or professional, way of being Christian. Being Christian is a grace-filled commitment to love human beings, especially those to whom we have responsibilities, as I do to the students of Keenan Hall. My life on this campus has no meaning, no identity, except in terms of the people to whom I offer my ministry, and that ministry involves far more than my function as a hall rector . . . At its best, my faith reflects the qualities—doubt, fear, passion, intensity, trust, courage, hope, grief—that are preoccupying the students, children, colleagues, and friends of the Notre Dame community. For as a Christian, I am here not only to witness to faith, but also to find it incarnate in the heartbeats that dance to the rhythms of grace.

—REV. ROBERT GRIFFIN, C.S.C.[8]

SPLENDID AS THE Dome may be by day, it is at night, against a blackened sky, that it shines with most brilliance. In all kinds of weather, whatever the hour of the day, the Dome is illuminated as the light of faith in a world of darkness. . . . Approaching the University by plane in the evening hours, the Dome is a guidepost not only for the pilot but also for the traveler, heart-weary away from home. Coming back from Chicago on the Tollway there is a rise in the road when suddenly and briefly the Dome can be seen in the distance. It is a most welcome sight in the late hours of the night, for we travel through this vale of tears always on the way to our heavenly home and guided by she who is "our life, our sweetness and our hope."

—Rev. Nicholas Ayo, C.S.C., '56, professor,
Program of Liberal Studies[9]

FAITH IS PROCLAIMED every day at Notre Dame by the imposing presence of Sacred Heart Basilica. It is there that Father Sorin met the community after the great fire and let his faith, undaunted by disaster, move mountains—in this case, mountains of bricks, some still warm, to build again, and this time bigger, the building that would be forever the pedestal for Mary, Notre Dame. When the price of complete restoration of the building, inside and out, was quoted, some suggested that it be torn down and that a new and bigger church could take its place. A wiser choice was made. Sacred Heart is the witness to a faith that inspired this place. Notre Dame men and women have worshiped here for a century and a quarter. Rockne's funeral was broadcast to millions on CBS from this church; Cardinal Eugenio Pacelli, later Pope Pius XII, prayed here. And so did thousands of tourists, students, parents, and townsfolk for more than a century.

Sacred Heart is eternally young, made so by the endless stream of weddings that need to be booked almost before an engagement ring is given and accepted. It is vivified by baptisms of future generations of Notre Dame students. It still echoes with the Sunday sermons of Father Bill Toohy, the Urchin's Mass of Father Griffin, the sounds of the Gospel choir, the glee club, the chorale. And every night, as another day draws to a close, the carillon sends through the campus the notes of the Alma Mater.

—JIM LANGFORD

IN LIEU OF the Greek system of fraternities and sororities, each of the single-sex dorms at Notre Dame has its own character and family identity. The dorm I lived in, Sorin College, enjoys many claims to distinction: It was Notre Dame's first residence hall outside of the main building; provided the piano that young alumni John F. and his brother Michael J. Shea, back on campus for a football game, used in 1908 to begin composing the "Notre Dame Victory March"; and housed such legendary Domers as Knute Rockne, Moose Krause, Paul Fenlon, Cardinal Father John O'Hara, C.S.C., Father John "Pops" Farley, C.S.C., and Father Edward "Monk" Malloy, C.S.C., who has lived in the first-floor northeast turret room since 1979.

But what truly makes Sorin Hall special is its history of being a close-knit community that studies, plays, and prays together. I remember vividly my first Mass in the Sorin chapel welcoming my freshman class and kicking off the new school year, and my last Mass as a student wishing the returning classes a good summer and the graduating seniors God's grace in the "real world." All the Masses in between brought me closer to God, made me a better person, and helped me forge lifelong friendships.

At the time I did not realize that while there are priests-in-residence at other Catholic institutions, the concept of having an active chapel in each individual residence hall is distinctively Notre Dame's. It is staggering to note that today sixty-eight Masses are celebrated each week in the dorms alone, with even more during football season. As Father Richard Warner, director of campus ministry and rector of Fisher Hall, has said, "Dorm Masses are a very special Notre Dame phenomenon. To build a space for worship into every residence hall is a strong statement about the nature of our community of faith."

What I never took for granted, however, were the power of the Mass and the experience of community. It was never weird to invite a friend or be invited by a friend to attend dorm Mass. In fact, it was a compliment, an expression that the friendship was open to deeper dimensions. Dorm Masses are earthy, simple, real. You can wear sweats and let your hair down. You can be yourself. Whether seated on the floor, in chairs, or on benches, you feel close to others in a way that is hard to describe or re-create outside of dorm life. Somehow you know that no matter what is going on in your life, there are others in the same situation right there with you. Somehow the homilies speak directly to you and help you enjoy the good and grow from the bad. Friends from your own dorm, and often from neighboring dorms, play instruments, sing in the choir, serve the Mass, give voice to the readings, distribute communion, and make announcements. The intentions are about everyday concerns and make prayer real while focusing the entire community's attention on what matters in life. On special occasions, Masses are offered for members of the community who are ill or who have died, to honor someone's success, to raise money for the poor or a special cause, or to celebrate feast days.

Upon graduation, many of us struggle to find churches that re-create our dorm Mass experience. We quickly realize that we are looking for the impossible. At the same time, we realize that having gone through the rites of passage associated with college and graduation, we are called to bring something of that same spirit to the places we go.

—JEREMY LANGFORD

NOTRE DAME PUTS a mark on your soul that heightens your sights and makes your values more secure.

I have traveled across the nation and dwelled in many places, and I know from cherished experience that Notre Dame is special. Students, faculty, and administrators come and go, yet there remains the continuity of a community striving for excellence. . . .

It is also a place where the liturgy is executed with dignity, and I cherished opportunities to preside at Mass in many residence halls. The students expected the liturgy to be well prepared. In those sacred moments, I saw Notre Dame men and women wait for the Word of God to open their hectic lives to deeper meaning and purpose.

—Monsignor Jack Egan (1917–2001), beloved priest of the Archdiocese of Chicago who spent thirteen years at Notre Dame (from 1970 to 1983) and fought for social justice his whole life[10]

NOTRE DAME PEOPLE are not complacent; they are afraid of complacency. But they are not afraid or ashamed of enthusiasm. They are capable of being enthusiasts in the deepest literal sense.

Notre Dame students are animated by a spiritual passion. I encounter this in the classroom every day, even among the large minority of students not formally attached to the Catholic Church. This intuitive response to God's will varies in intensity and its content differs from person to person. But a religious intuition and spiritual susceptibility, a capacity for enthusiasm, flourishes here in numberless ways.

—Professor Stephen Rogers, Program of Liberal Studies

I USED TO be impressed deeply at the sight of my players receiving Communion every morning, and finally I made a point of going to Mass with them on the morning of a game. I realized that it appeared more or less incongruous, when we arrived in town for a game, for the public to see my boys rushing off to church as soon as they got off the train, while their coach rode to the hotel and took his ease.

One night before a big game in the East, I was nervous and worried about the outcome the next day, and was unable to sleep. I tossed and rolled about the bed, and finally decided to get up and sit downstairs. About five or six o'clock in the morning, while pacing the lobby of the hotel, I unexpectedly ran into two of my own players hurrying out.

I asked them where they were going at such an hour, although I had a good idea. Within the next few minutes, my players continued hurrying out and I decided to go along with them. They didn't realize it; but these youngsters were making a powerful impression on me with their devotion, and when I saw all of them walking up to the Communion rail to receive, and realized the hours of sleep they had sacrificed, I understood for the first time what a powerful ally their religion was to them in their work on the football field. Later on, I had the happiness of joining my boys at the Communion rail.

—KNUTE ROCKNE, IN RESPONSE TO BEING ASKED
WHY HE BECAME A CATHOLIC[11]

MY FRIENDS, OUR religion, our faith does not take us out of life but energizes and gives meaning to everyday life. It links us in solidarity to a community that stretches back 2,000 years. This community has gone through history, ever changing and adapting, in one century never the same as before, its doors always open to the world. It has been sustained by men and women such as yourselves—the merciful, the single-hearted, the peacemakers. Dear friends, keep the faith, and in so doing live it and share it.

—REV. BILL MISCAMBLE, C.S.C., PROFESSOR OF HISTORY

HOPE

If it's God's will that I be cured, I will be. If not, I won't; obviously He has other plans for me. Whatever happens, I figure I have a right to ask only one thing: the strength to face up to it.

—FREDERICK B. SNITE, WHO AFTER GRADUATING FROM
NOTRE DAME IN 1933 CONTRACTED POLIO AND LIVED THE REST
OF HIS LIFE IN AN IRON LUNG

"WHAT THO THE odds be great or small, Old Notre Dame will win over all" isn't a boast; it is a hope and a promise not to settle for less than excellence. Hope feeds on faith, on a belief that who we are and what we do matters, that we can make a difference on the scale of human goodness. Every great venture starts with a vision; every successful venture requires the promise that only hope can provide. Hope rescues us from the routine and raises us from our failures. Hope depends not on luck, but on preparation and effort, on dreams that extend our reach and our ability to surprise ourselves.

For Notre Dame, Our Life, Our Sweetness, and Our Hope, the capital sin would be to settle for less than excellence. One cannot look up at the Dome without realizing that, indeed, the sky is the limit.

Many people wonder (or worry) about Notre Dame and that word, *Irish*. To us, it doesn't mean race exclusively; nor is it just another nickname. The fact is, it keeps alive the memory of a long, uphill fight for recognition against a spirit that was not always generous, nor even fair-minded. The Irish, as known at Notre Dame, has an authentic history and a meaning deeper even than race.

Notre Dame began athletic relations chiefly with local colleges founded by various denominations. Press reports would refer to the schools as the "Baptists" or the "Methodists," and the like. For Notre

Dame it was the "Catholics," or the "Irish." But the players were never all of Irish ancestry; nor were they all Catholics.

The usage was not original, but a continuing custom from earlier Colonial times. The bulk of the first Catholic immigrants were Irish—so that Catholics and Irish were identical in the public mind. It is sad to recall now, but few of the original states were without laws against them. Advertisements for "help wanted" commonly carried the restriction: "No Catholics. No Irish." The Puritans were the first to cry: "Stop the Irish!"

When the religious origin of other colleges lost its significance, the emphasis shifted to conventional names, and to their school colors. But history is recorded remembrance in our blessed heritage here at Notre Dame. Fighting Irish! It's more than a name; more than a people. It is the Faith!

In narrow, little New England, it began as a slur—a term of opprobrium. But we took it up and made of it a badge of honor—a symbol of fidelity and courage to everyone who suffers from discrimination; to everyone who has an uphill fight for the elemental decencies, and the basic Christian principles woven into the texture of our nation. Preserving this tradition, and this meaning of Irish, at Notre Dame does honor to every one of us. It explains why Lewinski belongs here; why Alessandrini is the Irish leader; why Schmaltz belongs here; why Bertrand, Moreau, Van Dyke, and Larson feel at home here as much as do Leahy and O'Brien.

YOU AND ST. PATRICK

Tomorrow, the world will be green for a day while we honor the patron saint of Erin. Bighearted people of all nationalities will pause to applaud the contribution of the Irish to the civilization of the world. Best of all contributions made was the Faith which they took with them wherever their wanderings took them. Patrick is a great saint of God; and therefore a great saint of the church. And if he belongs to the Church, then he belongs to you. That's why you should pray to St. Patrick, asking him to increase your Faith; bolster it; make it a living reality in your everyday life—keeping you aware that the trials and sufferings of this exile are as nothing when compared to the glory that awaits those who fight the good fight that overcomes the world!

Tomorrow you can take this one lesson from the Irish: they were never so poor in all their wanderings and sufferings that they bartered their Faith for the comforts of this life. They had little to take with them wherever they went; but the Faith was always the most precious of their paltry possessions. Their spirit has made it easier for you to practice your Faith here in America today. May the Fighting Irish always be with us!

—EXCERPTED FROM THE RELIGIOUS BULLETIN ISSUED THE DAY BEFORE
ST. PATRICK'S DAY 1953 BY REV. CHARLES M. CAREY, C.S.C.,
WHO WANTED STUDENTS TO KNOW HOW THE "FIGHTING IRISH"
NICKNAME WENT FROM A SLUR TO A BADGE OF HONOR AND A SYMBOL
OF HOPE, AND WHY EVERYONE SHOULD BE GLAD THAT
THE WORLD IS "GREEN FOR A DAY"[1]

TIME MARKED ITS ceaseless course through the terrible burning, even as it had done in the hours of peace, study and prayer. We shall never forget that bell, unruffled and peaceful, as it was heard, and barely heard, amid the crackling and roaring of the flames, the falling of walls, the noise of the engine, the rushing and hissing of water and the loud shouts of men—the peaceful but appalling sound of these sweet church bells striking the hours of God's ever passing time, His quiet, all-embracing Eternity.

—SCHOLASTIC, JUNE 1879, ACCOUNT OF THE GREAT FIRE THAT
DESTROYED THE MAIN BUILDING AND SEVERAL OTHER STRUCTURES,
LEAVING ONLY SACRED HEART CHURCH STANDING

IN A HUNDRED years, Notre Dame will still be Notre Dame. Some things will change, others will stay the same. Old faces will give way and new faces will take their place. Buildings will be built from the ancient yellow bricks of Sorin's time. The place will survive.

—REV. ROBERT GRIFFIN, C.S.C.

THE YEAR WAS 1937, the scene, Notre Dame Stadium; the game, a battle typical of those days between the Fighting Irish and Southern California. Tied 6–6 in the fourth quarter and deep in their own territory, Notre Dame calls on number 58, fullback Mario "Motts" Tonelli. He breaks through the line and races 70 yards before being tackled near the SC 15-yard line. Three plays later, he scores the winning touchdown.

Mario Tonelli had his class ring engraved with his initials, MGT, and his year of graduation,'39. He played a year of professional football with the Chicago Cardinals before joining the army in 1941 and being assigned to the Philippines. Then came December 7, 1941, and Pearl Harbor. Sergeant Tonelli, along with American and Philippine troops, was ordered by General Douglas MacArthur to retreat to the Bataan Peninsula to await reinforcements. The reinforcements never came, but the Japanese army did. And so began one of the most infamous and barbaric events in recent history, the sixty-five-mile-long Bataan Death March along steamy jungle paths with very little water or food and the certainty that anyone who fell or stopped would be bayoneted or shot on the spot. At one point, a guard spotted Tonelli's ring and demanded that he hand it over. It was not worth dying for, so he gave it over. Before long, a Japanese officer approached him and asked whether one of his men had taken something from him. He said, "My ring." The officer put the ring in Tonelli's hand and said, "Keep it hidden." He explained that he had graduated from Southern California and that he had seen Tonelli's run in the 1937 game. "I know what this ring means to you," he said.

Some 11,000 prisoners died on the march. That was only the beginning. Over the next two and a half years of imprisonment and forced labor, there were beatings, starvation, and humiliation enough to break most human spirits. But Tonelli's ring always reminded him to hope. In 1944, Tonelli, now a mere 100 pounds, was part of a group shipped to mainland Japan for slave labor. On arrival, he worked his way to the intake table to receive his identification number and prisoner clothes. The number assigned to him was 58, the same number he had worn on his Notre Dame jersey. He said later, "That's when I knew I'd make it."

Finally freed after the atomic attacks on Hiroshima and Nagasaki, Tonelli worked incessantly to regain his strength and weight. Two months after his liberation, he suited up for the Chicago Cardinals' game against Green Bay. But he soon decided to forgo football in favor of public service and politics in Chicago, a career he served for the rest of his working life. He kept the ring always with him. It had survived horror; so had he. Every day until his death on January 8, 2003, Mario Tonelli saw his survival as a victory and his Notre Dame ring as its trophy.

—JIM LANGFORD

THROUGHOUT THE GREATER part of his life, Frederick Snite was known as "The Man in the Iron Lung." His story was told in the December 6, 1946, *Scholastic*:

> On football weekends you would see Fred B. Snite in his house trailer–like vehicle parked on the sidelines. Through a specially built mirror attached to his iron lung, which he brought into the public limelight, he watched the game. Despite his handicap he followed the fortunes of the Fighting Irish, seeing all the Notre Dame home games he could and listening to away games by radio.
>
> Fred Snite was the scion of a wealthy Chicago financier, who graduated from Notre Dame in the spring

of 1933. Two years later he was ready to enter his father's business, but to celebrate the event properly, the elder Snite took his family . . . on a world cruise. Snite was to enter the Chicago loan firm upon his return. But things didn't work out that way; fate had smiled in another direction. In China, Fred Snite was suddenly taken ill while on a plane trip to Peiping. . . . Taken to a Peiping hospital after precious time had been lost and after a local physician had misdiagnosed his ailment, Snite was pronounced critically ill with the dreaded poliomyelitis, or infantile paralysis. Fortunately the only "iron lung" in China was at that time in Peiping. Snite, unable to speak or breathe without artificial aid, was placed in the lung, and little hope was held for his recovery.

However, the doctors didn't reckon with Snite's pluck. With splendid disregard for cynical predictions, Snite remained alive and within a few months he was not only talking again, but was speaking Chinese almost as fluently as a native. He never complained about his plight, but accepted it philosophically. In 1937, after his case had been making the headlines for a year, Snite was returned by boat to the United States. The following years he was again watching Notre Dame football . . . from a spot directly behind the goal posts.

The famed sportswriter Grantland Rice honored Snite by saying: "Condemned to spend a life of pain in a cumbersome Iron Lung, this Fifth Horseman of Notre Dame showed indomitable courage. His special trailer in which he traveled throughout the nation was a familiar sight at the north ramp of Notre Dame stadium at home games. He was, indeed, one of Notre Dame's all-time great competitors."

There was no room for self-pity or bitterness in his life, which, apart from almost complete confinement in the respirator, was surprisingly normal. He married Teresa Larkin in 1939, and they had three daughters. He became a symbol of the triumph of spirit over the body.

The image of "The Boiler Kid" was frequently seen in newspapers, magazines, and newsreels nationwide. He published a newsletter titled, appropriately, *Back Talk*, and his optimism encouraged countless other polio victims. At his funeral in 1954, at the age of forty-four, he was mourned by many more than the 1,500 who came to say farewell to this remarkable, dauntless young man.

Teresa Snite, Frederick's wife, . . . said there was no doubt that he had been inspired to go to Lourdes by the Notre Dame Grotto. In going there, she said, "he felt he had received a miracle of grace rather than a healing, a total acceptance that it was what God wanted him to do, that his respirator was his ticket to heaven."[2]

NOTRE DAME HAS many heroes, some sung, some unsung. For every story told here countless others are recounted among those who love the school. Who can forget the indomitable spirit of Rocky Bleier? Undersized, everyone said, except for his heart. He did not excel at any one facet of football; all he did was to find a way to win. When he was severely wounded in Vietnam, his hope to play in the NFL seemed relegated to the "What might have been" category. Except for Bleier's spirit and determination. After painful rehabilitation and rebuilding, Rocky made it with the Pittsburgh Steelers, where he was a valuable contributor to their dynasty years.

Or Adam Sargent, varsity lacrosse player at Notre Dame, left paralyzed from the chest down by an auto accident in 1997. Lots of people would have given up. But not "Sarge." Buoyed by his family and the Notre Dame family, especially his coach, Kevin Corrigan, he knew the fear of going from a strong twenty-one-year-old athlete to being dependent on others. His courage and equanimity led him back to campus to complete his double major in history and anthropology. Since graduation, Sarge has been a counselor in Notre Dame's Academic Services Department and works with some 120 student athletes. Pat Holmes, director of the department, notes that "Adam brings so many positives to his work, I couldn't list them all." Coach Corrigan adds, "He's one of my heroes. I've been with him in the best of times and the worst of times and I've never been anything but impressed with him."

More recently, the spirit of Notre Dame shines through the person of Danielle Green. Raised by her grandmother in a rough area of Chicago, Danielle resolved early in life that she would not fall into the trap of drugs or gangs; that she would make something of herself. Her basketball skills seemed to need only practice and perseverance to develop. She drew the attention of Notre Dame coach Muffet McGraw and accepted a scholarship to Notre Dame.

As a 5'7" guard she was fast, a good left-handed shooter and a playmaker. In her career at Notre Dame, she was twice named to the Big East Academic All-Star Team, and her 1,106 points scored ranks seventeenth on ND's all-time list. After Notre Dame, Danielle returned to Chicago, where she coached basketball for two years. Then she enlisted in the army, married her former coach, and, in January 2004, was shipped to Iraq. Three months later, while on security duty at a police headquarters in Baghdad, Danielle was hit by a missile fired from a nearby building. She lost her left arm—her shooting arm—and the hand that held her wedding ring. A soldier retrieved the ring for her. She was rushed to safety, then flown to Germany for surgery. The first face she saw was that of Dr. Tim Woods, a Notre Dame graduate, now a military surgeon. "I've always heard about the Notre Dame family," Danielle said, "but this is too much!" After surgery, she was flown back to the United States and reunited with her husband, whose ring she now wears on her right hand. Her dream is to be an academic sports counselor at the university level. Through it all, she still has the million-watt smile that has brightened the lives of those who know her. Asked whether she will still play basketball, Danielle responds with a grin, "Coach McGraw always told me I should learn to dribble with my right hand."

—JIM LANGFORD

WHEN CHRIS ZORICH took the field, he was one of the most feared noseguards in college football and defensive tackles in professional football. When he enters a room filled with children, he is one of the most beloved people in their lives. From his Chicago Bears uniform to his Santa Claus outfit, Zorich is a man with a mission: to help those in need. His passions for football and for life find their meaning in helping people. By all standards, Zorich is a walking paradox, a man who enjoyed driving quarterbacks into the ground as much as he enjoys delivering baskets of food to needy families. But when he is serving others, the fine line that separates his game face from his caregiver's face dissolves quickly.

Chris entered the world on March 13, 1969, the son of a poor Yugoslavian woman, Zora Zorich, who lived alone on the South Side of Chicago. Chris's father had run out on Zora upon learning that she was pregnant, leaving the expectant mother to fend for herself in a tiny apartment in one of the city's toughest neighborhoods. Despite her battle with diabetes and her meager income from government aid, Zora resolved to have her child and raise him well. Only her own desire to be a good mother and to share her love with her child improved the overwhelming odds against her. Outside her windows poverty, racism, gang warfare, crime, and hopelessness abounded. But inside her home thrived the indomitable powers of love and hope, which converted Chicago's mean streets into lessons in humanity for herself and her son.

From the very beginning, Chris experienced the searing sting of poverty. He learned what it was like to go hungry for days, to lie awake at night because the pain in his empty stomach was unbearable. When his clothes didn't fit right or were long out of style, it brought ridicule from his peers. He discovered how frustration can turn to tears by watching his mother sacrifice even the simplest of luxuries so that he could buy textbooks and school supplies. More than anything, he learned that without help, people like him would never make it.

Yet in the face of this hardship, Zorich found great joy in his relationship with his mother.

"My mom was and is my best friend. When I was growing up, we did everything together. She took care of me. Sometimes we didn't have food in the house, or in wintertime we didn't have heat. Sometimes we didn't have electricity. But my mom always kept a positive attitude. She didn't sit around crying or moaning about life. She did what she had to do. That would entail occasionally going to the local grocery store and digging through the garbage to find expired food that had been thrown away.

By the time Chris enrolled as a freshman at Chicago Vocation High School, he and his mom had made it through many tough years together. His mother looked out for him and had a say in everything he did. So when the head varsity football coach, John Potocki, asked the 250-pound Chris to join the team and put to use his obvious size advantage, the excited freshman raced home to get his mother's approval. "I took the release form home, but my mom wouldn't sign it," recalls a smiling Zorich. "When I asked her why, her exact words were 'Because I don't want my little baby getting hurt.' I was a big kid, but she still worried about me, so I didn't play."

Chris didn't give up on football, however. The next year, he brought the release form home again, and when his mom refused to sign it, the future star forged her signature and joined the team.

About halfway through the season, Zora discovered that her son was playing football against her wishes. "One day I wasn't thinking and brought my helmet home. My mom asked me what I was doing. We sat and talked about it, and I told her that football was good because it gave me something positive to do after school. On our streets were gunshots, gangbangers, drug dealers. We didn't have Boy Scouts or Little League. So football was the only positive thing I could identify with. After I explained why I wanted to play, my mom said it was all right."

For Chris, football was simply a sport he enjoyed that helped keep him off the streets. He never intended on playing beyond high school. In fact, he never even considered going to college. His main goal in life was to learn a trade so that he could get a job, save his money, and get his mother out of their neighborhood. Although life on the South Side was all Chris knew, he learned at an early age that his mom deserved better.

"When I was eight years old, my mom and I were walking down the street together. From across the street there were four or five guys throwing snowballs at us. They were throwing very hard. One hit me in the leg, and one hit my mother on the shoulder and in the face. I looked at her, and she started to cry. So I'm eight years old and thinking, 'What's going on? Why are they throwing snowballs at my mom? She's a great person.' It was because she was white in a predominantly black neighborhood. So at eight I wanted to get her out of there, but of course I couldn't do anything then, I was helpless."

Like so much of America, Chicago's South Side is divided by racial lines. The neighborhood simply would not accept a white woman, especially one who was raising a biracial child. And for Chris, living in between two races left him in a kind of no-man's-land. He and his mother were obvious targets for verbal and physical abuse from those in the neighborhood. They were mugged several times. People threw stones at them. Their apartment was broken into frequently and life was frustrating.

By the time Chris reached high school, he was angry. Not many things besides his mom could soothe his soul, but football provided an outlet, a release valve. Coach Potocki helped Chris convert his inner turmoil into talent.

His aggressive manner on the field earned Chris the title of team captain his senior year and drew the interest of a recruiter from Notre Dame.

The following year, a proud Chris Zorich enrolled at prestigious Notre Dame. As if in a dream, he walked the campus not as a visitor but as a student athlete. This time he had his mom's blessings to play football from the outset. Zora saw her son's football scholarship as a means to an end: to get a quality education that would prepare him for the rest of his life.

During the next four years, Chris earned a reputation as a fierce competitor. In an article titled "Hard Man, Soft Heart," *Sports Illustrated* called him the "toughest and most vicious player" in college football. He was the strongest man on the Irish squad, able to bench-press 470 pounds. And at 6'1", 277 pounds, his speed and uncanny instincts at nose tackle left opponents no choice but to double- and triple-team him every play. Throughout his career, Chris won many awards and accolades. He was selected an All-American for three consecutive years (1988–1990), was named Chevrolet's Defensive Player of the Year (1989), and twice won the Washington, D.C., Touchdown Club's Lineman of the Year Award (1989, 1990). During his senior year, he was named team captain, won the Lombardi Trophy as the nation's top college lineman, and finished his college career as the 1991 Orange Bowl's Most Valuable Player despite Notre Dame's loss to Colorado.

Off the field, he was well liked by everybody. His boisterous laugh could be heard from across the campus as he took delight in his friends. He was often spotted down by the lakes, feeding ducks and squirrels before games. He spoke of a generous God, read poetry, and picked flowers. Even his mother, whom he called every day just to say he loved her, once said, "Chris is a pussycat. He's a shy kid off the field."

For Zorich, life at Notre Dame was heaven. He always had food. He was popular. But most important to him and to his mother was his education. Even amid the hype surrounding his success as a football player, he let everyone know that his proudest achievement was yet to come: graduating in four years with a degree in American Studies and saying to his mother, "We did it!"

Then the unimaginable happened.

After the Orange Bowl, Chris called his mom from Miami and arranged to meet her at O'Hare Airport the day after the game. Leaving a day before the rest of the team, Chris boarded the plane and counted the minutes before he would wrap his arms around his mom. In the back of his mind was the exciting possibility that he would land a contract with an NFL team and get his mom out of the neighborhood. He knew his chances were good.

Chris arrived at O'Hare to find no Zora waiting for him. He knew something was wrong.

When he got to the apartment and knocked, there was no answer. He looked through the window and saw his mother lying on the floor. Chris kicked down the door and found that his mother was dead. And for that moment, so were all of Chris's dreams. Everything that had been so good meant nothing. Without Chris's knowing, Zora had gone to the hospital four times during the previous year. Something hadn't been right, but she didn't tell her son because she didn't want to worry him and spoil his season. A heart attack had claimed her life sometime after watching her son play his last game at the university they had both come to love.

"I grieved, but I was able to see how she dealt with adversity— she would face it, assess the problem and see what she had to do, and move on. I was conditioned by her. I couldn't wallow in sorrow by saying, 'She's never going to be here again; I'm not going to talk to her on the phone anymore.' It wasn't like that. When she died, I had no regrets whatsoever. Every time we talked on the phone, I'd say, 'Good-bye, Mom, I love you,' and she'd say, 'Good-bye, Chris, I love you too.' So when something like that is gone, it's not really gone. My mom's spirit is up here [points to his head] and in here [points to his heart]. I'll never be without my mom."

On a sunny spring day a few months after his mother's death, Chris graduated from Notre Dame. He knew his mom was watching, and he knew she was proud. Atop his graduation hat were words he'd made with masking tape that read, "Hi Mom."

Drafted by the Bears in 1991, Zorich built a solid career until he retired in 1998 to pursue a law degree at Notre Dame. He used his football money to help others. In 1993, he founded the Christopher Zorich Foundation to honor his mother and to offer diverse community-support programs, including the annual Zora Zorich Scholarships at the University of Notre Dame, Lewis University, and to a specified United Negro College Fund school in partnership with the Chicago Public Schools; youth programs providing cultural, educational, and entertainment activities; Thanksgiving grocery home deliveries to 1,500 Chicagoans; women's recognition on Mother's Day through flower corsage and cosmetics deliveries to shelters; and a holiday gift program providing gifts, and matching sponsors with disadvantaged children and families. To date, these combined programs have assisted more than 100,000 individuals.

In May of 2002, Chris received his law degree and currently works for the Chicago law firm of Schuyler, Roche & Zwirner, P.C. An active supporter of other community and civic organizations, he serves as a board member for numerous nonprofit organizations, including the Big Shoulders Fund, the Joffrey Ballet, KaBoom!, Special Children's Charities, and There Are Children Here. He is also a member of the Board of Trustees at Lewis University. Chris carries his mother's heart and bleeds gold and blue. He is part of the legacy of both.

—JEREMY LANGFORD

WHEN I WAS a student at Notre Dame, I made it a goal to seek out mentors on campus who could help me better understand the soul of the university and, ultimately, my own soul. At the top of my list was Lou Holtz, the legendary coach of the Fighting Irish football team. Not only had he won a national championship for the school in 1988, but he had authored several motivational books and was passionate about being a champion in life as much as he was in athletics. He demonstrated such skill in motivating and captivating others that corporations paid up to $15,000 to have him deliver keynote addresses. I barely had $15, let alone $15,000, as a college sopho-more, but in the summer of '93 I was determined to gain an audience with Sweet Lou.

After sending Holtz a letter introducing myself and simply saying I wanted twenty minutes of his time to learn more about his views on success, I became a success in pestering his secretary with follow-up calls. After weeks of my dogged persistence, Holtz's secretary left me a voice mail saying that her boss agreed to meet me. The time frame was even shorter than I had requested, fifteen minutes, and it had to be the next day or never.

I convinced a friend of mine, Ian Hernández, to join me for the meeting. Speaking with his trademark lisp, Coach Holtz greeted me with, "Shun, I've never shaken a hook before. How do you move those things?" I explained that when I move a shoulder, the strap har-ness that connected my arms across my back would pull the proper cable to move my hook or elbow joint. I also explained that the leg I wore contained a knee joint with a spring that allowed me to walk and run.

This launched a summary, at his request, of my views on over-coming adversity, maintaining a positive attitude, and never yielding to the temptation to give up. Holtz particularly liked it when I quoted from the book *Grit, Guts, & Genius*—a compilation of thoughts from motivational figures, including him: "Ability is what you're capable of doing. Motivation determines what you do. Attitude determines how well you do it."

But Holtz was not completely satisfied.

"Shun, I admire you, but you're forgetting one key component," said the fifty-five-year-old coach as he pulled up a chair next to wide-eyed Ian and me. "There's more to life than just overcoming chal-lenges. You do that out of necessity. I want you to learn how to live a life of excellence and how to *win*."

As he fixed a steely glare on us, Sweet Lou unleashed a passionate sermon on how the people he most admired were overachievers. He was one himself. Coming from a modest family in West Virginia, he had neither wealth nor great athletic skill yet trained himself to learn every position on his high school football team so that he could be inserted anywhere if a front-line starter needed rest or became injured. He finished 234th in a high school class of 278, yet was persistent in becoming a college football coach. His primary dream, though, was to be the head football coach at Notre Dame, and he held on to that goal with such conviction that whatever losing program he was reviving had to agree to insert a clause in his contract that allowed him to apply for the Fighting Irish job if it ever became available.

In late 1985, it became available. Holtz left another improbable success story at the University of Minnesota to take over Notre Dame's historic yet flagging program. The first thing he did was raise the standards whereby if star players were even late for team meetings, they didn't play. Now, if stringent academic standards were not met, they did not play. If a prized recruit did not demonstrate as much interest in receiving an education as he did playing in Notre Dame Stadium, Holtz would cancel his visit to the recruit's home.

"Shun, I raised the standards and you must do the same!"

He continued: "You've achieved a lot already, but I won't truly be impressed unless you overachieve. Raise the bar. Do *more* than what is expected of you."

"In times of crisis," he continued, "you can be the calmest person in the room if, while everyone is going berserk, you focus on What's Important Now and take it step by step. Same thing with personal adversity—if you get down, you shouldn't be down for long if you think about What's Important Now and go from there."

He kept it simple but kept it passionate. Holtz had no use for people, be they athletes or audience members, who pitied themselves or maintained a low standard for life goals. In his mind, "overachiever" was really a misnomer, because we all should strive to overachieve.

Holtz's final words to me were "Shun, I want you to keep in touch and tell me how you exceeded expectations set by yourself and others. I'm glad you don't allow others to feel sorry for you. Now go out and do more than that. Don't just live a life of overcoming, but of *excellence*."

—ALEX MONTOYA '96 IS A TRIPLE AMPUTEE FROM BIRTH WHO HAS MADE A CAREER OUT OF HELPING OTHERS[3]

YOUR YEARS AT Notre Dame have expanded both mind and heart. Your well-honed gifts will act as a beacon of hope for those you serve; and in turn, you will receive more blessings than you give.

—REV. MARK L. POORMAN, C.S.C., VICE PRESIDENT FOR STUDENT AFFAIRS, ADDRESSING GRADUATING STUDENTS

LOVE

*Since it was founded, the University has been abundantly peopled
with those willing to care. In all facets of life here, from feeding the
campus wildlife to caring for spiritual needs, someone is willing to
care; maybe not always many people, but always someone.*

—JIM GRESSEN, APRIL 26, 1974, SCHOLASTIC

NO VIRTUE IS more talked about, sought after, attempted, or
needed than love. It is the crescendo in the concert of the virtues.
We are told that when you come right down to it, there are three
virtues that matter most: faith, hope, and love. And the greatest of
these is love. Knowledge and love, the mind and heart, work in tan-
dem. The more we know, the more we are able to love; the more we
love, the more we gain a kind of intuitive knowledge. The goal of life
is happiness, and its road map is the kind of love that is practiced so
often and so well that it becomes a kind of second nature. The power
of truth is not unleashed simply by discovering or agreeing with it; we
need to *do* it, to feel it in our hearts, to empty the self and, in the
process, find a new fullness.

Service to others has always been a hallmark of Notre Dame. If
one could begin to assemble the narratives of goodness and giving
that belong to the administration, faculty, students, and staff of this
place, no binding could hold the resulting book. It would tell of
Vince McAloon taking the leftovers from the dining hall to the homeless every day during the Depression and its aftermath; it would
make note of the fact that thousands of students every year volunteer
their time and talents and love in programs that serve the young and
the old, the poor and homeless, the mentally and physically challenged, the helpless and homeless. The Center for Social Concerns
as a locus of these volunteers is a beacon of light in the community.
Fully 10 percent of the Notre Dame graduating class each year com-

mit to at least one full year of service. The following stories give a glimpse into the spirit of love that enlivens Notre Dame.

NOTRE DAME DU Lac has been given to us by the bishop only on condition that we build here a college. . . . This college will become one of the most powerful means of doing good in this country.

—Rev. Edward Sorin, C.S.C.

BROTHER HUGH AND Tubby, his dog, could be seen always together on the campus of the University of Notre Dame. Brother Hugh, stout and squat, was rector of Brownson Hall in the 1860s, a horse trader (so-called), a farmer, a philanthropist, a carpenter (when a stable had to be built), and as one admirer said, "An all-around wonderful man."

Brother Hugh has been dead some 14 years now; but he's still living within the hearts of many South Benders, and of all those who knew him. He was kind, gentle, and generous.

Brother Hugh was a great horse trader. At least he considered himself as such. Among those who knew horses, however, it was said that he didn't know a Cleveland Bay from a Clydesdale in respect to breeding, nor the gaskin from the stifle in regard to their anatomy. Once he traded a chestnut bay to a horseman in South Bend by the name of Abe Goldman; two years later, Abe traded the same bay back to Brother Hugh, who thought it was a new horse. (And such was his trading of quadrupeds.)

At one time Brother Hugh had five horses, but the small stables could hold only three. Something had to be done about this, and he did it. In the center of what is now known as Cartier Field, he built a rather crude stable from old planks, boards, and boxes. The students called it "Rockefeller Hall." Within the walls of this stable live not only horses, but men—derelict men. In those days, bums, tramps, and hoboes were common, much more so than they are now. These men would share the stable with the horses, or vice versa.

Brother Hugh never failed to give a meal to a man who wanted one, and to make sure that the man was hungry enough to eat it, he was given an extra appetite by working at some small menial task about the campus. These men were called "Tramps" by him. He distinguished between a tramp, who was a wanderer, but not afraid of work; a hobo, who would work occasionally and walk the rest of the time; and a bum, who would never work, and always wandered.

It was not long before every tramp in the country knew of Brother Hugh. Soon, the "waywarding" visitors were swarming over the campus. Brother Hugh again realized that something had to be done about this. He, therefore, received permission to convert an old rickety building, which was located on the spot the Huddle now rests upon, to a makeshift dining room for these men. It was not uncommon for him to feed 50 in an evening. This was also nicknamed by the students, and was commonly known as "The Privy Council."

The poor of South Bend will remember Brother Hugh for his charity, the tramps will remember him for his cooking, and the horsemen will remember him for his trading. Truly, he was "An all-around wonderful Man."

—FRANK ENGLISH, OCTOBER 30, 1942, SCHOLASTIC

WHERE FERVOR AND devotion reign, a sacrifice is a joy rather than an affliction.

—REV. EDWARD SORIN, C.S.C.

NO CAMPUS BUILDINGS are named after Sister M. Aloysius; no statue or plaque takes note of her 43 years at Notre Dame. Like the many dozens of nuns who cared for orphans in the Manual Labor School or taught in the grade school or labored as cooks, launderers, tailors, nurses, and general housekeepers for the men of Notre Dame,

Sister Aloysius has entered the shadowland of almost-forgotten female pioneers.

And a pioneer she was. An Irish lass named Honora Mulcaire who took final vows in 1875, Sister Aloysius rose high in the administrative structure of Father Sorin's multi-layered educational endeavors. For more than 40 years, she was in charge of the minims—the name given to the elementary school students at Notre Dame. That school existed from 1862 to 1929, and its "little princes" were favorites of Father Sorin.

By far her most famous student was Ben B. Lindsay, who later founded the juvenile court movement. When Sister Aloysius died, Judge Lindsay sent condolences to Notre Dame and passed along a compliment to warm a teacher's heart: Sister Aloysius, he wrote, "seemed to have discovered whatever small talents I had, and really opened the way for their development into any service that I may have helped to render in this world."

What Sister Aloysius did day in and day out, what she thought about what she did, how much authority she had and how she accepted her role is a story told in no history books. The few letters and anecdotes that do survive indicate both that she was quite willing to speak her mind—though well-loved, she was sometimes referred to as a tyrant—and that she had a lighthearted bent. In a note to Father Sorin, who was traveling at the time, the sister gave him a playful warning about the effect his absence would have on the "little princes" under her charge: "If you stay away any longer than the six weeks, the minims will become heretics—no confession and no invitation written on the blackboard to remind them."

When Sister Aloysius died of pneumonia in a harsh January 1916 winter, an obituary in *The Scholastic* read, "Just as Father Sorin and Father Walsh and Father Granger and Father Corby stand large and apart, so too, Sister Aloysius will hold her own chosen place in the gallery of Notre Dame's great ones forever and ever." The sentiment is as touching as it is ironic.

—CAROL SCHAAL '91[1]

NO WAY OF service is the only way or even the absolutely best way. You are not called to be Mother Teresa. You have to give you. You have to discover what the best, richest, wisest way to give yourself is in your circumstances . . . [because] the world has never had you and it does need you or God would not have made you.

—REV. MICHAEL HIMES, FORMER NOTRE DAME PROFESSOR OF
THEOLOGY NOW AT BOSTON COLLEGE

Hong Kong, December 2, 1960
Dear Father Hesburgh,
They've got me down. Flat on my back . . . with plaster, sand bags and hot water bottles. It took the last three instruments to do it however. I've contrived a way of pumping the bed up a bit so that, with a long reach, I can get to my typewriter . . . my mind . . . my brain . . . my fingers.

Two things prompt this note to you, sir. The first is that whenever my cancer acts up . . . and it is certainly "acting up" now, I turn inward a bit. Less do I think of my hospitals around the world, or of 94 doctors, fund raising and the like. More do I think of one divine Doctor, and my own personal fund of grace. Is it enough?

It has become pretty definite that the cancer has spread to the lumbar vertebrae, accounting for all the back problems over the last two months. I have monstrous phantoms . . . as all men do. But I try to exorcise them with all the fury of the middle ages. And inside and outside the wind blows.

But when the time comes, like now, then the storm around me does not matter. The winds within me do not matter. Nothing human or earthly can touch me. A wilder storm of peace gathers in my heart. What seems unpossessable, I can possess. What seems unfathomable, I fathom. What is unutterable, I utter. Because I can pray. I can communicate. How do people endure anything on earth if they cannot have God?

I realize the external symbols that surrounded one when he prays are not important. The stark wooden cross on an altar of boxes in Haiphong with a tortured priest . . . the magnificence of the Sacred Heart Bernini altar . . . they are essentially the same. Both are symbols. It is the Something Else there that counts.

But just now, and just so many times, how I long for the Grotto. Away from the Grotto, Dooley just prays. But at the Grotto, especially now when there must be snow everywhere and the lake is ice glass and that triangular fountain on the left is frozen solid and all the priests are bundled in their too-large, too-long old black coats and the students wear snow boots . . . if I could go to the Grotto now, then I think I could sing inside. I could be full of faith and poetry and loveliness and know more beauty, tenderness, and compassion. This is soggy sentimentalism, I know (old prayers from a hospital bed are just as pleasing to God as more youthful prayers from a Grotto on the lid of night).

But like telling a mother in labor, "It's okay, millions have endured the labor pains and survived happy . . . you will, too." It's consoling . . . but doesn't lessen the pain. Accordingly, knowing prayers from here are just as good as from the Grotto doesn't lessen my gnawing, yearning passion to be there.

I don't mean to ramble. Yes, I do.

The second reason I write to you just now is that I have in front of me the *Notre Dame Alumnus* of September 1960. And herein is a story. This is a Chinese hospital run by a Chinese division of Sisters of Charity (I think). Though my doctors are British, the hospital is as Chinese as Shark's Fin Soup. Every orderly, corpsman, nurse, and nun know of my work in Asia, and each has taken it upon themselves to personally "give" to the man they feel has given to their Asia. As a consequence I'm a bit smothered in tender, loving care.

With a triumphant smile this morning one of the nuns brought me some American magazines (which were limp with age and which I must hold horizontal above my head to read...) An old *National Geographic,* two older *Times,* and that unfortunate edition of *Life* . . . and with these, a copy of *Notre Dame Alumnus.* How did it ever get here?

So Father Hesburgh, Notre Dame is twice on my mind . . . and always in my heart. That Grotto is the rock to which my life is anchored. Do the students ever appreciate what they have, while they have it? I know I never did. Spent most of my time being angry at the clergy at school . . . 10 p.m. bed check, absurd for a 19-year-old veteran, etc., etc., etc.

Won't take any more of your time, did just want to communicate for a moment, and again offer my thanks to my beloved Notre Dame. Though I lack a certain buoyancy in my bones just now, I lack none in my spirit. I must return to the states very soon, and I hope to sneak into that Grotto . . . before the snow has melted.

My best wishes to the students, regards to the faculty, and respects to you.

Very sincerely,

Tom Dooley

—Dr. Thomas A. Dooley III '48 won worldwide recognition when he brought medical relief to Southeast Asians during the 1950s. He was presented with numerous humanitarian awards, including the Congressional Medal of Honor, the Legion of Merit Award, and the National Award of Vietnam, the country's highest honor bestowed upon a foreigner. He was the recipient of the first World Humanitarian Award. Dooley inspired President John F. Kennedy to establish the Peace Corps. He wrote this letter to Rev. Theodore Hesburgh six weeks before his premature death from cancer. The letter is mounted at the Grotto and is a testament to his remarkable spirit of charity and compassion.

ONE OF THE most popular holidays in America is Mother's Day. Its founder is a Notre Dame graduate and one of Notre Dame's greatest friends, Frank E. Hering. Frank was a prominent member of the Fraternal Order of Eagles and edited their national magazine. It was on February 7, 1904, that he addressed a convention of the Eagles in the English Opera House at Indianapolis. On that occasion, he chose to develop the theme that the great things of the world had been achieved by the devotion and love of mothers. It was a brilliant piece of oratory. He urged the Eagles at least to set aside one day a year for the honoring of motherhood. The young Mr. Hering probably did not suspect at the moment how that speech was to make history. In 1930, when the idea had been enthusiastically accepted by the whole nation, people began to wonder just who had started the idea. After an investigation by the War Mothers, it was discovered that Frank Hering was the first to propose such an anniversary. On Sunday, May 10, 1931, twenty-seven years after the occasion, the Order of Eagles unveiled a tablet in Indianapolis on the site of Frank Hering's address.[2]

WHEN THE FIRST-YEAR students arrive, the Sunday mass for the almost 2,000 students, plus parents, family, and friends of the new Domers, almost fills the basketball arena. I have found these moments ecstatic with happiness, albeit a bittersweet happiness. Good-bye-for-now weighs on the hearts of family members who may never before have lived apart. Hope abounds, nonetheless, and the arena could be christened the Joy Center. You can feel the love of parents for their children. They loved them and raised them through thick and thin to bring them here for this moment. They want them to learn to live their own life. They know to love them truly they must let them go. The mystery of love is always the mystery of the cross. Love requires sacrifice, sooner or later. . . . We must say goodbye to everything and everyone we love, in due time and due place. There is no joy without the cross, no eternal life with God in infinite joy without the passage of dying.

—REV. NICHOLAS AYO, C.S.C.[3]

TEXTS OF HERMAN Melville's *Billy Budd* lie spread on the table, as the students eagerly offer their opinions about the nature of goodness and depravity.

"It seems to me that Claggart was the embodiment of evil," says a student named Dennis, who refused to give his last name. Claggart is the master-at-arms in the novel who brings about his own death and the death of the title character.

Michael, another student who refused to give his last name, isn't buying the argument that the much-loved Billy Budd was a complete innocent. "People-pleasers find themselves in all kinds of trouble," he says.

The conversation bounces around the room of O'Shaughnessy Hall at the University of Notre Dame, with each of the seven men and three women students offering his or her take on the novel.

The students in this class are not the usual undergraduates. They are present and former residents of the Center for the Homeless in South Bend.

This is Great Books, a free college course started last fall for homeless center residents by Clark Power and Stephen Fallon, professors in the university's Program of Liberal Studies.

During eight-week sessions, participants read a series of assigned great works of philosophy and literature. Then they come to campus for two hours a week on Monday evenings and discuss that week's reading in a seminar-style class. A student earns one college credit for completing a session and a final written exam.

This session's reading list includes the Melville novel, Plato's *Apology of Socrates*, Shakespeare's *The Tempest*, selections from

Charles Darwin, readings from the Bible, selected poems of Wallace Stevens, and stories by such authors as Virginia Woolf and Gabriel García Márquez.

Last fall's sessions included works by Thomas Aquinas, Machiavelli, Martin Luther King, Alexis de Tocqueville, Homer, Sigmund Freud, and Frederick Douglass.

The students range in age from 20 to about 60 years old. They come from greatly varied life experiences—some have previously attended college, while others ended their formal education at high school.

Many of them have faced the challenge of substance addictions, and all have experienced the trauma of homelessness.

When planning the class, Fallon and Power encountered some skepticism from colleagues.

"People told us, 'These are difficult books. They won't be up to it,' which we didn't buy. Schools don't have a monopoly on brains," says Fallon. "I've always thought of education as a privilege, but I never thought it should be limited to the privileged."

"I love this class. It's a return to certain intellectual faculties I had forgotten I had," said Michael, a man of about 50 who moved out of the homeless center last August but shows up each week for the Great Books class.

The class focuses on large themes, such as justice and tyranny, self-discovery, or God and nature.

Billy Budd, the topic of a recent seminar, is about the tragedy of a young sailor forced into service aboard a British naval vessel in 1797.

The two professors get the discussion rolling by posing a question to the group about the reading.

The atmosphere around the table is informal, with some joking, but the students are eager to offer their comments and reflections.

Participants take the class seriously. All arrive with the material read, and sometimes reread. They often have underlined passages in their texts. . . .

The professors got the idea for the course from writings by Earl Shorris. Shorris was a student in a rigorous Great Books curriculum at the University of Chicago in the 1950s. He and others later started a Great Books course in New York City to provide education as a remedy for poverty.

Power and Fallon contacted Lou Nanni, [then] director of the Center for the Homeless and a Notre Dame graduate who majored in liberal studies. In the Program of Liberal Studies, students focus on classic writings and study them extensively in seminar-style classes.

The goal of the course is not just to expand the minds of participants, but to show them they have a stake in wider society, says Fallon. The class is designed to give a voice to the homeless and to help lead them further on their passage of self-discovery. . . .

Teaching the homeless center residents is different from teaching traditional undergraduates, says Power.

The homeless center residents "bring to the seminar life experiences our (undergraduate) students don't have," he says. "Books become a means for them to interpret their own past lives and help them look to the future."

Notre Dame students assist the program by providing transportation for participants and child care.

Each session is limited to about 15 students. There is a waiting list of center residents who hope to participate in the future. . . .

The professors have found the experience educational, as well. They discovered they enjoy rereading the great works of philosophy and literature and discussing them with adults of extensive life experience.

There are plans to expand the Great Books program . . . , recruiting other professors so several seminars can be offered simultaneously.

"This really is learning for learning's sake," says Power. "That's what they are teaching us."

—Margaret Fosmoe, '85[4]

WE SAT AT a table for two in the Oak Room, both sipping coffee while two cigarettes burned in the ash tray. When we had served meals together last year, I'd first had an inkling that Elizabeth Polonka's way of looking at Notre Dame was significantly different from most. She began with her conclusion even before I could utter a word: "I love this place, really."

There is nothing, as far as I can see, particularly appealing about dishing out eggs and bacon to disheveled, bleary-eyed, frequently gruff students at breakfast in the South Dining Hall. I hoped she could tell me what it is she sees, and even more, why Notre Dame means what it does to her.

Perhaps more than anything else, her stories about the South Dining Hall revealed a concern that students seldom realize exists. "Contact with students helps us all stay younger," she mused. "There are always those first days of school when we have to show the youngest ones how to go about serving themselves. I can always tell exactly what kind of parents each has, just by the way they treat others." And finally, "I guess I'm just lucky to have contact with all these beautiful people."

She has noticed a growing closeness between students and the staff, both in those with whom she works, and those she serves. Much of this stems from changes in the organization of the dining hall personnel. "There used to be an old-fashioned distance between them and us. But with student managers, authority is more distributed, interaction more pleasant for everyone."

A graduating senior probably summed it best when upon introducing her to his parents he said simply, "This is Elizabeth. She serves with the heart."

—FROM THE Scholastic, September 9, 1974

COLLEGE STUDENTS, BY nature, are inclined to think that they can change the world, but Notre Dame students are more inclined than most actually to try.

—KEVIN COYNE[5]

WHAT DO I hope for or ask of the class of '73? Why, only this: that using your private sources of grace, you establish absolutes of decency, gentleness, and service; and then that you live as witnesses of the truths you could die for.

—REV. ROBERT GRIFFIN, C.S.C.

I DON'T CONSIDER myself a typical Notre Dame graduate. I don't wear a class ring and I don't own a Fightin' Irish hat.

When I talk about the school, I never say stuff like "We need a better kicker" or "We should throw more to the tight end."

But try as you might, if you live on that campus, you often come to think of football players as heroes.

The guy from the *Rudy* movie, after all, was in my graduating class.

While I was a student, the football team won one national championship, in 1973. The year after I graduated, the Irish won another, in 1977.

Some refer to the 1970s as part of Notre Dame's glory years. I would agree.

It was a special time in a different way, too, because of guys like Al Sondej.

Al was a tall, muscular fellow, who stood outside the North Dining Hall every day with a milk jug, as I recall, asking students for spare change.

At first, he seemed creepy. It didn't look right for a student at a private university to be panhandling.

And for the first few weeks, we freshmen all would avoid him. We would use a different entrance, sneak out a different exit.

It took us a while to realize Big Al wasn't going to go away.

If you plunked a couple dimes into his jug, he would thank you. If you just walked by, he would nod anyway.

If you asked, and some people did, he would tell you he was raising money for Third World hunger relief.

By the time he graduated in 1974, he had raised $25,000, a dime here and a quarter there.

He also had told thousands of young men and women at this white, Catholic, upper-middle-class school about starving people with different skin colors, with different religious beliefs, on different continents.

I've thought about Al a lot during the past 30 years.

One of the bad things about graduating from college is that you lose touch with almost everyone you know.

You're lucky if you keep track of a roommate, a few friends, and maybe a professor or two.

Another bad thing that happens is that we lose touch with our dreams.

A lot of the guys who seemed interested in the big issues, like world hunger and social justice, end up in an office somewhere cutting million-dollar deals for people who already have plenty.

A lot of us who wore the peace patch in the '70s haven't said boo about Iraq or Afghanistan.

We still see the shriveled bodies on TV, so I knew Al hadn't solved world hunger.

No one would have had a right to complain if he had settled into a comfortable middle age. Maybe he ended up with one of those nice desk jobs, a house in Granger, an SUV, and a wad of credit card debt.

Through the wonders of technology, it wasn't that hard to find out.

I typed "Al Sondej Notre Dame" into the Search bracket of Google.com. Within seconds, I had my answer.

In the years soon after Notre Dame, Al continued working on some world hunger projects before returning to Hyattsville, Md.

There, he enrolled in a graduate program in geography. He worked on those studies part time for more than a decade while living at the Hyattsville Fire Department station house, where he volunteered.

Friends and colleagues had very nice things to say about his wit and intelligence and his genuine care for others in need.

All this was in a newspaper article, dated March 21, 1988, with the headline, "Student dies of burns sustained attempting rescue."

About two months before Al died, there was a fire. Al was told that people were trapped inside.

While he was inside searching for them, the blaze spread to the room he was in, setting his clothes on fire. He died because of complications from those burns.

It's sad, but it doesn't surprise me that Al died while trying to save someone else.

One thing I've learned over the years is that we're not all meant to be heroes.

Society would stop in its tracks if most of us didn't do our jobs, buy our cars, and raise our kids.

But I also know that when my old dorm pals and I get together, we've talked about dozens of Notre Dame quarterbacks, good and bad.

We've never spoken of Al Sondej. No one's made a movie about him.

Someday, for Christmas, I might get myself a class ring or a Notre Dame hat.

But first, I hope to have the courage to carry a milk jug.

—KEN BRADFORD '76[6]

AL SONDEJ '74 WAS A LEGENDARY PRESENCE ON CAMPUS,
NOT AS A FOOTBALL PLAYER OR STAR ATHLETE, THOUGH HE WAS BUILT
LIKE ONE, BUT AS A FUND-RAISER FOR CAUSES LIKE HUNGER RELIEF.
FATHER HESBURGH WAS SO TAKEN WITH AL'S DEDICATION AND IDEALISM
THAT HE SPONSORED AL ON A TRIP TO BANGLADESH TO WORK DIRECTLY
WITH PEOPLE HE HAD HELPED THROUGH DONATIONS FROM AFAR.
TWO YEARS AFTER HIS UNTIMELY DEATH IN 1988, THE NOTRE DAME
ALUMNI ASSOCIATION'S 85,000 MEMBERS HONORED AL SONDEJ FOR
HIS EFFORTS BY PRESENTING HIS FAMILY WITH THE DR. THOMAS
DOOLEY AWARD. THE RECIPIENT OF THE AWARD IS SOMEONE WHO
WORKS TO ALLOW OTHERS TO HAVE THE GIFT OF LIFE.

AS A STUDENT at Notre Dame, I was surrounded by others who were dedicated to community service, and I constantly heard stories from Notre Dame students and professors who had done international service abroad. These stories not only encouraged me to want to help others around the world, but provoked me to find answers to my questions about God.

When Notre Dame's International Summer Service Learning Program gave me the opportunity to teach in East Africa, I thought that I would find these answers. I thought that I would find answers about God, about service, and about life. I thought that spending my summer serving others, contemplating life in the middle of Africa, could propel me in a definite direction—closer to God. Now, as I leave Africa, I realize that I have not come away with these certainties. Instead, I have come away with even more questions.

As I board the Akamba bus this afternoon, making my final journey before returning from Africa to the U.S., I feel a rush of emotion. I know that I will miss each and every child that I have taught for the past two months. I know that I will miss the brothers and priests that I lived with, the teachers that I taught with, and the many friends that I made here in Uganda. I will miss all of them. During my time here, these people have shared their lives with me, showing me true love. The closest that I came to an answer here in Uganda was through these people. I am now certain that we express God's love through our relationships. In the end, the rules and regulations of religion fade away, and we are judged by how we have impacted the lives of others. The loving care and attention that people showed me here while I both taught and learned was exceptional.

My times of joy and times of pain here in Africa were only significant because of these people. While I think that I have impacted their lives positively over the past two months, I realize that my response will be even more important. I will find my answers in the changes that I can make when I return to America in the days to come. When I return, I have many decisions to make. Coming to

Africa, I felt young and free. As I return home, I feel the weight of responsibility on my shoulders. Now I hold myself accountable to live life in light of my recent experience in Africa, while leading others to do the same. As a student at Notre Dame, I know that I will have help along the way.

—FROM THE JOURNAL OF MICHAEL SWEIKAR '03, WHO PARTICIPATED IN NOTRE DAME'S INTERNATIONAL SUMMER SERVICE LEARNING PROGRAM

WHEN, TEN YEARS ago, Jill and I turned our fifteen acres into a place where children could come from the inner-city neighborhoods of South Bend and, sometimes, the public housing projects of Chicago, it was as a response to a number of things. Children at risk in the neighborhoods where they live need a safe and nurturing place to play, to be children. Grace, when it calls you, demands an answer. So does Alex Kotlowitz's book *There Are No Children Here*. The students in my Core Course at Notre Dame let the book sear their souls, and when they discussed it in class, concluded with a question: "What can I/we do about it?" The need, the grace, and the students somehow combined to cause a radical transformation in many lives, including our own. From private donors to local trust funds, to charitable organizations as far away as New Hampshire, California, and Maryland, funds came to support an inspiration, to make it real. Father Warner, Director of Campus Ministry at Notre Dame, helped immediately. But it was Notre Dame students who took on the challenge without flinching.

One of my Core students, Tony McCanta of Zahm Hall, was the first of a succession of student leaders who made the camp and its mission their own. His successor, Paul Nebosky, was named Notre Dame Volunteer of the Year for his work at TACH.

On the flagpole down the right-field line of the baseball field we built, a large flag emblazoned with a red Z pays tribute to the men of Zahm. Their stereotyped reputation as free-spirited is belied by the wondrous commitment, perseverance, and awesome care for the children who come to TACH five days a week from local agencies. To be sure, we celebrate the volunteers from Circle K, Farley, PE, Cavanaugh, Stanford, BP, and elsewhere, but it is Zahm men who coordinate the volunteers, find creative ways to raise money for food and supplies, and who make the daily trek, a half an hour each way, in the club wagon van donated to TACH by a Notre Dame graduate and trustee, John Jordan. To the hundreds and hundreds of Notre Dame students who have bicycled through the nine acres of woods, or played baseball, volleyball, basketball with the children, or joined them in the clubhouse for art and games, the theater building for an impromptu talent show, or the sandbox with shovels and imagination, you embody the spirit of Notre Dame. The children may not all know your names. But God and His Mother, Notre Dame, surely do.

You have seen and sensed how much these children cherish their time with you. You have heard some of their stories, and I have seen tears well up in your eyes as you try to retell them. Abuse and neglect, fear and anger should not be the daily bread of childhood.

And I know that sometimes you feel like throwing stones toward heaven as if to awaken God, demanding to know how God could let these things happen to children. But to ask the question is to risk having the same question asked of us. In our own way, playing with the children, teaching by example, affirming their smiles and talents, being available to them, we are the hands and the heart of the body of Christ on earth. Someone told me once that what we do is nice, but it is only a bandage, not a systemic cure. I responded that if you're bleeding, a bandage comes first; the systemic cure comes later.

I have watched you, sons and daughters of Notre Dame, over these ten years with more awe and inspiration than I could ever express to you. I have seen you work minor miracles, seen your love and goodness bring grace in the form of smiles and lessons and change in attitude to these children, so hungry for the presence you bring them.

Some of you actually changed your majors because of your experience at TACH. And you never had to secularize your motivation as you told others about it. One of you applied to the Harvard Law School by saying that he is a believing Roman Catholic and that this is what led him to TACH. His application recounted an experience that moves me still:

I don't cry much. It's not that I don't feel deeply or that I'm insensitive. Actually, most who are close to me would probably say the opposite is true. Maybe it's because I'm an ex-football player or because events over the years have upped the emotional quota that has to be reached before tears can fall. I just don't tend to cry a lot. But one April night during my junior year at Notre Dame, I wept.

While at Notre Dame I was privileged to work with at-risk kids at a wonderful place called There Are Children Here. This proved to be the source of some of my most amazing experiences at Notre Dame. One weekend, I was given the opportunity to work with kids from the projects in Chicago. Although I had already spent time with children from comparable situations in South Bend, I was not prepared emotionally for the experience. One little girl in particular stole my heart. Her name was Toni. She was a fifth-grader from a single parent family. She loved basketball, worked very hard in school, and had inquiring brown eyes. I remember hiding with her during a round of night-time "hide and seek." We had a chance to talk and look at the stars. I was inspired by her words and sweet disposition, her positive attitude and strength of character. You couldn't help but love her.

Later, I couldn't help wondering how many of these children would break out of their troubled circumstances.

As a volunteer at TACH, you hope they all will. Toni enlarged this hope. More than ever before I really wanted a kid to get a chance, to make it.

Toni cried when she said goodbye; she forced a smile through her tears and boarded a van back to Chicago. I was left standing there feeling overwhelmed. Later, in my room, I finally let go. It was then that I cried.

I consoled myself that someday I could do more about all of this. How could life ever change for kids like Toni? Maybe it was a lost cause. I refuse to believe that. I want to right the wrongs. I want to effect change. I want my life to make a difference.

Others have written to say that, in retrospect, TACH was the best part of their Notre Dame education. If so, it is only because you made it so. You are the ones who grew in both mind and heart at Notre Dame and who brought the gifts of intelligence and grace with you from campus to TACH. Our graduated volunteers are now doctors, lawyers, teachers, computer experts, professional athletes, community activists, social workers, and budding scholars. William James once wrote that "the greatest use in life is spending yourself in something that will outlast you." How wonderful it is that by the time you leave Notre Dame you have already done that!

IN LOVING GRATITUDE,
JIM LANGFORD

To whom much has been given, much is expected . . .

Having attended Notre Dame in the mid-eighties, I witnessed the continued infusion of female students within each freshman class, resulting in a 70/30 male-to-female ratio. While the campus was slowly transitioning to an equal-ratio environment, it remained a male-dominated campus. Despite the odds, I was fortunate enough to ultimately meet and grow in love with my best friend, Julie, while at Notre Dame. We were engaged at the Grotto and married at Sacred Heart Basilica. Together we embraced our alma mater and made it the cornerstone of our lives. No matter where we would end up in life, Notre Dame became a place we fondly called "home." We became active in two local alumni clubs in northeast Pennsylvania because we wanted to bring what we experienced at Notre Dame to others. Both clubs were relatively small in size but were built around a cadre of very special alumni and friends. The clubs diligently supported Notre Dame's mission but often struggled with limited alumni and/or resources. As club leaders, we continually sought ways to combine the available resources of both clubs to increase overall program awareness, participation, and support.

Nearly 80 percent of Notre Dame students regularly engage in community service during their undergraduate years. It should be no surprise that our alumni constituents conduct themselves similarly. In 1990, the Alumni Association officially established its Community Service Program, to assist members of the Notre Dame family in serving the global community.

In 1991, Julie and I initiated discussions with local hospital personnel to identify potential service opportunities for the two alumni clubs. Our discussions ultimately led us to Family House, a drug and alcohol recovery center for women with children. The agency, located in Allentown, offered women plagued with serious addictions an opportunity to rebuild their lives. It was an intense six-month program that provided the necessary hope and support for these recovering addicts but demanded much in return. Most of the Family House guests had little or no domestic skills. Many lived their lives on the streets, supporting their addictions through prostitution. For some residents, Family House represented their last chance to avoid an extensive sentence in prison or, even worse, a life back on the streets.

Since the concept of organized alumni service was still in its infancy during the early nineties, we decided to build our local programs around the existing strength of our student-led efforts back at Notre Dame. Working closely with Sue Cunningham, the director of Summer Service Programs (SSP) at the Center for Social Concerns, we introduced Notre Dame to Family House in the summer of 1992 with the inaugural SSP.

The SSP is an eight-week internship for Notre Dame students who devote their summer vacations to serving others in need. Local alumni clubs provide the necessary housing and transportation, along with scholarship support in exchange for the students' service. For the pilot program Julie and I offered to host our incoming student, a nineteen-year-old sophomore named Crissy, for the entire eight-week period. We instantly transitioned from (nearly) newlyweds with no children to "adoptive parents" with a teenage daughter that summer! Our new daughter taught us much, including just how important a role the alumni play in supporting the students during their internship!

In 1999, I was privileged to be elected onto the governing board of directors for the Alumni Association. The position offered greater exposure and governance of fifteen clubs within my region, while affording personal access to the dedicated people, programs, and departments that truly make Notre Dame such a special place. Within a year, I was presented with a life-changing opportunity that would affect both career and family—the opportunity to return to Notre Dame and work for the very place that had long served as the foundation of our lives. I accepted a position as the director for alumni service programs within the Alumni Association.

You often hear prospective students, families, and visitors explain that "special feeling" that seems to overwhelm them when they step onto the Notre Dame campus for the first time. It is affectionately called "the spirit of Our Lady—the spirit of Notre Dame," and it manifests itself in any number of ways. For some it resides in the ghosts and legends of our storied athletic programs or in the roar of the crowds on a Saturday afternoon during the fall football season.

For others the feelings emerge from the peaceful solitude experienced amid prayerful silence at the Grotto. Whatever its source, for many it is this welcoming spirit that sets our beloved university apart from the others. I personally like to think the spirit emerges out of the sense of "family" experienced by all who tread upon our ground. It us through this family that Our Lady's call to service manifests itself—through the actions of her students, alumni, and friends that give back to their communities in special ways.

Since my return to Notre Dame I have witnessed the continued joy of giving in the smiles and friendly embraces of those who have served, or in turn have been served by, our alumni efforts. The expanded arena now draws upon the lessons learned from earlier days to better assist alumni efforts throughout the world. I am continually inspired by the outpouring of care and love by members of the Notre Dame family within the global community. In each new case, the lessons learned remain similar, the lives of both the givers and receivers equally touched.

—SEAN P. O'BRIEN '86 MAINTAINS HIS ARCHITECTURAL LICENSE
WHILE CURRENTLY SERVING AS THE DIRECTOR OF NOTRE DAME'S
ALUMNI COMMUNITY SERVICE PROGRAMS. JULIE O'BRIEN '86
WORKS FROM THEIR INDIANA HOME AS AN ENVIRONMENTAL ENGINEER.
TOGETHER THEY ARE RAISING TWO CHILDREN, WHO THEY HOPE WILL
ONE DAY ATTEND THE UNIVERSITY OF NOTRE DAME. IN 1993,
SEAN AND JULIE WERE HONORED BY THE ALUMNI ASSOCIATION
WITH THE DR. THOMAS A. DOOLEY AWARD FOR
OUTSTANDING HUMANITARIAN SERVICE.

I CAME TO Notre Dame in 1964 on a football scholarship for Ara's first recruiting class. I graduated in 1968 and stayed for another year and got a master's of arts in teaching in 1969. While there are great memories of those years and of so many wonderful people, it's my experience of the University since moving back to South Bend, living in the community and working at LOGAN Center, that has given me a new perspective.

For me the spirit of Notre Dame is seen in the students, faculty, staff, and alumni who take to heart the Notre Dame message of service to others, caring about and feeling responsible to support our brothers and sisters in need. For over thirty-two years there has been an organized group of Notre Dame and St. Mary's students, at a rate of over a hundred a year, who volunteer in individual and group activities through LOGAN. The impact on the people we serve and on the students is too large to calculate, but it is truly enormous. And LOGAN is just one of many community organizations here in South Bend and around the country that benefit from the results of the Notre Dame spirit of service.

With the students in the lead, followed by the faculty, staff, and alumni, these Notre Dame People put the spirit of the message into action. As valuable as teaching, research, and striving to excel in athletics all are, the spirit of Notre Dame is service.

—Dan Harshman, Chief Executive Officer, LOGAN, Resources
and Opportunities for People with Disabilities

How is God better glorified than by intelligent and devoted service to others in the line of our chosen life's work. Neither God nor mankind is well served by mediocrity.

—Rev. Theodore M. Hesburgh, C.S.C.

INTERLUDE

NOTRE DAME'S SECOND FOUNDER:
REV. THEODORE M. HESBURGH, C.S.C.

WHEN THE DEFINITIVE history of Notre Dame, indeed of the American Catholic Church, is written, the name of Reverend Theodore Martin Hesburgh, C.S.C., will be front and center. This handsome, vital, tireless standard-bearer of moral values and human dignity has, for more than fifty years in public life, earned the respect and admiration of presidents and popes, educators and policy makers, students and strangers.

Named president of Notre Dame in 1952 at the age of thirty-five, Father Ted quickly let it be known that his dream for Notre Dame was inspired by a desire to make this small university into a place where truth would thrive, where excellence would always be the goal, and where zeal for justice on the part of the institution and its graduates would translate into real and effective influence in the world.

Shortly after he became president of Notre Dame, Father Ted was interviewed for an article in *Time* magazine. The writer asked him to pose for a picture holding a football. He declined. It wasn't that he didn't enjoy football, or the excellence of Notre Dame's tradition on the gridiron. It was that Notre Dame was much more than Saturdays and a stadium. And under his leadership and impetus, it would ever be more and more than that. Father Ted was not uninterested in athletics; not long ago, in fact, he served as co-chair of the Knight Commission on Intercollegiate Athletics, which produced a sweeping reform agenda for college sports. But he was never a one-dimensional person, and no one endeavor would be able to define or delimit the university he headed.

The same qualities of character, studiousness, and priestly belief in the cause of a better world that singled him out for the presidency of Notre Dame also brought him to the attention of leaders in the Church, higher education, and government. Although a man of clear convictions, he was able to get along with those holding differing views. Still, it was not hard to know what he stood for, and what he wouldn't stand for.

Father Ted earned an international reputation as a hardworking, fair-minded, and deeply committed person, both human and humane. It will take historians years of research and reflection to uncover the expanse and extent of his remarkable contributions to his church, university, country, and the world. The facts are well known: Father Ted has held fifteen appointments from presidents of the United States involving such crucial matters as civil rights, atomic energy, Third World development, immigration, and post-Vietnam reconciliation. What is important is that whatever and wherever he served, he always did so as a priest. When the great French Dominican preacher Lacordaire celebrated the ideal of the priesthood at Notre Dame Cathedral in Paris more than a century ago by saying that the priest "is a member of every family, yet belonging to none," he might have been writing an encomium for Father Ted. *Priest* is how he defines himself:

If there is any center in my life, anything that is inseparable from my identity, it is my priesthood. That is the ground of my being. In the midst of a busy schedule, almost incessant study and preparation for commission meetings, flights, phone calls, talks, and similar responsibilities, it would have been easy—and perhaps forgivable—to omit the daily recitation of the divine office prayers or the celebration of the Mass. But I don't think I ever willingly missed praying the office, and with only two or three exceptions, I celebrated Mass every day. Steadfastness of devotions every day makes one mindful that no matter what pressures or deliberations have to be faced, they have behind them a will and care firmly rooted in the love of God and humankind, and a commitment that comes from deep within one's own identity.[1]

Father Ted estimated not long ago that he had logged nearly 20 million miles as he brought Catholic thought and Notre Dame to every corner of the earth. He was presented with the Presidential Medal of Freedom in 1964 and the Congressional Gold Medal in 2000. The fact that he has been awarded 150 honorary degrees by institutions of higher education, the most ever awarded to an American, attests to the respect and admiration he has earned. He said recently, "Faith has always been the lens through which I focused on what I saw, what I wished for and worked for, whether as a member of some high-powered commission or in a simple encounter with a campesino family in rural Chile."[2]

That faith was nurtured during his student days at Notre Dame and in his thirty-five years as its president. Even a visionary like Father Sorin could not have foreseen the heights the University would reach under Father Hesburgh's leadership. Under Father Ted's direction, Notre Dame has grown into the premier Catholic university in the world, a qualitative growth that merits Father Ted's being described as "Notre Dame's second founder." His signature is on more than 75,000 Notre Dame diplomas, his influence on many more students than that. He was never too busy to greet a group of students who, seeing the light on in his office late at night, would bypass the locked doors of the Main Building and climb the fire escape to his office on the third floor. They would come there to talk about their problems and hopes. He was there for them.

Father Ted said once, "My basic principle is that you don't make decisions because they are easy; you don't make them because they are cheap; you don't make them because they are popular; you make them because they are right." With that, Father Sorin would have agreed. Cloaked by Mary's mantle, Sorin, the visionary, sometimes maverick, is on one side; Hesburgh, the visionary, diplomat, is on the other. Both priests. Both dreamers and doers.

Father Hesburgh's is the kind of knowledge that feeds constantly on ideas, interaction, and experience. It comes from books and from our own story and the story of others. This kind of learning never ends, even when it crosses the point where fact and experience, hypotheses and dreams, certainty and doubt, possibilities and probabilities fuse together in what can truly be called wisdom. Wisdom does not come from knowledge only. Its other parent is love. And its gift is action in a common cause much larger than self. That sounds like our own Father Theodore Hesburgh. His mark is on this campus, this country, and this world: God, Country, Notre Dame, and beyond.

—JIM LANGFORD

COMMUNITY

*For those nurtured on its campus and proud of its tradition and
spirit, Notre Dame evokes a sense of family. Whatever one's origins
or time of matriculation or employment, there is a bond that links
the generations and makes them comfortable with the symbols,
sites, and songs of the place.*

—REV. EDWARD A. MALLOY, C.S.C.[1]

FROM THE SMALL band of brothers who helped Father Sorin
launch this place, to its present status as the largest employer in
the area, community has always been essential to Notre Dame's definition. The one-word description or metaphor that stands for the
bond formed by Notre Dame's embrace of its people has always been
"family."

You see it and feel it on campus, from friendly hellos on the side-
walks to campuswide concern for a Domer facing serious illness. And
you see it in the 248 local alumni clubs around the world, each of
which undertakes projects to help others in their own communities,
and many of which provide scholarships so that local students can
attend Notre Dame. The Notre Dame Alumni Association sponsors
continuing education, summer volunteer camps, working with Habi-
tat for Humanity, and a network where Domers offer assistance to
brothers and sisters in the family. This community is a family based
not in genes but in concern and care, love and support, respect and
responsibility. As in every family, there are dysfunctions at times, disagreements, and even discord. Somehow, the family stays close-knit;
weakness and failure are cared for and carried by the stronger. Notre
Dame is our Mother. To be part of this place is to belong to a family
where everybody knows her name.

The Athletic Department uses "No Place Like Notre Dame" as
its slogan on all the publications it issues. Game programs, media

guides, pocket schedules, and letterheads all have it emblazoned upon them. It certainly catches the eye as well as the heart.

⌒

I always wondered about the pull this University of Our Lady has on people. It is especially noticeable the first week in June when graduates return for their reunion. The men from the fifty-year-and-above group often come back early. The reunion officially begins Friday and ends Sunday, but these men arrive Wednesday and leave Tuesday.

You see them walking the Main Quad with a very patient spouse in tow. They are wearing their reunion baseball caps perched at a jaunty angle atop their heads. The style is reminiscent of the campaign hats they wore during World War II. You could easily picture them in the caps of their branch of service.

These men visit the Administration Building, Sacred Heart, and the Grotto. They go to their old residence halls and eat in South Dining Hall. They make these visits often during their stay, including one grand "last look" before going home.

As he neared graduation, a student once wrote home to his mom how much he was going to miss this place. He found it hard to believe that his time here was coming to an end. He mused in ink that if he could stretch out his education another six or seven years, he would gladly do so because he loved this place so much!

That lad was Neal Gillespie, and he wrote in the early 1850s.

Notre Dame was just a few small buildings then, with swampy ground surrounded by henhouses, outhouses, pigsties, and cow sheds. At best the food was bad and the water worse. Yet somehow this place had a grip on his heart and he could not shake it. Mr. Gillespie later returned to Notre Dame and became the first graduate to be ordained a Holy Cross priest. His sister came also. She was to become Mother Angela Gillespie of St. Mary's College.

In June of 1961, when I was a nine-year-old third-grader, I came to Notre Dame for the first time—for the ordination of my cousin,

Tom Chambers, as a Holy Cross priest in Sacred Heart Church. I fell in love with the place.

As we were leaving Sunday morning, I tried to pull one of those whiny-kid routines. My dad would have none of it. He grabbed me by the arm and said, "Do you want something to cry about?" I got the message and sat in the car.

I knew I would be back. Nine years and two months later, in August of 1970, I came back as a freshman. Basically, I have been here ever since.

Some friends of mine from the far southern end of Indiana brought their son to campus for the first time. This lad was genetically predisposed to be a Domer, no doubt about it. On both sides of the family tree, Notre Dame and St. Mary's branches abound. Household talk contained many references to the campus.

As they pulled up to the Main Circle by the Law School on a football Friday in September, the car was barely turned off before junior was out the back door running on the lawn. Wearing a blue Notre Dame football jersey, he tossed his NERF football up in the air, caught it, ran, tackled himself, and in a matter of minutes was covered in grass stains and sweat.

His mom said, "Christopher, calm down. You have the whole weekend!" He responded passionately, "Mom, I've waited my whole life for this." Chris was just a bit shy of his third birthday.

While catching an early-morning breakfast in New Orleans before flying home, I had an insight into why Notre Dame has such a hold on so many of us.

"Mothers" is an old eatery above the French Quarter. It is a cafeteria where you order at the counter and they bring you your meal. An elderly lady with a beaming smile looked at me and took my order. With that wonderful New Orleans accent, she asked me, "Do you want grits or do you want biscuits?" Because her front teeth were someplace else, it sounded like, "Do you want grithhs or do you want bithhcuithhs?"

As she asked the question, her smile grew bigger and her eyes brighter. Even though she may ask that question of many patrons every morning, she was intent and really interested in what I wanted. I responded by saying, "Ma'am, can I just stand here and listen to you talk?" She giggled and said, "Oh, honey, you something else." I ordered biscuits.

Watching while I ate, I saw that each person who came to her got the same smile and intent look. It was very early on a Monday morning. People came into that place looking tired and grumpy. Those fortunate enough to place their orders with her came away with a smile.

It dawned on me that she was not just feeding people. This lady was doing much more than that. She was nourishing them.

That is what makes Notre Dame such a different kind of place. Those fortunate enough to come here are not merely fed, they are nourished. Mentally, physically, emotionally, and spiritually we are nourished. The totality of one's personhood is attended to here. Few places in this world do that.

This to me is the essence of the Notre Dame Spirit. It is not athletics or the greatest fight song ever written. It is the nourishment received that keeps us coming back. We fill our tanks when we visit so we can leave refreshed, renewed, and recharged.

Father Charles Carey, C.S.C., died in 1998. He was a priest for more than sixty years, all of them at Notre Dame. He was asked once why he never lived at any other place. He responded, "I came here to the high school seminary in 1922 when I was fourteen years old. Why would I ever want to leave?"

No place like Notre Dame.

—REV. WILLIAM SEETCH, C.S.C.,
RELIGIOUS SUPERIOR, CORBY HALL RESIDENCE

FROM 1849 UNTIL the magnificent South Dining Hall was built in 1927, the daily meals for all Notre Dame students were prepared by Holy Cross brothers and sisters in a two-story building just northwest of the Main Building. Under the direction of Brother Willibrord, a team of bakers produced more than 300 loaves of bread and more than 3,000 each of buns and cookies daily. The "Notre Dame buns" were famous among the students, who said they were delicious the first day, good the second, and ideal for building material the third. Also beloved by students were the sisters—like Martha, Lourdes, and Bertina—who prepared meals with love and delighted in making fresh pies and pastries for the young men in their care. Truly a community effort, meals in the early days were prepared from start to finish without the aid of appliances and had to be made fresh each day because there was no refrigeration. The dining halls have carried on the community spirit through the hard work of those who prepare the food and the table fellowship enjoyed by the students.

I DON'T KNOW to this day why I chose Notre Dame. I just thought I'd like to go there, and that was all right with my father. I'm delighted Notre Dame accepted me. I love the place.

—EDWIN O'CONNOR '39, AUTHOR OF *THE EDGE OF SADNESS* AND
THE LAST HURRAH

SINCE THE DAY an exultant Sorin and his friends placed their vision and their swath of frozen Indiana wilderness under the protection of Our Lady, Notre Dame, whether thought of as a university, a place, a gathering of generations, or all three of these things, has been the beneficiary of what Professor Edward Fischer called "a long-descending blessing." Beginning that day, Notre Dame has played an irreplaceable role in the affairs of the Church, nation, and world. It has often been a glorious role, ample with heroism. One thinks of the courage and compassion of Father William Corby's ministry amid the carnage of Gettysburg; the unyielding intellectual integrity of Fathers John Zahm and Julius Nieuwland; Knute Rockne's inspirational exuberance; Dr. Tom Dooley's single-hearted devotion to the poor of Southeast Asia and his cheerfully accepted death. . . .

The paradox at the center of its community had made Notre Dame, during its finest moments, a place of peculiarly Catholic hospitality to which any soul open and honest enough could fairly lay claim. G. K. Chesterton noticed and spoke about this years ago. On his first visit to America, Chesterton said, he had been struck by the country's enormity and distance from what was familiar and dear to him. "I did not feel like that at all when I came to America the second time," he told the Notre Dame students he had come to teach. "If you want to know why I felt different, the reason is in the name of your University. That name was quite sufficient as far as I was concerned. It would not have mattered if it had been in the mountains of the moon. Where she has erected her pillars, all men are at home, and I know that I should not find strangers."

—Michael Garvey '74, Assistant Director,
News and Information, Notre Dame[2]

DEAR MR. EDITOR:
You can scarcely realize how anxiously an old student like myself looks for the mail that is expected to bring the SCHOLASTIC. I shall long regret that I was not aware of its existence, until last "Commencement day," had I been, I would, most assuredly have had it since the day it was christened. Suffice to state, that the moment I saw its pretty *form* and well filled *corpus*, I became a life subscriber, and now feel more than half tempted to become a "life contributor,"—*permissu Editorum-orum,* of course.

Could you not, Mr Editor, devise some plan to induce a few more of the old students, who reside *extra muros Col-*

legii, to take *one* or *both* of the aforegoing resolutions, at the beginning of the present year. Every old student, worthy of the name, must feel a certain interest in all, or much of what transpires within the hollowed precincts of his *Alma Mater* and in the adventures, *per mare, per terras* of those, with whom, in days of yore, he shared the joys and sorrows of College life.

Professors, tutors, prefects, brothers, one and all, together with the Seniors, Juniors, aye, and the little Minims too, will be only too glad to hear through the SCHOLASTIC, of our wanderings and ponderings, and out o' the way loiterings on the world's high-way.

Come, rouse ye! ye old fogies who anxiously wait for each coming number of the SCHOLASTIC and who never dream of penning a line for it; let us hear of your whereabouts! Heretofore your communications, with one or two exceptions, have appeared *rari nantes in gurgite vasto.* It is high time to make up for past carelessness—to repair the broken links of "friendship's chain." Where are you? What doing? How have you been treated by Madame Fortune, since last you supped with us on "College Commons"?

—LETTER TO THE EDITOR FROM SYRACUSE, NEW YORK,
PUBLISHED IN THE *SCHOLASTIC*, JANUARY 14, 1871

IF WE, YOUNG and old, can agree on those basic values that make human life worth living, then perhaps we can pool our efforts to redeem the time. It still won't be easy, but it can be done.

—REV. THEODORE M. HESBURGH, C.S.C.

WOMEN STUDENTS HAD studied at Notre Dame since 1918, the year female religious were admitted to the summer advanced-studies program. Women were able to enroll in the graduate school from its beginning in 1932, and occasionally a laywoman had been allowed to study for her bachelor's degree. Essentially, though, the University named for the Mother of God remained a male bastion for 130 years. Following the social upheavals of the 1960s, that changed.

Unsuccessful attempts had been made in the early '60s to convince several Midwestern Catholic women's colleges, including Barat College in Lake Forest, Illinois, and Rosary College in River Forest, Illinois, to relocate to Notre Dame. Then university officials turned to their neighbors across the road at Saint Mary's College. In 1965 a Co-Exchange program was started: Notre Dame students could attend classes for credit at Saint Mary's and vice versa. By 1970, a merger seemed likely. Sister Alma Peter, C.S.C., acting president of Saint Mary's and that school's liaison for the merger plan, was made a vice president in the Notre Dame administrative table in anticipation of the merger. . . .

But the merger was not to be. In the end, the crucial issue became one of identity: In the joining of the institutions, it was obvious that the smaller of the two, Saint Mary's, had the most to lose. . . .

In November 1971, the two institutions called off the wedding. At the same time, Notre Dame officials announced a plan to admit a limited number of women undergraduates for the next academic year. The following fall, the first 325 female undergraduates—the majority of them transfer students—began classes at Notre Dame.

With co-education, Notre Dame was able to double its pool of applicants and thus raise admission standards even higher than they already were. The move upgraded the academic environment and improved the overall quality of student life. The ratio of women to men students gradually was decreased. . . .

"It was more a symbolic thing," Father Hesburgh later said. "It raised the quality of students and of student life. The roughness that comes with an all-male campus is gone."

—MARGARET FOSMOE '85[3]

NOTRE DAME IS a place, a sequence in time, an immediate living fact all wrapped round with people.

—PROFESSOR RICHARD SULLIVAN

I NEVER TIRE of this campus so full of familiar things and the recurring cycles of the academic year. In a world that has grown more chaotic since Father Sorin's time, Notre Dame retains its freshness because, for the most part, it has kept its tranquility. Visitors are impressed with the serenity they sense here. It is a tranquility that comes in part from the design of the campus; as I said earlier, in moving from one quad to another, an ordered arrangement always meets the eye.

Notre Dame has always had a reverence for trees. No tree is cut down unless it is so diseased that nothing else can be done with it. Three oaks and a crabapple were in the way when the Snite Museum of Art was begun, and so a professional was brought in to move them with great care to the back of the arts and letters building. When the library, fourteen stories tall, rose on old Cartier Field it looked severe, sitting there in the wide open space of a football field with no transition between it and the ground. By planting around it dozens of large trees, called "instant forest," and a multitude of shrubs and ground cover, the severity was replaced by a softening effect. And with those plantings, the serenity spread eastward across the campus.

These acres reflect different moods, depending on the time of day and the season of the year. On a cool, sweet morning in early June there is nothing in the world more lovely. On an October afternoon, with the lake reflecting bright colors and the Dome shimmering in the Indian summer sun, the whole world hums with contentment. When an August night is filled with the whir of crickets and cicadas, it hints of autumn and of time running out.

Without care all loveliness turns shabby. Visitors here comment on how well kept everything is. Thanks to twenty-two groundskeep-

ers and 253 housekeepers, its well-keptness contributes to the aura
of calm.

—PROFESSOR EDWARD FISCHER[4]

THE FOUNDATIONAL LOVE for thousands of families, religious
vows, and forms of self-giving more difficult to categorize has been
received or discovered during strolls around the lakes.

—MICHAEL GARVEY

WHEN PEOPLE COME back here and say, "You have the same size
student body. How come there have been so many buildings constructed?" I answer, "It wasn't for any frivolous purpose but because
we are trying to provide an environment for faculty, students, and
staff that is first-class, and a beautiful campus that can be a delightful place to live and work, where the accoutrements, the natural
environment, and the relationship between one building and another
all fit the kind of institution we are."

—REV. EDWARD A. MALLOY, C.S.C., FROM HIS EIGHTEENTH AND FINAL
ANNUAL ADDRESS TO THE FACULTY, OCTOBER 5, 2004

BY THIS POINT, your minivans and SUVs are unloaded, you've
seen the movie *Rudy* and perhaps the theme song is still lingering in
your subconscious. Class of 2007, you probably never imagined
you'd be woken up this early on a Saturday morning while in college,
let alone we'd have you singing such a diverse number of cheesy
dorm songs. Yes! It does feels like summer camp . . . and parents,
you're probably still praying that if your son is living in Zahm Hall it
will be the best four years of his life—not the best seven years.

When I recall my initial moments as a first-year student, I am
flooded with a multitude of emotions: excitement . . . anxiety . . . fear

. . . anticipation . . . readiness. I was initially overwhelmed to see the small army of Badin Hall women all outfitted in the same dorm paraphernalia. They were eagerly awaiting my arrival—energized to carry all my clothes, the refrigerator, even the futon—up four flights of stairs to my tiny dorm room. Well, I had learned a valuable piece of information on my move-in day, which I am certain all of you are now quite aware of: The Admissions Office is not joking about the size of that dorm room. The U-Haul truck I packed to the brim was larger than the actual room I was to share with two people for the upcoming year. So on my first day of First Year Orientation, I was forced to prioritize and decide which items were to stay and which I must send home. One dorm accessory I had to eliminate was a full-length mirror.

It was not until last summer that I began to ponder the implications of forgoing the full-length mirror my first year. A little over a year ago, I was blessed with the opportunity to volunteer with Mother Teresa's sisters in Calcutta, India. It was the vitality of this University that fostered my desire to share meaningful moments with the poorest of the poor. It was the spirituality Notre Dame offered that sparked my strong devotion to Mother Teresa—and it was the Center for Social Concerns (an organization on campus devoted to social outreach) that brought this ministry to fruition. I mention this facet of my life with you today because it links back to those initial days my first year.

While in Calcutta, I was able to work in Kalighat, Mother Teresa's home for the destitute and dying. We ministered in a way that built the culture of life by caring for the abandoned until their last breath. After a few weeks of service in this home for the dying, I observed something unique about my surroundings. There were no mirrors in Kalighat. No mirrors . . . I was puzzled by this and located a sister to inquire the reason. She smiled at my realization and informed me that Mother Teresa's home was intended to be a place without mirrors. "Without mirrors we are forced to see our reflection through the eyes of others," she said. Without mirrors we must begin the process of allowing others to challenge us—mold us—and become integral factors in our vocational journey.

My thoughts drifted back to those first days at Notre Dame, a period of my life when I had to abandon the full-length mirror in my dorm room. The perceptive Calcutta nun's wisdom can be a challenge for all of us today. At this moment, it is tempting to stare in the mirror. Oftentimes, when fearful of new situations, we place shells around ourselves and turn inward, merely looking at our own perspective and reflection. However, we are called to action—to be doers—to allow the inspiring community around us to serve as a catalyst of our growth and development. This involves discarding our personal mirrors and looking to the eyes of others.

Class of 2007, you were selected from a record number of 12,096 applicants. Eighty-four percent of you participated in community service in high school, and more than 70 percent took part in varsity sports. You join us from all fifty states and thirty-six other countries. It is tempting to hear such vast statistics and become overwhelmed. I recall receiving such numbers as a first-year student and feeling paralyzed.

I was wait-listed at this University, and it terrified me to contemplate that I was one of the final twenty students admitted to my class. However, the predominant component of my maturation at Notre Dame has been the continuous process of discarding mirrors—those fears and insecurities in my life—and accepting the opportunities this University so generously provides.

When the Class of 2003's valedictorian stood on this stage this past May, she posed a challenge to her classmates. Quoting Pope John Paul II and Christ Himself, she stated: "DO NOT BE AFRAID!" Just as our outgoing graduates were urged not to allow fear to overwhelm the illuminated path ahead, you too must hold a similar disposition.

"Do not be afraid." Do not be afraid to look to the reflections of the Notre Dame community . . . Sign up for the retreat at Campus

Ministry . . . Be a hall commissioner . . . Join student government . . . Cherish late-night discussions . . . Dress to the theme of your dorm dances . . . And at the football games, cheer cheer and wake up the echoes . . . Be malleable . . . Integrate your life.

This is your time. You have four sacred years ahead of you. Now is the time to abandon your mirror and look outward. Allow the people you live with in community—your rectors and your advisors—to challenge you, to guide you, to aid your growth. . . .

The evening I was elected president of my class, I ventured down to the Grotto and lit a candle for my classmates. Throughout my service in this leadership position—and now years after—I have kept a candle lit in that same location day after day.

Now over the past years I've become a bit lax on the whole donation policy with lighting Grotto candles. I should not be admitting this in front of President Malloy, but by this time I have accumulated a hefty tab at the Grotto. My justification is that the tuition pays it off!!!

Last night I decided to light an additional candle—in a spot directly above the location I have kindled for the past three years. Class of 2007, this is your candle! I promise to keep this candle glowing throughout the duration of your first year.

There are no mirrors at the Grotto, only reflections. Allow the light of this candle to serve as a reminder to seek the challenges and reflections from the inspiring community around you. Class of 2007: I welcome you to the Notre Dame family.

—FIRST YEAR ORIENTATION IS AN IMPORTANT TWO-DAY EVENT AT NOTRE DAME. SPEAKERS BEFORE THE ASSEMBLED NEW STUDENTS AND THEIR PARENTS ALWAYS GET A RESPECTFUL HEARING, BUT NOW AND THEN SOMEONE GENUINELY STIRS THE EMOTIONS AND CREATES WHAT HAS COME TO BE KNOWN AS A "NOTRE DAME MOMENT." ON SATURDAY, AUGUST 23, 2003, IN THE JOYCE CENTER, SENIOR KERI OXLEY OF FREMONT, OHIO, BROUGHT THE CROWD OF ABOUT 6,000 TO ITS FEET WITH A SUSTAINED OVATION AFTER HER ACCOUNT OF WHAT THE UNIVERSITY HAS MEANT TO HER AND WHAT IT CAN MEAN TO THEM. THE PREVIOUS IS AN ABRIDGED VERSION OF HER SPEECH.

ON SATURDAY WE gathered in the library auditorium to learn the university's policy on admissions. We heard that of 8,000 applications for the freshman class, 1,275 men and 500 women were accepted.

While affection for Notre Dame is not inscribed in the genes and passed on in the gene pool, still one out of every four freshmen is the offspring of an alumnus. Alumni whose offspring are not accepted often show strong reactions, said the director of admissions. One father thought that his daughter should have been admitted because of when and where she had been conceived: the weekend of the Michigan State game in the Morris Inn.

Seminars that day ranged from estate planning to stress management, from career planning to the emerging woman. Most popular were the tours of the Snite Museum of Art, where guides showed some of the 17,000 pieces from the collection valued at $30 million.

For our class photo we gathered, as the printed program directed, "on the bleachers near the beer tent." Class photos used to be taken on the long stone steps in front of the old library when we were still lithe and lean. Faces are broader now and weight in the shoulders has slipped downward "on the bleachers near the beer tent." The photos of our forty-fifth reunion suggest that none of us will ever again, on the Feast of San Firmin, run with the bulls at Pamplona. As the Second Law of Thermodynamics warns, everything is running down.

How the bells did peal that Saturday night! When Father Sorin planned Sacred Heart Church, in 1871, the naysayers must have considered him mad to build such a great edifice in the remoteness of northern Indiana. But now it could be larger, especially on reunion weekend, when alumni overflow from every door.

Father Sorin was much a part of the Solemn Mass; his chair, chalice, and paten were used in the liturgy. A brass quintet played, the alumni choir sang, and the 2,929 pipes of the great organ did their best.

After Mass a kilty band—six bagpipers and five drums—led the alumni down the main quad past Father Sorin's statue, past O'Shaughnessy Hall, and on beyond the stadium to the Athletic and Convocation Center where the round tables, with eight seats to a table, stretched on and on across the gigantic hall. There 2,478 grads sat down to a banquet. They had come from forty-seven states and Scotland, Guatemala, Uganda, Canada, Mexico, and the Virgin Islands. The banquet came to a close with thirty-five former members of the Glee Club singing "Notre Dame, Our Mother" and "The Victory March."

At ten o'clock we stepped out into a chilly night. It felt more like a football weekend than an alumni reunion. The moon was full and clear, and yellow spotlights made the Dome more golden still.

Voices in the night air were mostly young. Few at the reunion went back far enough or remember when the campus bakery specialized in what was called the Notre Dame bun, a celebrated geological specimen. The crusty beige object had the shell of a turtle and the interior of caulking compound. A student once pasted a stamp on one, added his girl's address, and sent it through the mail.

Under the circus tent that Saturday night there was enough drinking to soften the present, but still a miasma of sadness hung in the air. Things that pierce the memory deeply—old photo albums, old yearbooks, old hardships—bring an uneasy mirth. We laugh when we are reminded that God has the knack of planned obsolescence.

Clustered in small groups on folding chairs, friends for many years took out memories and passed them around. The memories, blurred enough by now to be attractive, created a freemasonry that made us feel we still hold more in common than we really do. This was the time to enjoy the modified reminiscences of youth, not authenticate them. A stickler for facts is as out of place at an alumni reunion as Roman numerals on a scoreboard. Legends are not born in the midst of cross-references. And besides, to have delightful memories is to be written in the book of the blessed.

Who would want to check too closely the story about how an unsuspecting prof carried the exam answers from a student in the front row to one in the back row: "There's this Holy Cross priest, see, who paces the aisle reading his breviary during exams. He always does that, paces the aisle, and everybody knows it. So this smart student up front uses a safety pin to hook the answers onto the priest's cincture. Get the picture? The dumb student lifts them off when the priest makes his turn at the back of the room."

Alumni reunions are more restrained than they used to be. At one time they were the greatest breakdown in order since the collapse of Pax Romana. A recurring theme used to be "how we raised hell and slid a block under it."

Why are things more restrained? Could it be *accidie?* Or the presence of wives? Or is there really such a thing as the perfectibility of man?

Sunday dawned a blue and gold day. In the morning sunshine three of us walked past Father Sorin's statue talking about how evocative a visit to the community cemetery can be. Names that we saw first in the college catalog are now on stone crosses.

We recalled the Holy Cross Fathers who meant something in our lives. In fusty classrooms under the Dome they passed along a trend of mind that is more important than data. By hinting that creation is the husk of something infinite, they opened windows onto a long view, framing problems of the day in light of eternity.

One priest used to harp on the difference between inclinations and principles. Another passed along a practical wisdom that went beyond books, for it came from spiritual experience. Most had the old-fashioned notion—it dates back to Quintilian—that the teacher must accept responsibility not only for what a student learns but what he becomes.

They made us see it is possible to live in a way we had never considered. While trying to impose order and lucidity on our minds, they showed us how to detect the center of gravity in certain situations.

What an uphill job they had, trying to help us separate sense from nonsense! Our best teachers knew that true education means teaching things that are worth being in love with.

At a reunion, vivid comradery fades fast. The flow of reminiscence runs dry. The most garrulous is talked out. After a certain number of years, it takes courage to attend an alumni weekend. You face reflections of your mortality, seeing in others what is happening to yourself. It becomes more of a spiritual retreat than a lively celebration once you admit that not far downstream looms the Ultimate Tax Shelter. And yet those of us at the forty-fifth reunion said, "See you at the fiftieth." Such promises grow more chancy through the years.

We parted feeling more finite, knowing our horizons will move in like the wood of Dunsinane. In some well-worn classroom under the Dome we heard about "this mortal coil," but what did that mean at twenty. Now we were paying attention while the lessons were being taught.

"See you at the fiftieth!"

With the permission of God, of course.

—PROFESSOR EDWARD FISCHER[5]

. . . A UNIVERSITY SUCH as Notre Dame is bricks and books, classrooms and laboratories. But it is, above all, people. Some come here for four years, perhaps to return only in spirit, while others' very lives revolve around this place. I like to think that Notre Dame makes its mark on all who come here, and not a few make their mark on Notre Dame.

—REV. THEODORE M. HESBURGH, C.S.C.

SEARCHING FOR THE way, trying not to trip in the dark; will we ever get there?

It's a cool, drizzly October night in a patch of Michigan woods,

all wet leaves and rotting boughs under our flashlights. I'm suppos-
edly night-orienteering with the Boy Scouts, but most of my mind
frets anxiously for Griff, who lies dying at Holy Cross House a hundred miles away. My dear old ghostly father, as I name him, will soon
be a ghost himself. I want to sit beside him, maybe hold his hand and
read him some Gerard Manley Hopkins. Perhaps something of my
presence will sift down through the fitful, troubled torpor which has
settled on him as he strains not to go gentle into that good night.

But first these boys want to show me their stuff. All they have is
a compass and a list of numbers to navigate the dark wilderness. But
the one landmark, that big rock at the edge of the clearing, is your
best friend, because if you can't fix your position at the start then
each subsequent bearing will be a little bit off course, and each succeeding step a little more off course, magnifying your error, carrying
you further away from our goal.

I suppose that Father Robert Griffin, C.S.C., was just such a
landmark for me and countless other Notre Dame students. He
would never actually point out the way, but he was fixed and solid,
holding a true position from which I knew the possible coordinates.
Griff died on October 20, and I feel as if every step of my adult life
was his gift. Now that I'm on my own, can I find the way through the
darkness, with only his written words left behind?

> Death is a bully whose nose should be
> tweaked, and I hope to be one of the
> tweakers. I grow weary of fearing death, for
> myself and for my friends. I become
> embarrassed for God; death makes such a
> fool of Him. I want to be present at death's
> judgement; I want to hear God say that death
> must die. I want to be present at
> resurrections that defeat death's victories. I
> want to see the fallen sparrows renewed in

their flight. I want to greet death, when he
comes irresistibly, with insolence and
swagger, as though I were a baggy-pants
clown to whom the final snickers belong.

He did look clownish, I guess: surely the most awkward man on
campus. Large and heavy, baby-faced even when unshaved, unkempt
hair escaping from a shabby cap, elephant trousers, flecked with cig-
arette ash, a cocker spaniel named Darby O'Gill yanking its leash
between the ankles, Griff would shamble across the North Quad
with a wobbly vagueness, a frumpy black-clad reject from Macy's
parade.

He was chaplain of the University for 30 years, but it's almost
impossible to identify Griff with any formal organization. His post
simply meant that he was the best listener in the world, and he
seemed happiest when listening to those on the fringes. He celebrated a Mass for children with mimes and mummers and teddy bear
picnics on the altar. He ran a coffee-house-cum-study-hall in the
bowels of the student center from midnight until dawn, a haven for
insomniacs and the depressed. He spent his summers in the skuzzier
parts of Manhattan, ministering to alcoholics and druggies and to the
prostitutes whom he called joy maidens.

A missionary to the lonely, nobody has ever loved us so much.
Griff wrote once, "You cannot sing a night song until the hour before
dawn, when the darkness has nearly ended. Then, when loneliness
has worn you out, you understand, in an insight as spontaneous as
laughter, that God has been keeping watch." Griff taught us to sing
night songs of faith in the basement of LaFortune. Even in his last
hours of consciousness he insisted on counseling me on my recently
failed marriage, as lovingly alert and keenly sympathetic as when I
sat at his feet 20 years ago, righting the wrongs of creation with me
at midnight over a cup of cocoa. His was the simple but ineluctably
vital ministry of being there.

Faith teaches that there is an eternal
Heartbeat in me that belongs to God; it keeps
me from getting weary when I need to care.
Yet sometimes the best I can do is give a
professional attention, wanting to care
deeply, yet knowing that in all my attention
there is nothing really personal. Eventually,
with God's help, I touch the place where the
nerve ends quiver; I find the spot where the
pain shows through. Then my experience is
like that of Thomas, when he put his finger
into the side of Christ; a personal bond is
established because I know how someone has
suffered. Is caring, then, a personal response,
a special cherishing of the person cared for?
Sometimes not, I suppose, but I've never
found a person whom I needed to love whom
I couldn't love, if I am patient enough.

Lovely, Griff. Maybe you should be missed most as the late Laureate of the Dome, for your golden prose interrogated and enveloped and chronicled our lives: dozens of columns for *Our Sunday Visitor, Scholastic,* and this magazine, the stuff of journalism awards, essays collected into two books. But for me your best legacy is the 25 years' worth of weekly "Letters to a Lonely God" that ran in the Friday *Observer.* How I delight to follow the gentle movement of your thought, that Senecan amble that takes us to questions and issues via the roads and by-ways of your singular experience. Your speculations appear seamlessly to embrace most of writing and culture—the Gospels, Graham Greene, *Saturday Night Fever,* Teilhard de Chardin, Henry V, Jimmy Swaggart, Dr. Seuss—always outlining a significant argument, but soft-spokenly, glowing with a lucid periodicity of prose.

Such a lively stylist, Griff. But what you write! When I was younger I undervalued you, for you have always wrestled so honestly for the Truth, and I was mostly charmed by the style. Some years ago, for instance, you wrote on Tom the gay Catholic, and it's so loving a response—your critical faculties of discernment are agile and strong, yet you reach out first, and then utter the truth that you must. You grasp exactly the psychological and spiritual dimensions of Tom's issues, but when you write you give the impression of listening rather than that of sternly preaching. Of course my fellow Griff-groupies and I loved you years ago for this patient attentiveness—but what awes me now as a reader is how sharp an observer of contemporary life you remain, and how true an ear for the voice of humanity you retain. All this, and preaching the Truth besides. You never shunned the hard urgent topics—gay Catholics, women wanting the priesthood. Always "with it" and relevant, to be sure: but it's the Gospel you preach, always by reaching out rather than ramming down. Isn't ours the faith that is built upon questions left dangling in the air? You served as our apostle of the unanswered questions, Griff, and, God in heaven, you did a lovely job of it.

> Death, when it comes unexpectedly, must
> always seem like a horror. But if death comes
> when you are waiting for it, hoping for it, it
> must seem as welcome as a mother's hug. Of
> it death comes to say: "Not now, not yet. I'll
> be waiting someplace up the road, but I don't
> want you to be afraid of going home with a
> friend"—such a death, comforting as a night
> sky full of stars, must seem like the dark
> angel at God's hand, the messenger of his
> hidden mercies.

Mercies, yes, but they don't feel like they're for me right now. "When it is a drizzly November in my soul," says Ishmael in *Moby*

Dick, "I put out to sea," and we have each one our own solitary, exigent navigations which we must make the best of, howsoever drizzly we feel. Orienteering is always tough, so very tough. I wish to God I had a better compass and a clearer path. But once, I knew exactly where I was.

—LUIS GAMEZ '79[6]

THE PAST FEW weeks have been for me a time of unusual highs and lows.

The lows didn't surprise me. Three weeks in a hospital, even with kind, professional care, becomes a drag—all those strange, undignified things being done to you according to a schedule which could make sense only to a computer.

The high moments came unexpectedly, gradually developing into a pattern.

From the beginning, there was a steady flow of visitors: family, members of my religious community, and then many friends, people with whom I have worked, people whose lives, joys, and sorrows I've shared in the past.

They kept coming, usually for only a brief visit, but the intensity of concern, the things said, told me that there was something more going on than the kind-but-customary expression of sympathy.

I was deeply moved by many of these visits, but also somewhat puzzled. A friendship might go back many years; we had shared efforts, celebrations, griefs. A lasting warmth remains when we get together.

But this didn't seem to explain the obvious intensity of many of these people as they expressed their hopes for me, their concern and love.

Then, in the early morning hours, when I couldn't get to sleep, I suddenly realized what was happening.

These people were a recapitulation of 31 years of my priesthood.

Their visits were an incomplete but representative snapshot album touching all those years of my priestly life.

It has been an unusual pattern. All this time lived on one campus, in one city. Never assigned to ordinary parish duties. I had come to know most of these people as we worked together on projects we considered important . . . or because they came to me with particular questions they wanted to discuss.

These people, in their hospital visits, calls, notes, made reference to things I had said or done, things which had slipped from my memory or which I never saw as particularly helpful.

These men and women were and are my friends, but the pattern which emerged during these early morning thoughts made it clear that my presence to them, at special moments in their lives, had been more than the support of a caring friend.

For many, it was hard to formulate, but somehow I had represented God's presence to them through the life of the church.

This pattern of memories revealed an experience most priests have had in isolated incidents. After dealing with a painful, complicated problem in confession or direction, he will see that something he said or the way he said it had been just right for this person at this time.

But he will be left wondering: Where did that approach come from? I never considered it before. It didn't come from teachers or from reading.

And then he realizes, he knows, that his guidance had come from God in a special way. He knows that God had used him, as priest, to touch the life of this person.

I have long recognized and treasured such special moments in which I was convinced that God has used me as an instrument of His presence in these lives which He touches.

These visits, the memories they elicited, the tone of my friends' response to my situation, showed that the same kind of mediation took place far more consistently than I had realized. Without my awareness, in many activities and associations which I had regarded as routine, God had been touching these lives through my identity as priest.

When I finally dropped off to sleep in the hours before dawn, it was with a special gratitude for the gift which these people have given me in their visits, in their concern for my illness. Their words, their support, their friendship are very important, but this was the gift of enabling me to see all my life as a priest in a different perspective, with a consistency not dependent on my efforts and skills.

It showed me that in spite of my failures and fumbling, God had regularly used me as a channel of His presence in the lives of others.

For me, that is a profoundly reassuring conviction at this time. It links the reality of these 31 years to the hope and vision which drew me to this life.

Whatever else comes, I shall treasure this insight from my time in the hospital.

—Rev John L. Reedy, C.S.C., served as publisher of
Ave Maria Press from 1953 until his death on December 2,
1983. In his thirty-one years of service as a priest, he was active
in Catholic journalism and publishing and received the 1966
Catholic Press Association award for outstanding service.
This article for Our Sunday Visitor was written
a week before his death.

It is the capacity for human decency that does distinguish us, that makes Notre Dame unique as a community of teachers and students. . . .

—Professor Frank O'Malley

The spirit of Notre Dame, that real but elusive property that defines the place and its people, is perhaps never more revealed or revealing than when one of its own meets with triumph or tragedy.

The celebrations of special honors or athletic victories are easily obvious. But volumes could be filled with narratives of the Notre Dame spirit as exemplified in the stories of those who find its strength in their living or their dying. Let some of the more recent ones stand for the hundreds that could be told.

No one who was connected to Notre Dame in 2000–2001 will forget the courage of sophomore Conor Murphy of Zahm Hall, nor the outpouring of love from the entire Notre Dame community when he was diagnosed with leukemia.

Conor had told people that he was studying politics because he wanted to be President of the United States, not for power or to rule, but to serve by reminding the world of the rights of human dignity and the need for solidarity in working to improve the lives of people everywhere. He was an idealist with the charisma to inspire others. And when it was clear that his life was in danger, it was his friends, his dormmates, his university brothers and sisters who learned from him the meaning of steadfast faith and courage. At his urging, 610 people joined the National Marrow Donor Program at a drive held on campus.

When Conor died on the last day of January 2001, there was a sadness across the whole campus. He left a legacy that no one who knew him and few who knew about him will forget. He had wanted to inspire others to live well and to care. He succeeded.

BY EERIE COINCIDENCE, there is another story of loss to leukemia of another Notre Damer, this one a fourteen-year-old San Diego, California, boy who was adopted by the Notre Dame community he had chosen to be his own. In September of 2000, Scott Delgadillo and his family came to Notre Dame thanks to the Make-A-Wish Foundation. He was met by many people at Notre Dame, including Father Monk Malloy, President, and head football coach Bob Davie. Davie invited Scott to speak at the pep rally before the Purdue game.

"I was nervous at first . . . I looked all around and saw Rudy, I looked at the players, all the cheerleaders and the band. I kind of took a deep breath and started speaking," he later told the *San Diego Union-Tribune*. His words inspired many. When he returned home, hundreds of letters and e-mails poured in. His leukemia went into remission, and he was able to speak at the breakfast on the morning after the ND–Southern Cal game. But the disease returned and claimed his life on January 29, 2001. Eight weeks earlier, he had sent a thank-you to the Notre Dame community through Jennifer Laiber of the Public Relations and Information Department. In it he said:

> . . . My love for the University of Notre Dame has grown more and more especially since my trip because of the inspiration it has given me. Notre Dame is a very special place . . .
>
> Every night I thank God for all the nice people that have sent me their prayers. I also thank God for all the nice people I have met at Notre Dame like Joey Getherall, Shane Walton, Coach Bob Davie, Father Edward Malloy, Rudy Reuttiger, the entire football team and Jennifer Laiber. These people in some way have made my wish an on-going process and have affected my life in a positive way. These people as well as the whole ND family, in some way made me feel like I was a special kid. I thank these people that I have met at Notre Dame and my recent trip to the ND vs. USC game. You all have made me feel great inside and all the well wishers have played a big part in that too. Fortunately, the Notre Dame family has so many members with warm hearts. My family: Carmen, Henry, Eric and myself would like to wish everybody Happy Holidays and gratitude for your support. GO IRISH!

—SCOTT DELGADILLO, DECEMBER 2, 2000

THE FIRST DAY of college was as scary as it was exhilarating. As incoming freshmen, we were informed of our dorm, room number, and roommate assignments just before the fall term. Back then, we were permitted to rank our top three dorm preferences, but we could not select our rooms or roommates. I was fortunate to get my top choice of Sorin Hall, the oldest dorm on campus, and was eager to meet my roommate and other guys in the dorm.

As we all descended onto campus and gathered with the rector and resident assistants for "freshman orientation," we had the chance to size each other up. One of the first people I met was Andy Pauline from Potomac, Maryland. We became instant friends, sharing similar stories of high school; love of books, music, and sports; and an overall enthusiasm for the next four years. Within the first week of school, other guys in the dorm thought Andy and I had known each other all our lives.

While we had just met, two of Andy's best friends from high school—Tom Gerth and Jay Kelly—were also assigned to Sorin. All graduates of Georgetown Preparatory School in Maryland, Tom was from Rockville, Maryland, while Jay had been a boarding student from Flint, Michigan. It did not take long for me to build friendships with Tom and Jay, which made people wonder even more how long we'd all known one another.

Throughout freshman year, the four of us were pretty much inseparable. Being from South Bend myself, I loved being pals with these East Coasters. I was so interested in where they came from and they were so willing to show me, that for spring break that year we all drove out to a frozen Maryland in Tom's Volkswagen Rabbit. While I loved my first tour of Washington, D.C., I loved even more seeing Georgetown Prep, especially the sports facilities that had made Andy, Tom, and Jay heroes in their own minds! It was also a joy to meet Andy's and Tom's families, where Jay had been so welcome when he was a boarder at Georgetown.

Late freshman year, Jay developed a severe pain in his right leg. It got so bad that he could not play sports and had to drop out of Bookstore Basketball, a tournament he desperately wanted to play in. Eventually, he could not walk without limping and had to go to the doctor. He was told that it was either a pulled muscle or a pinched nerve. The pain did not subside by the end of the semester, so we all prayed that Jay would get better over the summer. At first he was told that special exercises would help rid him of the pain and get him going again, but there was no diagnosis. But by the middle of summer the worst came true: Jay was diagnosed with Ewing's sarcoma, a rare form of cancer. The pain in his leg was caused by a tumor along his side and back. I will never forget the round of phone calls between Andy, Jay, and another of our close friends, Terrence Murphy. Jay was in real trouble, and we were all trying to digest the news and be there for him.

Jay was well into chemotherapy when school started up again. He was unable to make it back to Notre Dame for the first semester because he was going through testing and treatment in Boston and recovering in Flint. All of us wanted to be there for Jay as often as possible, so we took road trips to Flint and made sure that Jay's friends all over campus stayed in touch with him. During fall break of that year, 1989, Jay was in Boston for radical surgery to remove the tumor. Andy, Tom, and I drove to Maryland and then took the train to Boston for a day visit with Jay. It was very tough to see him in such bad shape, but his faith, humor, and strength gave us all courage enough to process the situation and hang out with him just like old times.

When we got back to campus, we missed Jay more than ever and were all questioning our faith in new ways. Why Jay? Why now?

One fall evening, Andy and I did the only thing that made sense in the midst of our confusion and sorrow: We went down to the Grotto to pray for Jay, for his family, for us all. Walking silently down the hill from Corby Hall toward the Grotto, we were ushered into this sacred cove by the gentle sound of wind whistling through the few living leaves clinging to tree limbs no longer able to sustain them. To our left was the statue of Dr. Tom Dooley, to our right was the Grotto.

Instinctively, we bowed our heads as we approached the cave of candles. Then each of us entered, lit a candle, returned to the kneelers, and prayed. After what seemed hours, we stood and made our way over to the bench near the Dooley statue and sat next to one another. As we looked at the Grotto from this distance, we both noticed that many other candles had been lit by many other people with many different prayers. And for a brief moment, all those individual candles joined with all the candles that have flickered here for over a century and made the Grotto glow with the fire of faith that we experience only rarely in life. The Grotto became a beacon of truth that told us we were not alone, Jay was not alone. Mary, our Mother, was watching over us all.

Later on, Jay made a few visits to campus, but he was not able to enroll in classes. Instead, he went to a local college in his hometown and worked at rehab with a determination I had never seen before.

Throughout that summer, Jay held out hope that he would be able to come back to campus for junior year and continue his education. But he was only able to enroll in classes for a brief while before having to go back to Flint for more tests and treatment. During one of his extended stays, Andy and I were studying with him when I could no longer hold back asking, "Jay, are you mad at God?" With a look of calm understanding, he said, "There have been times throughout this whole thing when I've gotten mad, even at God. But I always come back to God. What upsets me most is that I have so much I want to give. But no matter how much I don't understand all of this, in the end God is all we've really got. And the time we have here is a blessing and a gift."

When Jay died on July 15, 1991, I tried to remember his words. Like the candles at the Grotto on that autumn night, they spoke a truth that taught me that life is indeed a gift and that we are never alone, even in our darkest hour.

—JEREMY LANGFORD

ON A WIND-SWEPT promontory of the Flint Hills, out of sight of any vestige of human habitation, lies the twisted wreckage of a giant Fokker, its three motors buried deep in the stony soil, which carried to death Knute Rockne, the Viking of football, two pilots, and five other passengers.

The Flint Hills, marking the boundary between the cornfields of Eastern Kansas and the ocean of wheat to the west, are a lonely and desolate out-cropping of hard limestone ridges which run two hundred miles from north to south across the state. A few isolated villages and ranch houses dot its gentle valleys and every spring hundreds of thousands of cattle come up from the Texas ranges to be fattened for market on the virgin prairie sod, untouched by plow, which in a few weeks will be green with the spring rains.

A few miles away, almost within sight of the twisted fuselage of the trimotored Fokker, run the abandoned ruts of the old stage road cut by stage coaches in the eighteen-fifties and sixties, which ran between the ancient federal military posts of Fort Leavenworth and Fort Sill, five hundred miles apart.

Among the first to reach the wreckage was R. Z. Blackburn, who was feeding his cattle in a pasture. He heard the roar of the morning mail plane. It is just at this point in the Flint Hills that the old stage road, marked by furrows in the prairie sod, intersects with the transcontinental air mail line marked by flashing beacon lights, running between Kansas City and Wichita.

The hum of airplane motors was a familiar sound to Blackburn. Today the plane was invisible above the gray clouds which hung a scant one thousand feet above the Flint Hills. After dying away in the fog, the hum returned and attracted his attention. Something apparently was wrong with the regular morning mail plane. He looked up from his work in time to see the silver Fokker drop like a plummet from the low-hanging clouds. Behind it fluttered a severed silver wing.

Its motors still roaring, the Fokker disappeared behind a hill, there was a splintering thud and the motors ceased. Blackburn saw the severed wing twisting, lighting down through the air. It came to ground a half a mile to the east of the plane.

Leaving his work, Blackburn hurried over the hill, but first to reach the scene was Edward Baker, a ranchman's son, who was finishing his chores when he saw the roaring Fokker spin down from the low clouds.

One look at the twisted wreckage lying strangely silent on the brow of the hill, and Edward turned his wiry little cow pony back toward the ranch, where the news of the disaster reached Cottonwood Falls via a humming rural telephone line.

News via the rural telephone party wires travels fast, even in Flint Hills. Almost before the two ambulances arrived from Cottonwood Falls, the ranchmen were galloping over the hills toward the stony promontory on which the plane lay in the stillness on the prairie. But an hour later the world closed in. First, two ambulances arrived and picked up the mangled bodies.

Then streams of motor cars from the nearby villages of Bazaar, Matfield Green, Cottonwood Falls and Strong City were on roads. Ranchers' wives and children trudging from the road in the valley to the scene of the wreck were guided by the tail of the plane, jutting high from the hill on the horizon.

The sheriff, the county attorney, the coroner, and the village correspondents for the big town newspapers rushed to see the scene.

A team of mules from a ranch pulled the remainder of the fuselage from the holes plowed in the ground. Three more bodies were separated from the wreckage.

An hour passed, then early in the afternoon as the news spread to the cities that a mail plane was down and Knute Rockne was dead,

to hide their gloom and heart-break, for if they had talked, they would have wept.

It was on Holy Saturday, April 3rd, that Rockne was buried from the campus church. Since there could be no mass of Requiem that day, the services were held in the afternoon. The public manifested so great a desire to participate in these services that it was impossible to accommodate all. Hence, the Columbia Broadcasting Company asked and obtained permission to send to the nation the events as they took place in the Church of the Sacred Heart. Loud speakers were employed on the campus also, so that the throngs outside might follow the funeral services.

Rockne's coffin was carried into the church by six of his players: Carideo, Shwartz, Mullins, Brill, Conley, and Yarr. At the portal, waiting to receive the body, was Most Reverend John Noll, Bishop of Fort Wayne, and the attending clergy. When the holy water had been sprinkled, there burst from the throats of the Moreau Seminary choir, under the direction of Father James Connerton, a song that was strong, poignant, solemn. People from every part of the land wrote to say they had never heard music so beautiful, so moving.

—PROFESSOR AND HISTORIAN ARTHUR HOPE, C.S.C.[7]

WE CAN HAVE a personal relationship with the Lord, but never an individual one. We go to God with our brothers and sisters or we don't go at all. He planned it this way, and we can't go with them unless we know and care for them, until there is no more strength or life in us.

—MONSIGNOR JOHN J. EGAN, FORMER SPECIAL ASSISTANT TO THE PRESIDENT, NOTRE DAME

I LOVE NOTRE Dame very, very much.

—VICTOR COUCH, A WELL-KNOWN MEMBER OF THE NOTRE DAME COMMUNITY WHO SERVED AS A STADIUM USHER FOR SIXTY YEARS

HUMOR

Sorry, Professor, but if we do this for you, we'll have to do it for everyone on the faculty.

—BROTHER IN CHARGE OF THE NOTRE DAME FARM,
REFUSING TO PROVIDE TEMPORARY BOARDING FOR A HORSE
OWNED BY PROFESSOR EDWARD FISCHER IN 1966

HUMOR IS A vital virtue in every healthy family. Notre Dame has always had an abundance of characters and incongruity, so that fun and laughter are always part of the present and past of this place. Student pranks of old still liven up reunions; people still recall moments like a professor asking a student who had given a wrong answer, "How did *you* ever get into Notre Dame?" and the response, "I said lots of rosaries." They still talk about the students in one dorm playing "Pistol Packin' Mama" repeatedly out their window directly across from the window of their rival hall's rector until he could stand it no more and burst through the door to confiscate it, only to have the students report him to security. The annual Keenan Revue pokes fun at any and all.

There is and has always been a certain spirit of playfulness that has always been at the heart of Notre Dame. In the early years, it might have been the sight of Father Sorin playing marbles with the minims, the grade school students who were part of Notre Dame until the 1920s, or delighting in seeing their joy at the bicycles he brought for them all the way from France. Students in the fifties will remember the humorous barbs that punctuated every movie shown in Washington Hall. Tales of blind dates gone awry, stories of what really happens in the pileup following a fumble in football, imitations of teachers and coaches, all provide the laughter and light touch that remind us not to take ourselves too seriously.

February 24, 1933

Dear *Scholastic* Editor,

A few of the fellows in our hall were having a discussion
the other day, and we decided that to abolish 8 o'clock
classes would be a great benefit to all the students, and
would necessitate no great changes in the University
routine.

To make up for the 8 o'clock classes, it would be quite
simple to have general classes at 4:15 in the afternoon. No
one would mind this.

The advantages of such a plan are innumerable. That
well-known lethargy which features the 8 o'clock class
would be gone; students would get plenty of sleep; professors are less inclined to irritableness at 9 than they are at 8;
the cold, dreary trudge to the dining hall in the dead of
night would be a thing of the past. Out of a group of students going cheery-eyed about their business when the sun
is high in the heavens, a new Notre Dame would emerge.

—L.G.B.

THERE'S PRESSURE IN every coaching job, but winning makes it
a lot easier to accept. Fortunately, we have been winning. But like
one fan told me, we're with you Ara, win or tie. You notice he didn't
say anything about losing.

—ARA PARSEGHIAN

SOME OF THE most hilarious Notre Dame stories come from the
era of Frank Leahy's legendary teams. Tough taskmasters like Leahy
always need foils, free spirits who keep their teammates smiling
through the torment of practices. In Leahy's day, Saturdays seemed
like a light drill compared to the practice-makes-perfect motif of the

grueling practices every other day. Many of these stories are chronicled in Jack Connor's book *Leahy's Lads*.

To this day, Leahy's former players gather at least once a year to celebrate their four National Championships, their deep bond of friendship, and to share memories. Creighton Miller, star halfback from 1941 to 1943, inducted into the College Football Hall of Fame in 1976, was always in demand to retell a story from the 1943 National Championship season. Connor recorded it:

It was a surprisingly balmy November day that Saturday as the Notre Dame team prepared to battle [Northwestern] for its eighth straight victory. Before the game even got underway, Miller provided some extra color.

He had obtained four tickets for good friends who lived in nearby Winnetka. During the pre-game warm-up Miller spotted his friends in 50-yard-line seats situated close to the playing field. When Leahy gave the signal for the team to return to the visiting locker room, Miller went over to the stands to say a quick hello. In the meantime, the Notre Dame team exited the field via an unusual exit route peculiar to Dyche Stadium. To get to the locker rooms below the stands it was necessary to first exit the field at the 10-yard line, go up the steps to a ramp, then take the Ramp down below the stands to the unmarked visiting team locker room.

When Miller had finished his short visit with his friends, he glanced to where the players had been only to find that they were already out of sight. He now had to make a decision. If he went back on the field to the 10-yard line, all the people in the stands would see the recognizable number 37 on his jersey and wonder what Creighton Miller was doing alone on the field. He thought that would be embarrassing, so he opted to take the closest ramp which was higher up on the 50-yard line. This ramp took him underneath the stands, but the problem now was to locate the correct door. To his dismay, there were numerous unmarked doors. He tried a couple of doors, knocked on them, but no luck. He hurriedly knocked on a few more doors with no success. By this time, Miller is starting to get panicky as he can imagine what Leahy must be thinking about his absence such a short time before kickoff.

He had an idea. He would ask a concessionaire for directions. Surely, one of these guys would know where the visiting locker room was located. As he anxiously looked for a stand he could not help but notice that people were looking at him in a strange way. He recalls thinking, "I am sure these people are wondering what kind of jerk wears a football uniform to a game."

He spotted a hot dog stand and with no pretense of politeness pushed his way through the crowd to the head of the line. He asked the man working the stand if he knew where the visiting locker room was. The attendant, thinking that Miller was a weird fan dressed as a player, replied, "That uniform doesn't cut any mustard with me, fella, get back to the end of the line." Miller went to the end of the line to wait his turn. As he was about third in line he saw Father John Cavanaugh, the vice president of Notre Dame in charge of athletics, approaching him. He tried to hide behind one of the fans, but Father Cavanaugh had already spotted him. Father Cavanaugh inquired what Miller was doing standing in a hot dog line just before game time. As Miller started to explain, Father Cavanaugh cut him short and turned to the distinguished-looking gentleman with him, the president of Northwestern, and said, "Remember our conversation at lunch yesterday when I predicted that Northwestern should do well against Notre Dame? Well, here we have one of our starting halfbacks in a hot dog line with just five minutes to game time. See what I mean?"

To Miller's relief, a student manager whom Leahy had sent looking for the missing Miller, suddenly appeared and told him that Leahy wanted him right away. The manager escorted him to the visiting team locker room. As soon as they entered the room, Leahy rushed up to Miller and asked, "Oh, Creighton Miller, where have you been? Where could you possibly go with that uniform on?" Before he could answer, Leahy hastily added, "No, don't tell me. Just don't say anything. I don't think I want to know. I just don't want to know."

Miller had a much easier time on the playing field than he did under the stands as he gained 151 yards running and scored a touchdown as Notre Dame rolled over Northwestern by a 25–6 score.[1]

Without a doubt, one of the greatest characters ever to wear the uniform of the Fighting Irish was Zygmont Pierre "Ziggie" Czarobski, starting tackle on the National Championship teams of 1943 and, after military service, of '46 and '47. Ziggie's sense of humor was always at the ready; he brought good cheer everywhere he went. He was a born emcee, a comic, and an All-American tackle. Czarobski made friends wherever he went; his antics brought humor even to the most punishing practices or exquisite banquets. He was like a Lou Costello, but with muscle and better lines. Leahy's players will tell you to this day that Ziggie was the spirit who made Leahy possible; all Leahy with no Ziggie to break up the intensity would have driven even stars into the dirt. Czarobski simply dominated the Notre Dame campus in his time. The stories were legion. Like the day Leahy assembled his squad after a four-hour practice and told them that it seemed like he had to start over with them, had to remind them of the fundamentals. "Lads," he said, "this is a football." And then Ziggie's voice: "Hold on, Coach, I'm trying to take notes."

And everyone heard the story from one of Leahy's famous pregame premonitions of disaster. He told Ziggie that the tackle he would be playing against was 6'6", 260 pounds, mean, and a Phi Beta Kappa. "Zygmont," he asked, "how are you going to handle him?" To which Ziggie replied, "No problem, Coach, I'll just hit him a couple of times and he'll be as dumb as I am." Comic relief . . . but Ziggie was far from dumb.

Perhaps he was at his legendary best at pep rallies. The student body could not wait to hear Ziggie. All he needed to do was to begin his comments with "It behooves me greatly . . ." and the crowd would go berserk. Eventually, he wrote a column for the *Scholastic* under those four words. Jack Connor describes the fallout from one of Ziggy's pep rally performances:

Before the Purdue game, the pep rally had such a big crowd that the students were out of doors and surrounding the fieldhouse. Most of the new ones came to hear Ziggie. The word had spread. When captain George Connor finished his brief remarks, he asked the crowd from whom they wanted to hear; the response was deafening, "Ziggie!"

After one of his crazy stories, Ziggie waited until the laughter subsided, then turned around and looked directly at Freddie Miller sitting in the first row. Miller was the president and owner of Miller Brewing Company in Milwaukee. He was also a former Notre Dame All-American tackle and one of the university's biggest benefactors.

Without saying a word Ziggie turned back to the crowd. He then said, "Looking around reminds me of two brothers that owned a brewery in Milwaukee, Wisconsin. One day they received a letter from the United States Bureau of Standards in Washington wanting to know the alcoholic content of their beer. The brothers packaged a bottle of their beer and sent it off to Washington to be tested. In a few days the brothers received a telegram from the Bureau of Standards that said, 'Dear Sirs: Please rest this horse for six weeks.'"

Pandemonium broke out as the students laughed, hooted, and yelled. Miller turned five shades of red and Leahy almost dove under his seat. From that point on, the pep rally was in such chaos one had to wonder if the old fieldhouse walls would hold up.

That Monday after the Purdue game, Father Kehoe, the prefect of discipline for the university, sought out Connor. Father Kehoe opened the discussion: "George, I don't want you to call on Ziggie anymore at the pep rallies; his carrying on is really getting out of hand."

"I couldn't do that, Father, everyone expects him to speak," replied George.

"You're going to have to," said Father Kehoe. "He insulted one of the university's biggest supporters, and his antics have the students getting too wild. I'm afraid he just can't speak at future rallies."

"If Ziggie doesn't speak, Father, there is no team, and if there is no team, there is no pep rally."[2]

Father Kehoe backed down. The pep rallies continued to feature Ziggie, and he continued to write his column "It Behooves Me Greatly." We still have pep rallies, but we no longer have Ziggie. That genial man devoted much of his life to raising funds for Maryville Academy, a place for at-risk children run by Father John Smyth, the former Notre Dame All-American basketball star. Even in death, Ziggie provided a last laugh. His funeral was so emotional that as the service ended everyone rushed out of the church so they could gather outside and tell Ziggie stories. Everyone. Even the pallbearers. Only one thing was still inside: the casket with Ziggie in it. Probably smiling.

NOT ALL INTERACTIONS between rectors and students involve disorders or tragedies, of course. Farley rector Etheridge recalls the time one of her residents came to her in tears because a drunken male visitor had eaten her goldfish.

Sister Jean Lenz, OSF, assistant vice president of student affairs and one of Notre Dame's first female rectors, headed Farley from 1973 to 1983. She says, "I always told [residents] they could come to me with any good news, too." Which they did—sharing delights such as a marriage proposal or word of acceptance into graduate school.

Lenz enjoys special fame among rectors for how she handled an unusual situation in the mid-1970s. One spring evening around midnight she received a call from a priest across campus warning that a group of some 400 male students was making its way toward the North Quad. Suspecting mischief afoot, she put down the theology papers she was correcting, went to the hall entrance, and opened the door to have a look around.

"Oh, my God, it's sister!" shouted one of the students, who, like the rest of the multitude, was naked.

Momentarily speechless, the nun recovered enough composure to assure the streakers, "You are not getting in here like that!"—at which point someone in the mob suggested they terrorize Lyons Hall instead.

—ED COHEN, ASSOCIATE EDITOR, NOTRE DAME MAGAZINE[3]

HUNDREDS OF ALUMNI returned to the University of Notre Dame this weekend to recount old stories, recall cherished memories, and relive their college years for a couple of days—but some had taller tales to tell and more daring days to dwell on than others.

For Drs. Ed Manier, Will Santoro, and Cam Witzleben, their 50th reunion also marks the 50th anniversary of a prank they played to cap off their time at Notre Dame, a story that each man remembers a little differently.

It's an adventure they've dubbed "The Great Sorin Caper," and they tell it with such glee that those listening might swear it continues even 50 years later.

And, according to one of the men, it does.

It all began when Witzleben, now professor emeritus of pediatric pathology at the University of Pennsylvania Medical School, discovered a 3-foot replica of a statue of the Rev. Edward Sorin on the steps of the old post office the night before Christmas vacation. The bronze statue of the university founder normally resided in the lobby of Sorin Hall.

"It was somewhat of a campus joke to move it around, but we made a Mark Twain story of it," said Manier, professor of philosophy at Notre Dame.

Faced with what Witzleben called the opportunity of a lifetime, he and Manier deliberated over what to do with the statue.

"I was the brains of the operation," Manier insisted.

Since the ground was frozen, he suggested burying it in a sand-trap on the Notre Dame golf course.

When Manier and Witzleben went home for Christmas, they asked friends in the armed services who were returning to their posts abroad to send postcards back to South Bend from the missing statue.

The *Tribune*, the Rev. Charles McCarragher, then prefect of discipline, and senior class President Kerwin Fulton all received postcards from Sorin, commenting on his supposed visits with the emperor of Japan, the queen of England, and the pope.

Telegrams also bearing "Sorin's" signature arrived from locations including Washington, D.C., and Miami, and a committee was formed at the university to investigate the disappearance.

In a *Tribune* interview in January 1953, McCarragher questioned the newsworthiness of the prank.

"It has a certain amount of news value, I suppose, for a certain type of disordered mind," he said.

Meanwhile, the ground on the golf course was thawing, and the men feared their prank would come to a premature end.

"Spring came, and we were afraid someone would unearth Sorin, so we dug him up one night," Manier said. "Everything was done at night."

The next day, Manier and Witzleben delivered the statue to a friend's house in Chicago but later decided it needed to be returned before graduation.

"Getting the statue back was a tale from Huck Finn," Manier said.

In April, they retrieved the statue from Chicago, hitchhiked with it to Michigan City, and left it in a locker at a bus station there until they could come back for it in June.

"I had the idea to have a fantastic party when the statue returned the night before commencement," said Manier.

He printed and distributed signs in every downtown bar, advising students that Sorin would appear in the Main Circle the night before graduation. A huge crowd showed up, he said, and the men of Sorin Hall carried the statue back to its rightful home triumphantly.

But can anyone trust that the statue the pranksters returned was the original?

Not according to Santoro, who has his own version of what happened to Sorin, something he revealed to his partners in crime for the first time this weekend.

"The statue was missing from December to June, but it didn't actually just languish in the locker," said Santoro, director emeritus of a psychiatric outpatient center in Los Angeles.

Postcards weren't outlandish enough to achieve notoriety, Santoro concluded.

"I decided the statue should really travel the world. So I shipped it to France and then to Spain across the French Riviera. From there it went to Venice and then to Florence," he said.

In Florence, Santoro said he commissioned an Italian woman to make a copy of the statue and to ship the copy back to the United States, where he returned it to the bus station locker.

"It's a fake in Sorin [Hall]," Santoro pronounced with a mysterious gleam in his eye.

Santoro claimed the original had sunk with the Italian ocean liner Andrea Doria in 1956, after he had asked a friend in Florence to bring it back home.

While the details remain elusive, the disappearance of the Sorin statue from December 1952 to June 1953 amounts to a significant contribution to the university's history, the men said.

And regardless, it's a prank that's keeping three clever alumni entertained 50 years later.

—LAUREN BECK, *SOUTH BEND TRIBUNE* STAFF WRITER[4]

ANOTHER STORY THAT I passed along to Dick was about Walter O'Keefe, a student here in the early 1920s who later appeared in Broadway musicals and was a personality in broadcasting.

While O'Keefe was living in Sorin Hall, the prefect of discipline laid down the law at the close of evening prayers in chapel: "I wish you fellows had more imagination! It gets tiresome hearing the same lame excuses over and over. If when you got into trouble you could give me a fresh alibi, one I have never heard, I might let you off the hook."

O'Keefe was already in trouble. Because of a transgression he was campused, meaning he should not go south of Cedar Grove Cemetery until next semester. But a dance band was playing in South Bend, one that he just had to hear. Temptation triumphed, and Walter was caught coming out of the Oliver Hotel.

When appearing before the prefect of discipline the next morning, he said: "Father, you told us that if someone gave you an excuse you have never heard before you might let him off the hook. Well, I wanted to go to town and felt I had a good reason. I came here to ask your permission, but you were not in. I went to talk to the president, but he wasn't in either. So I decided to try the founder, and went out to Father Sorin's statue, and said, 'Father, may I go to town?' There was no answer and so I took silence for consent."

I heard O'Keefe tell that anecdote on the radio in 1946. Nearly two decades later, in Hollywood, I asked him if the prefect of discipline had reacted with good grace.

"Oh, yes! He admitted he had never heard that one before. As I was leaving the office he added, 'And I had better never hear it again!'"

—PROFESSOR EDWARD FISCHER[5]

"WHO WANTS TO listen to a policeman telling everyone to behave themselves?" Tim McCarthy asked himself. He knew the answer.

The year was 1960, and McCarthy had just been promoted from trooper in the Indiana State Police to safety education sergeant. One of his new responsibilities was to make an announcement at Notre Dame home football games reminding people to drive safely on the way home, but after two games he knew people weren't paying attention.

He decided to change that by adding something to the message.

At the first home game in 1961, the message was about drinking and driving, and McCarthy ended by saying, "The automobile replaced the horse, but the driver should stay on the wagon."

More than 220 stadium announcements later, fans in Notre Dame Stadium fall silent in eager anticipation during the fourth quarter when they hear, "May I have your attention, please. This is Tim McCarthy for the Indiana State Police."

They know what's coming: a reminder to drive carefully and courteously on the way home, punctuated by an often groan-inducing play on words.

McCarthy says he got the wordplay idea from a friend of his, Chicago policeman Len Baldy, who used the device in the helicopter traffic reports he did for a radio station. Baldy gave McCarthy a few ideas to try at the Notre Dame games.

After running through these and receiving a good response, it was up to McCarthy to keep the tradition alive.

Early on, the safety sergeant worried that the gag might be taken as trivializing the hard and dangerous work the state police perform, so he reverted to announcing the messages straight. But fans kept asking for the punch lines. McCarthy says he knew then that if he reinstated the punch lines, fans would listen more closely than ever.

These days when he makes the announcements, McCarthy identifies himself as "for" the Indiana State Police rather than "of" because he retired from the force in December 1978 after being elected sheriff of Porter County. He later was appointed county tax assessor. In 1999 he retired from political life to form his own company, which does tax appraisal work for assessors.

The 68-year-old admits he still gets the jitters when he steps up to the mike. He says it's not easy coming up with new plays on words, so he keeps an ear out for them throughout the year. He gets a kick out of fans' reactions and says he doesn't mind when the lines aren't met with applause.

"I've been booed a few times, but that's OK because I knew they listened to the safety announcement."

McCarthy says he has been contacted by the Seattle Supersonics (ND alumni work for the team), the Chicago Bears, and other nationally recognized sports teams interested in having him make announcements for them. But the loyal Notre Dame fan has yet to take his safety-minded wordplay on the road.

TIM MCCARTHY'S
PERSONAL TOP TEN

10. "Don't let your day go down the drain by forgetting today's safety plug."

9. "When it is only coffee for the road . . . there's always grounds for safety."

8. "It takes a strong heart to drive on clogged arteries."

7. "No one relishes a pickled driver."

6. "Anyone whose driving sparkles . . . is a real gem."

5. "Keep your driving well polished to avoid having a bad finish."

4. "Horsing around in traffic after dark could become a real nightmare."

3. "You can always bank on safety . . . for your best interest."

2. "Drinking drivers are like light bulbs: The first to get turned on are the first to burn out."

1. "Anyone who tries to bolt through traffic . . . is a real nut."

—KRISTY KATZMANN[6]

PRAYERS WORK BETTER when the players are big.

—FRANK LEAHY, AS QUOTED ON THE COVER OF *TIME* MAGAZINE, OCTOBER 14, 1946

STANDING IN THE WINGS, Kevin Carney looked pleased as he watched the Keenan Revue Band and Keenan Revue Dancers rehearse the opening number for this year's show.

The band pounded out its cover of "Basketcase," and a dozen residents of the men's dorm jogged on stage wearing T-shirts and warm-up pants. As part of the customary show-opener, off came the T-shirts, which were then rubbed front to back between their legs like floss between teeth. Several gyrations later, the routine led into pelvic thrusts.

"You wouldn't think you'd have to spend a week and a half choreographing pelvic thrusts," Carney, this year's director, observed to me wryly, "but you have to have perfect pelvic thrusts if you're going to be in the Keenan Revue."

I've attended the Keenan Revue for the past seven years, and I'm always alternately appalled and amused, but mostly impressed.

The Revue began as a hall talent show in the dorm basement in 1977, something to break up the dreary chill of South Bend's winter. It's grown into the most popular hall-organized event of the year, selling out three shows in Saint Mary's 1,300-seat O'Laughlin Auditorium at the end of January. Actually "sell-out" is a misnomer. Keenan gives away all the tickets, mostly to Notre Dame and Saint Mary's students who wait in long lines to get them.

This year I dropped in on some of the rehearsals to see how the show is put together. Astonishingly quickly, I found out. Though they get started on the standard opening and closing musical numbers a little early, the rest of the acts audition less than a week before opening night. Selections are made on a Sunday night, the cast rehearses Monday, Tuesday, and Wednesday, and the curtain goes up Thursday for the first of three straight nights.

The show consists mostly of comedy skits and musical numbers with an occasional juggler, magician, or other specialty act. It's a testament to the talent of the Notre Dame student body that residents of a single hall—guys randomly thrown together by computer—can put together a two-hour show of this quality in so short a time.

And it's amazing Notre Dame and Saint Mary's let them. With a show designed exclusively by males age 18 to 22, the humor is predictably sophomoric and often crude. Carney, a senior pre-med major, made his mark last year with a number called "Taco Bell's Cannon"— the gentle "Pachelbel's Canon," standard in weddings, performed to recorded sounds of flatulence. One of this year's acts featured a man being kicked in the crotch multiple times by, among other characters, the Pope. But the Keenan Revue is undeniably an artifact of the campus culture, and not in an entirely embarrassing way.

One of the more interesting aspects of the show is its complex treatment of the Catholic faith. Although not exactly reverent, the humor reveals respect, knowledge, pride. In a sketch from 1992, the announcers at a football game between the Old Testament and New Testament marvel at Lazarus, "who seemed dead out there in the first half" but after a halftime talk with Jesus "has really come to life."

The Revue is often criticized for playing on stereotypes, which it does; "Making Fun of You Since 1977" is its slogan. Perpetual targets include the girls (never "women") of the residence halls Breen-Phillips (fat), Farley (smokers), Pasquerilla West (hairy). The virility of the men of rival Zahm Hall is relentlessly questioned.

The show's victims don't all suffer this abuse gladly, but mostly they do. Last year in a referendum, Saint Mary's students—continually depicted as dumb and easy—voted overwhelmingly to let the show continue to be performed in O'Laughlin.

Former hall residents help keep the tradition going. Every August, the producer—this year it was junior David Cantos—mails appeals to 3,000 Keenan alums. Their donations, along with sales of ads in the show program and souvenir T-shirts, provide the bulk of the estimated $11,000 it costs to produce the Revue. Residents also pass the hat at each show. In his appeal to audience members this year, Carney said people often ask why the hall doesn't just charge a dollar for tickets.

"We don't want to do that. We want to keep it completely free, our gift to campus," he said. "Plus everybody would be coming back on Monday like, 'Dude, I want my dollar back.'"

—ED COHEN, ASSOCIATE EDITOR, *NOTRE DAME MAGAZINE*[7]

MOOSE KRAUSE'S SENSE of humor was legendary. While he poked fun at others, one of his favorite targets was himself. Relaying one of his favorite stories, Krause remembered that during some of the most difficult times with the football program, he found himself sick in the hospital with pneumonia. A note from Father Joyce heartened him. "It said, 'We want to wish you a speedy return to health,'" Krause said. "'The vote was four-to-three by the faculty board.'"

A group of school principals in Columbus, Ohio, once invited him to give a speech about education, Krause said, and he left the podium proud of how well he made his point. "The next day, on my way back to South Bend," he said, "I picked up a Columbus newspaper and the headline read, 'Moose Krause's speech shows need for education.'"

That provided a nice segue into his larger point about the lessons of athletics and their place in a liberal education. "I'm a normal guy, I hate to lose," Krause said, but he placed more importance on the value of competition than the thrill of victory.

Krause's sense of perspective came from a lifetime of personal losses that shaped his outlook on life far more than his victories. Growing up in the Back of the Yards, he had little more than faith to sustain him, the one constant in his life whether he lost a football game or his father. Enduring the Depression and the murder of his father, collecting the remains of fallen soldiers—Krause had seen worse than a 2–8 record.

—JASON KELLY[8]

January 14, 1922
Dear *Scholastic* Editor,
There are two types of individuals entering the gymnasium these wintry, unpleasant days; the one type goes there to use the gymnasium, the other merely to look on. There is a place for each. Those using either the apparatus room or the track should be dressed suitably in either tennis shoes

or spikes for the latter. Those acting in the role of spectators will kindly remain in the gallery.

The gallery and the track hall are large enough and
comfortable enough for all interested. Both places, the
track and the apparatus room floor, are for exercise, not not
for loafing; besides loafers get in the way of those wishing
to get the most out of college. You are requested to conform
with these remarks for the benefit of others and yourself,
incidentally.

B.H.B. Lange, C.S.C.
K.K. Rockne, Director

There was one game in particular during my playing days at Notre
Dame that stands out in my memory. This was the Army game in
1933. The cadets were favored by about thirty points. The Irish
played their hearts out and we won 13–12. That day I managed to
deflect, not block cleanly, about eight punts. These deflections so
shook up the Army that they changed formations and started putting
two players in their backfield on punt formations. Their job was to
block our great end, Wayne Millner, and me.

Late in the game we were behind by a touchdown and Army
went into punt formation. Wayne and I set up a play. At the snap I
ran in, jumped over the first back, grabbed the second, and all three
of us went down in a heap. Millner blocked the punt with his
knees—he had so much time to get in. The ball bounced into the
end zone where Jim Harris and I fell on it. We were both holding the
ball but the officials gave the touchdown to Harris.

I never scored a point in my college career but I always maintained that three of those six points should have been credited to me.

There were some memorable occasions when I returned to Notre
Dame as a coach. I handled the team a few times when Frank Leahy
was ill, once at USC in 1946. I gave the team a rousing pep talk

before the game and I topped it off by pointing at the door and shouting, "Now get out there and beat 'em!" The team was on its way out of the dressing room when Lujack came up to me and told me I'd forgotten to name a starting line-up. "Everybody starts!" I shouted. I was the most excited person in that dressing room. Somehow we got eleven people on the field, and we absolutely clobbered the Trojans, 26–6. That victory clinched a National Championship for us.

—ED "MOOSE" KRAUSE[9]

INTERLUDE

FULFILLING THE PROMISE:
NOTRE DAME TODAY AND TOMORROW

BY REV. EDWARD A. MALLOY, C.S.C.

IF YOU WILL allow me, I would like to look back a bit, because I think it's not only acceptable to be nostalgic, but also pertinent to the University's future.

I have always thought my first and fundamental responsibility to be the maintenance of Notre Dame as a Catholic university. I really do believe that our distinctiveness is our greatest strength. To be Catholic, of course, is not reducible to being any one thing. It includes our insistence upon a core curriculum with required courses in philosophy and theology. It insists upon a connection among all fields of knowledge. We may not be wise enough to see it all the time, but we believe that within the Catholic tradition every approach to the truth is a way to God. A Catholic university, of course, needs to be an exciting and stimulating place of learning. The various fields of endeavor here must try to draw a connection between teaching and scholarship and a fundamental commitment to communally held transcendental values. . . . For Notre Dame to be a Catholic university requires many different things. It has to do with the way in which our centers and institutes manifest our curiosity about and our interest in things that are religious, specifically Church oriented and conducive toward interaction with the grand religious traditions of others. Many of the ventures that Father Ted Hesburgh initiated, particularly the many institutes he helped establish, justify Notre Dame's claim to be a Catholic university and a place where the Church does her thinking and converses with the broader society. So often when I have gone to meetings of my peers in higher education, they have turned to me at some critical point and asked, "What does Notre Dame do about that?" or "Do you have a set of scholars or a program or some way that you can assist us in thinking about comparable matters within our own institutional context?" We are a Catholic university when we try to be in connection with other institutions of higher education around the world, particularly other Catholic institutions. Our affiliations both within the United States and elsewhere allow us to play a leadership role that I hope we can continue to play in the future. . . . No matter where you look on our campus, the Catholicism of the school should be apparent. . . .

The role of the Congregation of Holy Cross is essential to our Catholic mission and identity, which is why I'm delighted that my successor is a fellow Holy Cross priest and a distinguished scholar in his own right. It is, in my judgment, very important for the well-being of the institution not simply to have an isolated person in a position of power and influence, but to recognize the collective strength which the Congregation of Holy Cross and particularly its Indiana Province brings to this University. Not only are we the founders of Notre Dame, but we are also deeply involved in every dimension of the life here, and as we look forward we hope we can continue to recruit young people prepared to participate in our mission.

A second of my priorities concerned the debate throughout academia on the relationship between teaching and research. I am pleased by the way in which our aspiration for excellence in teaching has been passed on from one generation to the next, particularly the fine work of the Kaneb Center and the manner in which the Kaneb Awards allow us to honor excellent teaching across all the disciplines. Even as we hire, we try to show those who come to us— whether they are junior faculty or senior faculty—that teaching counts here and is one of the ways in which they will be evaluated. It's taken seriously in the promotion process, and I know that the Provost's Advisory Committee and the deans and the departments take teaching more and more seriously as part of the portfolio by which we evaluate people coming along. Students, of course, wonder whether their assessments are taken seriously, and, as far as I'm concerned, they are. Faculty worry about whether the instruments we use to evaluate teaching are adequate to the task. If they are not, then we need to find better ones, but we must not retreat from our insistence upon evaluating quality teaching. We must simply do it better than anyone else. I believe ours is an excellent teaching institution in all its dimensions: the lectures, the seminars, class discussion work groups, collaborative research, on-site computer-generated opportunities, and feedback from faculty. I think we are learning from each other, and I hope that tradition will continue. . . .

Another of my priorities was that we be a fully coeducational institution and that we take on the challenge of diversity in a way that we lacked the will or the resources to do until recently. I feel that we are making progress in both regards. It is now taken for granted here, as it wasn't before, that women should be vice presidents, serve as deans and as directors, and play very influential roles in department leadership as well. Many of the best-recognized and -appreciated faculty here at Notre Dame are women. May their numbers increase. It takes effort, goodwill, and astuteness to find out where the best faculty women are, and we have to continue to work hard at a supportive environment for women faculty. I think we have made progress, but that, too, needs to be monitored and we have a long way to go. . . . We need to be focused on the coeducation dimension moving forward. The same thing, of course, applies to student life and the opportunities for leadership in every student organization and in student government. We are making steady progress, but this priority requires constant affirmation.

When it comes to underrepresented minorities, I always feel a prisoner of census categories because so many people who come to us today have multiple backgrounds and multiple histories, ethnically, racially, and even religiously, which is why, in talking about diversity, you are often talking about the diversity of an individual person as well. In census categories, we have moved from under-

graduate classes with 7.5 percent underrepresented minorities eighteen years ago to approximately 21 percent in the last two classes.
This reflects hard work in the recruiting efforts, in the welcoming
process, and in the creation of support structures across the board.
As many of you know, I teach a seminar each semester which looks a
bit like a Rainbow Coalition, and when I walk in, the nice thing is
that I can't predict by looking at people and gauging their ethnic or
racial history what grades they are going to get. In my experience, all
stereotypes break down in that kind of learning environment. That's
as true this semester as it has been every other semester. The people
who are coming here from underrepresented groups come with high
aspirations for themselves, and we need to do everything we can to
foster those high expectations and to give them all of the skills necessary to succeed in the challenging world in which we live. They
clearly contribute to the quality of our learning environment, and not
simply to the academic side of the University, but to everything that
has to do with student life. . . .

I'm also excited about our development as an international institution. I have traveled a lot and have seen some of the great universities of the world. We have relationships with many of them, and
many others would like to have a formal agreement with us. We have
quite a few international centers where our students and some of our
faculty go for study. Almost all of the students come back with a different perspective on reality and a level of confidence about being
able to negotiate a complex and interesting world in a way that they
didn't possess before they went. There are always questions about
costs and about rigor and about learning another language as part of
that experience. One of the goals which I have mentioned many
times is for every Notre Dame undergraduate to graduate bilingual.
We are far from that. If I had to live my life all over again, I would
want to be fluent in at least four languages. . . . What a wonderful gift
to possess, to have been there and to have sensed with all of one's
senses what it's like in another culture of violence or a culture of

prosperity. Wherever we might go, there are lessons to be learned and ways in which to bring back to the University what we've learned. We have graduates living and working in just about every part of the world, and we have tried to establish Notre Dame clubs and to gain financial contributions from some of those graduates in order to recruit undergraduate international students from a wider socioeconomic background. And, of course, in our various professional programs like the MBA and law programs, in architecture, in the MDiv program, as well as in the graduate school, the presence of international opportunities and international students and faculty is a rich gift to the institution. . . .

As a university we have promoted closer bonds with our surrounding communities through a number of initiatives: the South Bend Center for the Homeless, the Robinson Community Learning Center, with the Chapin Street Health Clinic, and a lot of other wonderful outreach programs to members of our community who are in need. I think we have had a good relationship with the city governments and the county commissioners and all of those who are in representative positions, not only at the local level but at the state and national level as well.

To be a good citizen and to be concerned about the quality of life of everyone here is an important dimension of what it means to be a major institutional actor. We are not a bank. We are not a for-profit organization that can provide huge sums of money for some of these activities, but we can partner and we can make a difference. These positive changes allow us to attract people who otherwise might not be interested in coming here. The closing of Juniper and the straightening of Notre Dame Avenue and Angela is another part of this long development of our relationships with the neighborhoods around us. We have been able, in the midst of all these developments, to foster the centrality of the residential tradition here at Notre Dame.

I live in a dorm myself, and during the last couple of weeks I have been able to have informal discussions with residents of three of our undergraduate dorms and to hear students talk about what's on their minds and to marvel at how bright and talented and eager and energetic they are. We are blessed in the quality of students we have, but when you see them in their living situations, you also recognize how blessed we are to have dedicated rectors and assistant rectors who carry the burden of the day and, most of all, night. If you are not ready to go to bed at 3 or 4 o'clock in the morning, then it's not a job for you, particularly on the weekends. The rectors are the people who console in time of grief, confront when people need to be held accountable, and help people recover after things have not gone well. They help create a sense of community. They foster the liturgical life of the campus community, and they encourage people who are gifted to serve those less fortunate than themselves. This is a tremendously hard-to-describe phenomenon, and it has made Notre Dame a special kind of place. I am proud that many of us who are Holy Cross live either in positions of authority in the dorms or in-residence, like myself and Father Jenkins. It allows us, I hope, to manifest an interest in our students and to be in touch with the kinds of things that keep them up at night or that worry them about their futures and about our world. But it also allows us to try to tap in to all their potential and capacity to make a wonderful difference in the future. When people ask about Notre Dame's loyalty, about the mystique of Notre Dame, I tell them it is really made up of many separate elements, but I think no part of it is more critical than the residential tradition of the institution. It's funny that often the students who complain the most about the rules when they are here later want their kids to come here, and I have been around long enough to watch that phenomenon. In fact, I can remember that the parents of the students who are here now got in the same trouble that their kids get in, but that is a story for another day. We have all the support services under Student Affairs here: Campus Ministry, the Center for Social Concerns, the outreach activities like the Alliance for Catholic Education, and all of the ways in which we try to create a campus environment that prays together, plays together, studies together, and serves together. It seems to me that each one of these is integral to what makes Notre Dame a special and distinctive kind of institution. . . .

A note about athletics: Notre Dame has a storied tradition in athletics and, most of you know, I was a student-athlete myself. It was my vehicle for coming to Notre Dame, and I never could have afforded to come otherwise. I am very comfortable in the world of intercollegiate athletics, and I have tried to play a leadership role in its various dimensions. It is, however, an area where passion reigns supreme—sometimes irrational passion. It is very important for us to keep a sense of perspective. We certainly want all of our athletic programs to excel, just as we want the bands and the Glee Club and the other choral groups and the student government and the student publications to excel. We want them all to be excellent in their own modes of operation. Thus it is in athletics: It's a field which is highly competitive, not only sport to sport but also in the way that it's structured. I believe we have in place here a model administrative structure for overseeing and promoting athletics. . . . We are a place that takes academics seriously, that gives a meaningful degree, that tries to play by the rules, and that tries to support our student-athletes so that they can have a meaningful experience here. Still, any of us traveling or meeting with faculty from elsewhere will invariably find that every other dimension of Notre Dame's excellence is subsumed within the question: "How's the football team going to be?" I use such informal banter as an opportunity to talk about everything else, but we must remember that it isn't going to go away. Let's recognize what an integral part of our history intercollegiate athletics is. It gives us a visibility and a presence which provide a vehicle to tell the fuller story. . . .

Finally, I would like to speak about the colleagues that I have enjoyed through the years. This is a place, as I have explained to many who have come here from elsewhere, that is not governed by memos and formal letters, but by relationships fostered in informal environments, such as over a meal like those we have been able to share in recent years when new faculty convene for a welcoming retreat up at Lake Michigan, or when we bring the academic administrators to Chicago to spend time together. Such occasions are worth their weight in gold because they help us get to know and to understand each other. This is a place where people quickly develop lifelong friendships and where they are motivated to serve the common good by the human dynamics of this place. . . .

—Excerpted from President Malloy's
eighteenth and final annual address to the faculty,
delivered October 5, 2004

MIND

An education that is complete is one in which the hands and
heart are engaged as much as the mind. We want to let our students
try their learning in the world and so make prayers
of their educations.

—REV. BASIL MOREAU, C.S.C., FOUNDER OF HOLY CROSS

THERE ARE IRREFUTABLE signs pointing to the respect now accorded Notre Dame in the academic world. Notre Dame ranks eighteenth in the 2004 *U.S.News & World Report* national universities rankings. But a new system, differently weighted, has Notre Dame eleventh among doctoral-granting institutions. The quality of students enrolling at Notre Dame equals that of the finest universities in America. The University continues to attract outstanding senior and junior scholars to its faculty, with a concurrent increase in outside research funding and publication. Currently, twenty-eight Notre Dame graduates are presidents of institutions of higher education. James Witherbee, the only U.S. astronaut to command five space flights, is a 1971 graduate of Notre Dame. U.S. Circuit Court of Appeals Judge Ann Clare Williams is a 1975 graduate of the Notre Dame Law School. Dennis Jacobs, Professor of Chemistry, was named U.S. Professor of the Year in 2002. Notre Dame leads the nation in National Endowment for the Humanities grants in the past six years, with twenty grants made to Notre Dame faculty.

No university has achieved lasting greatness without major financial resources. Dramatic and continuing support for Notre Dame's mission to become a great Catholic university has fueled what otherwise could not have happened.

All of this would have delighted and probably shocked Father Sorin, who dared to call his tiny school a university in 1842. What has happened at Notre Dame, especially since World War II, has not been simply growth but evolution. Some things do not change, such as dedication to catholicity and a commitment to good teaching. But this is in every way a contemporary university with excellent and always-improving facilities. The new Marie P. DeBartolo Center for Performing Arts is arguably the best facility of its kind on any campus in America. The dream of a Catholic university, tied to its roots and tradition, but open to the needs of its time and able to address them, is now a reality.

It is worth noting the University's presidents who have, over the years, made Notre Dame what it is today;

Rev. Edward Sorin (founder)	1842–1865
Rev. Patrick Dillon	1865–1866
Rev. William Corby	1866–1872
Rev. Auguste Lemonnier	1872–1874
Rev. Patrick Colovin	1874–1877
Rev. William Corby (second time)	1877–1881
Rev. Thomas E. Walsh	1881–1893
Rev. Andrew Morrissey	1893–1905
Rev. John W. Cavanaugh	1905–1919
Rev. James A. Burns	1919–1922
Rev. Matthew J. Walsh	1922–1928
Rev. Charles L. O'Donnell	1928–1934
Rev. John F. O'Hara	1934–1940
Rev. J. Hugh O'Donnell	1940–1946
Rev. John J. Cavanaugh	1946–1952
Rev. Theodore M. Hesburgh	1952–1987
Rev. Edward A. Malloy	1986–2005
Rev. John I. Jenkins	2005–

A DROLL AXIOM has it that any institution's golden age is the one that included you. That's natural and necessary. Without it there would be no golden anything, no greatness, no sense of identification that outlasts the years and their diversions.

Notre Dame is famous for it. The place inculcates that sense in its daughters and sons and nourishes it: Yours *was* the golden age.

It may be inevitable as sentiment, but it is not always true.

Notre Dame's century and a half did include such an age: the time between the two World Wars, roughly the 1920s and '30s. It was the time when Notre Dame went national in a dozen ways beyond the football legend that grew to overshadow its other virtues and achievements.

The period was one of stunning growth—physically, academically, intellectually. But The Time Between the Wars brought more than growth. It also brought a profound change of direction.

None of it was the work of a single mind, nor was there any master plan. All that went before the time was necessary prologue; all that followed was made possible by that remarkable period. When World War I ended, Notre Dame was a provincial sectarian college of modest reputation and goals. By the time America was shocked into World War II, the campus under the Golden Dome was a national institution.

If there was no single moving force, there were plenty of heroes. Knute Kenneth Rockne springs first to the minds of too many. He was part of it, the stuff of legends—but legend springs from myth, and there was nothing mythical about the men who led Notre Dame's coming of age. They were brilliant; they had courage; they were ready. Rockne was one of their valuable assets, but never the guide or the soul. Perhaps it was Father Burns.

James Aloysius Burns, C.S.C., may be Notre Dame's most underrated hero, the least celebrated of her great captains. No residence hall bears his name; no famous biography records his triumphs. He is in the books, of course; he is listed as the 10th president, which is akin to noting that A. Lincoln was the 16th president of the United States.

You can argue endlessly whether Burns was merely there at the right time or caused the time to happen. It doesn't matter. He was the pilot of the great change.

He organized the colleges into departments with deans and chairs, bringing order to chaos. He established the credit-hour system, designed by Father Matthew Schumacher, that's still essentially in use. He went looking for good lay professors and paid them decently. He strengthened the studies already offered, and he added more.

Burns relied on more than the loyalty of the lay faculty to help with the revolution. He had a cadre of young Holy Cross priests who were genuine scholars, and that too was his doing. From 1900 until his election as president in 1919, he had been superior of the Holy Cross School of Theology in Washington, where he urged, prodded, and coaxed the brighter seminarians into intellectual development beyond the requirements of preparation for the priesthood.

Some of these younger men were on the Notre Dame faculty when Burns returned to the campus at the end of World War I; others flocked back. They gave strong political and intellectual support to his determination to make the place more than a finishing school for good Catholic boys, to make it a genuine university dedicated to intellectual development.

He phased out the manual labor school and the prep school, moves that made sense but also made enemies. That may explain his brief presidency. He served from 1919 to 1922, then was rejected for a second term—so he could concentrate on fund-raising, according to Father Arthur Hope in *Notre Dame: One Hundred Years*. Perhaps.

Hope's history is crammed with dates and facts and sugary platitudes. He so avoided discussion of the infighting that involves any human organization that his chronicle is incomplete. Even so, he was right about the fund-raising. . . .

Burns was aware before he ever took the presidency of the need for organized funding and the 20th-century use of those funds. The result is a Burns legacy: He fought for the establishment of an investment board that included laymen, then convinced his religious colleagues to turn over to the new board, heavy with experienced businessmen, the control and administration of University funds. That was as much the beginning of the new Notre Dame as were Burns's academic reforms.

The board met first in January 1921, and Burns set out immediately to raise some money for the members to administer. The Rockefeller and Carnegie Foundations liked his message and offered $250,000 and $75,000, respectively—if he could raise an additional $750,000. He did. That million-plus was Notre Dame's first endowment, even as the two foundation grants were the first major outside money.

The Burns career manifests a trait associated with great men, the knack for finding, even in mid-life, talents one didn't know one had. Ascetic and reserved by nature, he became the first of the University's great salesmen. The new money didn't last long because the needs were daunting. Almost everything about Notre Dame was inadequate when The Great War ended. Applications exceeded available places. "Not enough places" has been a chronic problem at Notre Dame; it is not new, later myth to the contrary.

TO MATTHEW WALSH, C.S.C., successor to Burns and president for most of the '20s, fell the job of building to meet these needs. He built. The splendor of the south quad, the stunning mall that stretches east from the Rockne Memorial, is the result of that extraordinary effort. It wasn't a development, it was an explosion. It was not a new aspect of the old campus, it was a new dimension.

Walsh wanted most of his students on campus. When he took office, only a few hundred were residents; more than 1,100 found what lodging they could in South Bend. Walsh and his advisors did the expedient thing: They erected two temporary dormitories on the east end near the gymnasium. Then they got to work on the real buildings.

The administration commissioned two gifted members of the architecture faculty, Professors Francis Kervick and Vincent Fagan, to design a cluster of three large, permanent resident halls south and southwest of the old library. Excavation for Howard Hall started in the summer of 1924, and by November of the next year Morrissey and Lyons were under construction as well. They formed an aesthetic entity with the Morrissey tower as the focal point.

By then there was no stopping. A showplace dining hall went up on the southwest corner of the campus. It opened in 1927, two main wings each 220 feet by 62 feet with terrazzo floors and oaken wainscoting on the walls (yes, that's real oak).

That's when the central heating system developed. Father Thomas Steiner, dean of the college of engineering and later provincial superior of the order, designed an arrangement of easy-access underground conduits to carry steam to each building. It worked, allowing the headlong growth to continue without pause.

When ground was broken for Alumni and Dillon Halls and Cushing Hall of Engineering in 1931, the new law building had been open for a semester. The commerce building was dedicated in 1932. It rolled on that way as a tide does; except for the World War II years, it never really stopped.

Bricks and mortar do not make a golden age, certainly not in terms of a university. The greatness of those years is keyed to the fact that the Burns spirit of university was carried on by his successors. The buildings are impressive; the mall is majestic. But they were the physical manifestations, not ends in themselves.

The academic reforms continued, too. The Walsh administration pared the numbers of credit hours needed for a degree but reorganized those hours and set up the system of a major study sequence. It was a task, because there'd been no real system at all before.

In his book, Stritch describes it as a "muddle." Hard as it is to believe, the college of arts and letters in 1924 still offered seven different degrees. Within two years, that was reduced to the one proper degree: Bachelor of Arts.

Not all of it was easy. Out went the ancient requirement of studying classical Latin or Greek, which the new leaders considered a sterile and unrewarding use of time on the college level. This was heresy to the 1920s version of the Old Boys. But the reforms stuck; the movement was a tide, not an aberration.

Nor was it a work of a few. Those early disciples of Burns were now deans and department heads, and they were believers. What they believed was that changes in courses and curricula were essential to the realization of their ideal of a university. Naturally, the faculty they built shared the dream.

Walsh doubled the size of that faculty to 180 by 1928, and salaries of lay professors improved steadily. Walsh and his fellow clerics understood that while man does not live by bread alone, it comes in handy when feeding a family. Faculty morale improved along with faculty quality.

Gifted teachers signed on in music and the other arts, in letters and engineering, in the business disciplines. It was an exciting time. There was a surging interest by faculty and students in serious scholarship and in experimenting, too. The wide interest may have been new, but not the questing for knowledge.

Notre Dame had, in fact, a tradition of that, especially in the physical sciences. Father John A. Zahm is the most celebrated example. He joined the order about 1870 and apparently mastered one science after another with dazzling speed. He developed a national reputation and lectured and taught with an éclat that made him a guru to his students.

Father Julius Nieuwland followed him as a priest-scientist of international fame—a science scholar who was honored in his later years by half a dozen world organizations for his experiments and discoveries. As a teacher, though, Nieuwland had his weaknesses.

He was impatient with mediocrity and gave most of his time to the very bright—a serious flaw in any instructor of undergraduate students. The same trait made him a notable teacher of graduates; he excelled in it, especially in chemistry, and his efforts, starting at the end of World War I, developed the first really important graduate studies at Notre Dame.

Those efforts began in science and engineering and grew slowly through the '20s. Organization did not come until the return of Father Philip Moore in 1933 to be secretary of the Committee on Graduate Study. Moore was a medieval scholar and a planner, and he spent the next two decades developing a graduate school. Through all the years, however, Notre Dame's fame as an American institution rested solidly on the strength of her undergraduate education.

That status grew in the 1920s to be immense and national. It was a time when America was forced to look at its Catholic citizens as more than hod carriers, when Notre Dame undergraduates burned with ambition and energy. In the Roaring '20s they rejected second-class status. The new dynamism prompted them to reach for excellence in several ways. The most spectacular had nothing to do with scholarship. It was football, of course.

Football and Knute Rockne. The man and the moment. They were one of life's perfect matings. Pious sentimentalists saw the hand of God; skeptics called it coincidence. It was an immeasurable benefit to Notre Dame.

The end of World War I triggered an eruption of interest in sports across the land. People wanted an end to "grim"; the new message was "Ain't we got fun?" Baseball players, prize fighters, and race horses were more celebrated than the American presidents (especially those presidents).

Times were rich, prosperity seemed endless, and dollars by the millions poured into sports. And there was Rockne and the little school somewhere in Indiana. It pains scholars to think about it; it shortchanges the memory of the men who built the place as a center of higher learning. Nevertheless it is true that Rockne and The Game thrust Notre Dame into the national consciousness.

He was no public relations creation. He was good and he knew it, and he inspired that same confidence in the young men who played for him. His own story delighted writers and fans: a penniless Norwegian immigrant who worked his way through Notre Dame on odd jobs and football and was bright enough to be offered a chemistry instructorship at graduation.

Rockne played the game well, but he also thought about it. He reasoned that there was too much emphasis on size. He substituted speed and perfect execution, and the rest, as they say, is . . . well known.

He began as head coach in 1918 with an indifferent season. Then he rolled, helped in the next two seasons by a so-so scholar named George Gipp who electrified crowds and stunned opponents. After that it was mostly Rockne. His teams won 105 games, lost 12, and tied five times. A notable sports scribe of the time hung the appellation "Four Horsemen" on the 1924 backfield, and legend was born. Rockne's 1928 "Win one for the Gipper" speech helped it grow. Even his death did. He went down in a plane crash in March 1931 at the crest of his fame, generating front-page headlines and radio bulletins. He was national and so was Notre Dame.

Scholars can sulk about the football connection. Notre Dame's detractors, many of them stuffed with malice and misinformation, can jeer. Football is a cultural fact on the South Bend campus. In the surge of those golden years it was a sociological phenomenon. To millions of Catholics of German, Irish, Italian, and Slavic ancestry, Notre Dame was a proud symbol of arrival. An Irish-Catholic boy growing up in Brooklyn in the Depression 1930s looked west, not east, for his Mecca.

So The Game has been more than a game to the people who adopted a slur, Fighting Irish, for their nickname. The intellectuals and planners who built a genuine university used it as an effective tool to continue the building. Cavanaugh, Zahm, and Breen-Philips Halls went up in the '30s. So did the football stadium.

Clamor for it started in the '20s, but Father Walsh told the zealots, "not before more necessary buildings are completed." History at times does repeat itself, to the amusement, or perhaps distraction, of the current leadership.

The growth was more than physical. The two decades featured a parade of notable visitors and lecturers. Franklin Roosevelt and Al Smith came, of course. So did William Butler Yeats, the Irish poet and Nobel laureate, and G. K. Chesterton, Yves Simon, Jacques Maritain, Karl Menger, and F. A. Hermens.

Notre Dame attracted foreign scholars and many stayed. Political philosopher Waldemar Furian was a familiar campus figure long after World War II. He was, in 1939, the first editor of Notre Dame's impressive *Review of Politics*, a continuing contribution to American political philosophy.

Much, perhaps too much, has been written about the 1924 brawl between students and the Ku Klux Klan when domers administered thrashings to the human refuse arriving with their bed sheets for a South Bend parade. Although it became part of the lore of the place, it was incidental, symbolic of a bigotry that was dying, imperceptibly at first but surely.

American Catholics and Notre Dame already were moving into the mainstream. When the '30s ended and a nightmare fell upon the world, they were already a strong part of the whole. After the war there was no doubt.

No age stands alone, separated from the years before and after. Father Burns came to Notre Dame a decade before the death of Sorin the Founder. He became the Sorin product who pointed Notre Dame toward its modern role.

The University's Time Between the Wars turned out leaders in every field of human endeavor, and among them was Theodore Martin Hesburgh, C.S.C., the giant of the postwar era. He too is a link, a product of the '30s, a part of the golden age of awakening that made possible today's Notre Dame.

—JOHN POWERS, WHO RETIRED IN 1990 AS EXECUTIVE EDITOR OF
THE *SOUTH BEND TRIBUNE* [1]

I WILL FOREVER be grateful to my parents for making it possible for me to go to Notre Dame, for it truly changed my life.

I was born in Detroit, the second of six children, to Emily and Joe Saracino. Dad was born in Flatbush, New York, the son of Sicilian immigrants, and Mom (one of eleven children) was raised on a farm in a small German community in the middle of Wisconsin. Mom and Dad met in Detroit, where Dad was going to school full time during the day and working the forty-hour-per-week "graveyard shift" on the assembly line at Ford Motor Company.

It is hard to believe that forty years ago I began my undergraduate studies at Notre Dame. And I have come full circle, as my office now is right next to the classroom where I took English Literature as a freshman. That class truly had a profound impact on me and began my "Notre Dame experience." I remember the professor looking directly at me and asking what it meant when Huck Finn was floating down the river and clouds were forming overhead. I quickly froze and then stammered, "It meant it was going to rain." When the classmates' laughter ended, the professor kindly responded that "perhaps the clouds signified the coming storms in his life." Now, I still can't say I totally agree with him; but I honestly believe I haven't read a book in the same way since! Notre Dame opened up the world to me by challenging me to look at things differently. The books I read, the discussions I participated in, the people I met, the different music I heard, the places I saw. Notre Dame changed my life profoundly and permanently for the better. I am forever grateful that I am a member of the Notre Dame family.

It is humbling and daunting to oversee the Admissions Office at this time in our history. I accepted the invitation to return to my Alma Mater in 1997 because I saw that we were now committed to make the Notre Dame "dream" possible for all students regardless of whether they could afford it or not. While away from Notre Dame for twenty years from 1977 to 1997 (working at Santa Clara University), it hurt me to see many outstanding young men and women who wanted Notre Dame but were unable to attend because of insufficient financial assistance. For the 2004–05 academic year, Notre Dame awarded almost sixty million dollars of our own money to our undergraduates, all based upon each student's demonstrated financial need.

What this current dramatic commitment from Notre Dame means is that anyone who is outstanding enough in terms of academic talent and personal character to be admitted can make the dream of attending Notre Dame possible regardless of his or her personal socio-economic background. Our current first-year class reflects this financial commitment in that it is the most talented and truly diverse class in the University's history. In addition to the geographic diversity within the United States (which we have always had), we now have more international students and a significant increase in ethnic, racial, and socio-economic diversity. From hall rectors, faculty, staff, and students I have heard more comments than ever before on what an impressive class this is and how much Notre Dame has become even better because of these students.

I also consider myself blessed that all three of our children graduated from Notre Dame. In 1991, my daughter Christina's first e-mail from Notre Dame arrived in our San Jose home, and the time stamp was 3:00 A.M.! Her message went on and on about what happened that day with her roommate Tamara from Puerto Rico, her class discussions, jogging around the lakes after dinner with new friends. She ended her three-screen e-mail with a simple statement, which was *Thanks for making this possible for me, Dad. Your opportunities to learn here at Notre Dame are only limited by your need for sleep.*

As more people hear of the wonderful things occurring here, the quantity and quality of the applicants have increased dramatically. For example, the average SAT score for the roughly 12,000 applicants this year was higher than the average score for the entering freshmen in 1995! And, at the same time, the level of community service and other extracurricular involvement by the students seeking admission to Notre Dame is greater than ever before. I honestly wonder when many of these young people sleep!

That is what gets me out of bed each morning! To try and reach the very best individuals with the story of Notre Dame. And, at the same time, I want my office to always treat each and every person who comes in contact with Notre Dame through us with respect and dignity. To "tell the story of Notre Dame" to the next generation of students who will become new members of the Notre Dame Family . . . that is what I want to continue to do. Notre Dame is a special place, a special community.

When I retire in about eight years, I hope to be remembered as someone who loved Notre Dame deeply and made Notre Dame a better Notre Dame.

—DANIEL SARACINO, FACULTY ASSISTANT PROVOST, ADMISSIONS,
UNIVERSITY OF NOTRE DAME

IT WAS SPRING semester 1974, and I was a senior still looking for answers. I had majored in English, had read plenty of books, had gotten into plenty of talks about God and the world and the meaning of life. By second semester senior year, all of my friends were locked into a job or law school or a career in medicine. And I was still trying to figure it out, still trying to get the most out of my Notre Dame education so I could walk into the real world with a good sense of myself and it and how I should fit in.

Freshman biology had taught me some stuff. Mark Twain and Tom Werge had taught me some other things. I had studied Willa

Cather and Taoism and Shakespeare and the koans of Thomas Merton. I had talked late into the night over beer and pizza, walked the lakes, sometimes went to Mass in the Farley Hall chapel. Collegiate seminar, that "great books" course once required of Arts and Letters students, was also a Farley experience for me.

Each Monday night for two semesters, fifteen or twenty of us met in the Farley Hall lounge for three hours to explore the week's readings. Two students presented papers, led the discussion, *and* contributed a couple of gallons of wine to make sure the conversations went well. We talked Plato and Freud, Black Elk and Confucius, Thomas Aquinas and Karl Marx. Here we were—dirtballs, hippies, and pseudo-intellectuals—talking about war and peace and God, evolution, the role of government and how to get along . . . then going back upstairs to test our good intentions in the smelly, warty mix of all-male communal living.

But it was the second semester senior year when the prize of Notre Dame appeared to me. Each afternoon, MWF, I went to Chris Anderson's abnormal psych class. There I learned the truth about human nature—stimulus-response and B. F. Skinner, the mechanistic body, behavioral conditioning, brain chemistry, and the neuroses of the religious. And I walked out of there thinking, yes, that is all there is, that is the human species, there is no soul, the rest is all delusion.

And then I walked over to Father John Dunne's theology class and listened to his lectures on the spiritual essence of life, the unseen and invisible, the mystical and the supernatural, and his moving examination of the path of the heart's desire. And as he paced back and forth, delivering truths like nuggets of flame, citing the guidance of Rilke, Kierkegaard, and Kazantzakis, he would lift us and inspire, and paint whole new vistas of the wonders of infinite human nature.

For thirty years now, that juxtaposition has stood for me as the most eloquent definition of my Notre Dame education—the sometimes uncomfortable meeting of the intellectual and the spiritual, the crossing of the worldly and eternal, the dazzling facets of truth that come from living the right questions. Notre Dame is a place where the ultimate and most elemental answers matter.

—KERRY TEMPLE '74, EDITOR OF NOTRE DAME MAGAZINE

I TRY NOT just to teach what they need to know, but to light a fire in the gut.

—REV. WILSON MISCAMBLE, C.S.C.

THE ULTIMATE GOAL of a liberal education is *not* to get a better job. Rather, it is to become a better person, to better know thyself. That's what we do at Our Lady's University, and that's why Notre Dame is a special teaching place.

—GEORGE HOWARD, PROFESSOR OF PSYCHOLOGY, NOTRE DAME

FOR THE PAST 13 years, I have been teaching introductory and intermediate language and culture classes at Notre Dame. Each of those years I have thought, "God and the computer were really kind to me this year. I've never had a class like this one." . . . What a journey we make together. The syllabus shows a starting and an ending point, but we take detours over mountains (things we try that are harder than any of us thought could be achieved), into deserts (my ideas that produce nothing but dust—but at least we tried something new), into ruts (we all have our off days), and on scenic routes that break us out of the routine. Somehow the students are the leaders. Rather than teach them, I show them how to learn; and they do, exceeding my expectations and making me race to catch up.

—BARBARA MANGIONE, ASSISTANT PROFESSIONAL SPECIALIST,
DEPARTMENT OF ROMANCE LANGUAGES AND LITERATURES,
NOTRE DAME[2]

I BELIEVE THAT it is essential that we take our place among the great and influential universities of our country. From their very inception, Catholic universities have been tied to the aspirations of American Catholics. During the nineteenth century and the first half of the twentieth century, these have been the aspirations of an immigrant people. Now, as these aspirations are changing, we must be responsive to new challenges for leadership at a higher level of academe. We must become increasingly influential in our society on the one hand and in our Church on the other, through highly creative contributions to the arts and sciences, technology, the professions, and public service. We have a special responsibility to encourage increased participation of Catholics in the intellectual life. We still have to ask the rhetorical question posed by John Tracy Ellis in the 1950s: "Where are the Catholic intellectuals?" We must emphasize the fact that the quest for knowledge is part of our search for God and therefore a natural source for sanctifying our lives. . . . At a Catholic university we have a special challenge to make sure the door between the life of the mind and the life of the spirit is kept wide open.

—PROFESSOR TIMOTHY O'MEARA, HOWARD J. KENNA PROFESSOR OF
MATHEMATICS, AND PROVOST OF THE UNIVERSITY OF NOTRE DAME
FROM 1978 TO 1996

IN MY THIRTY years as a professor of chemical engineering at Notre Dame, I have discovered that in many ways, a teacher's lessons are rarely confined to the constructs of the classroom. Chemical engineering does not lend itself to fostering the kind of spirited student debates found in other subjects at Notre Dame. More than any specific student or event, the memories I have of my teaching career are more collective, encompassing the thousand or so students I have subjected to the rigorous study of scientific principles framed in the precise language of mathematics. Yet despite the size of the classes or the complexity of the material, I have realized that both my students and I unconsciously record in our notebooks a few special unexpected formulas we discover that equate to our own lives.

One of the most significant lessons I strive to teach undergraduates is to conquer their fear of being questioned in front of the class. To teach this lesson, I use the Socratic style of questioning students in class throughout my lectures. To avoid playing favorites or targeting select individuals, I've implemented several methods to deliver my questions as randomly and fairly as possible. It seems no matter what I try, students are not happy about being questioned in class. Yet, as I constantly remind the students, being on the spot and answering a query in front of their peers is perhaps the best experience they may have in my course. I try to prepare students for life after graduation and to show them that while intimidating, defending your answers in front of a group will prove invaluable after graduation. From the professor's classroom perspective, it is easy to quickly spot the future winners in the game of life—they are not necessarily the students with the best GPA, but those that handle themselves best in front of their peers and potential colleagues.

As the years go by, professors occasionally reunite with former students, and the things my students remember most are not assignments or even chemical engineering marvels, but casual comments I made off the cuff that may have only indirectly related to what was going on in class. Likewise, what I remember most about them are not situations rooted in painstakingly developed equations or difficult class work. I remember the students with wide eyes who came to my office crying for help and wanting to talk about personal problems of depression or lost loves, financial difficulties, gender identity, family problems, and death. An unannounced visit by these students revealed to me the otherwise covert problems far more complex than those posed in class, and often intertwined with the student's struggle to find a direction in their lives while juggling a whole range of problems affecting their academic performance and their future. The counseling of students is an unseen aspect of the teaching experience, which does not get publicized and never makes it to the University's obligatory Teaching Evaluations. It is a silent and unspoken role, as most of these situations cannot be discussed beyond the fleeting moment in which they happened. To fill this role of counselor and mentor, I often find myself tapping into the closest related experience I have ever had—which is, of course, being a parent. The experience of raising four children has helped guide me to know when to be tough with my students and when to make exceptions, when to simply listen and when to point out the way. Teaching is not just the passing of technical and scholarly information, but also the counseling and guidance of our students in the hopes of steering them into the future in quite the same way as our own children, and with similar care and concern.

The parental counseling role sometimes takes on an especially appropriate and literal significance. One of the best benefits Notre Dame provides to the faculty is the tuition-waiver program for all qualifying faculty children after a certain period of committed employment. As a result, I am extremely fortunate to have had all of my children attend Notre Dame. As some of my colleagues whose kids have attended Notre Dame have experienced, I ended up having one of my kids, Eduardo, in class because he was majoring in the field in which I teach. At Notre Dame, there is pressure to perform well as a teacher and provide students with the premier education they expect. Adding one's own son to the mix adds an extra dimension to this responsibility. Children are the ultimate critics; they are well acquainted with their parents' antics and theatrics, which in my case I use to spice up a rather dry subject. Something as simple as a smirk on my son's face would illustrate to everyone else in the class that he knew a different side of the story that he had heard before in another context. A worrisome face would telegraph a potential mistake on my part and would send me into a flurry of silent double-guessing, trying to figure out what error I may have committed before the eyes of my students. Like most parents, I have learned my parenting skills by trying various communication strategies with my children and learning from their responses. These skills are fine-tuned to a further extent through the professor's dual role dubbed *in loco parentis* by University officials. I clearly remember a senior who, after a few beers at the graduation farewell party, told me with a bit of critical scorn and contempt, "You sound like my father." While to him that may have seemed like a well-placed barb, I know I could not have received a better compliment.

It is nearly impossible to capture the essence of the teacher/pseudo-parent/counselor relationship between professors and their students. Each student who graduates from Notre Dame leaves with the Spirit of the University indelibly imprinted on their soul. A large part of this Spirit is embedded in the multifaceted Notre Dame teacher-to-student experience forged in and out of the classrooms. In my case, this experience was made all the more special when, as a father, I shared it with my son. For this reason, my most prized memento as an educator is a poem by my son that hangs on my office wall. The poem invariably captures the attention of students and visitors who come to see me. It is a frequent visitor to the copy machine down the hall because it is a tribute to ND parents. It reads:

"Son," my Father said to me
"Remember that some things you are given only one of,
And you must take care of them or lose them.
You have only one body,
Care for it as it carries you.
You only have one mind,
Fill it with wonder and watch wonderful things result.
And you only have one life,
Live it like no other so that it may be for others."
And as I hugged him, through wisecracks and clichés,
I realized that there was something else I only have one of.

—JUAN EDUARDO WOLF '93

—EDUARDO E. WOLF, PROFESSOR
(EDITING TOUCHES BY CAROL '01, CATHY '95, JUAN EDUARDO '93,
AND CHRISTINA '02 WOLF)

OF THE MANY privileges that the teaching profession offers, I can think of none greater than catalyzing and witnessing remarkable transformations in students.

—DENNIS JACOBS, PROFESSOR OF CHEMISTRY AND BIOCHEMISTRY,
U.S. PROFESSOR OF THE YEAR IN 2002, VICE PRESIDENT AND
ASSOCIATE PROVOST, NOTRE DAME[3]

SOME PEOPLE DREAM about how they'd change their lives if they won a lottery. Not Edward Cronin, associate professor emeritus in Notre Dame's Program of Liberal Studies. He knows exactly what he'd do: just what he's been doing for half a century. "If I won a million dollars, I might be late to class the next day from spending so many hours in the chapel, but I'd be there, and I'd be there the next day and the day after that."

In his 50-year career, Cronin has taught everything from economics to philosophy, but his passion is literature and his specialty James Joyce. Despite his 74 years, he says, "No one can make me feel old. I suppose teaching the children of former students would make any rational person feel old, but I find it invigorating to have a fresh start."

He cites love of learning as "the most important thing my students can gain from being in my classroom," and his presentations come laced with humor. After a stimulating lecture, he'll sometimes "confide" to students that he bought the notes from another professor—for 25 cents.

Cronin denigrates his ability as lecturer, pointing out that as a husband and father he could never talk long without being interrupted, so he never got used to lecturing. Even when he taught a class of 300 at the University of Minnesota, "I'd find the handful of students who would talk with me and let them represent the whole class."

No matter. Former students find his teaching methods memorable. "He was a great teacher, who could cajole, entice, intimidate, or embarrass his students into learning," says Andy Panelli '77. Moreover, in the Program of Liberal Studies, where 25 students constitute a large class, learning is a two-way street. Cronin keeps a large yellow notepad handy and invites students to record their wisdom on it. Over the years, he says he's learned as much about Joyce's *Ulysses* as he's taught, and far more from his students than from scholars.

Few students, however, win arguments with Cronin. Panelli recalls Cronin listening intently, gradually stretching his suspenders as a student expounded his argument. When the student reached his conclusion, *thwack* went the suspenders. Then Cronin would say, "See!" and launch into an organized rebuttal.

He's called "a tough old bird" by a former student who once taught Cronin's granddaughter. He insists that his students turn in seven themes per semester, on time, and rewrite until what they've written sounds like English. He introduced one class for sophomores by saying, "This class will be many things to you. What it will *not* be is a 'spill your guts' creative writing class. You will learn to write even if it kills us both."

Though he's been called "B-minus Cronin," a former student remembers him as scrupulously fair: "He even changed my grade once after I pointed out how my sentence structure had improved. If I'd said I needed a B to get into med school, he would have been unimpressed."

Students today, says Cronin, show one significant difference from those he taught years ago. "When I began teaching, if I mentioned a great author, many of the students would have read his work. Now many haven't even heard of him. Nor can I assume they know how to write a sentence."

Students may tremble at entering the "confessional" in which Cronin critiques their written sins, but they often line up outside his door during office hours. "Occasionally one comes with a concern more significant than a comma splice," says Cronin, who compares his listening role to that of a bartender. . . .

He credits two deceased Notre Dame professors, James Withey and Leo L. Ward, C.S.C., with teaching him the craft of writing. Withey gave his freshmen a writing assignment every day and unfailingly returned each essay the following day. "Father Ward would rub his head until just the right word came out," chuckles Cronin. "That's why my hair is thin on top."

In graduate school, one professor taught him to read closely and document the author's intention; another who was terribly disorganized communicated great enthusiasm. "By dang it, Cronin," he'd say, "listen to that! Isn't that beautiful?"

After graduation from Notre Dame in 1938, Cronin earned graduate degrees from the Universities of Chicago and Minnesota. His first job was at Chicago's Bryant & Stratton Business College, where his salary was $1,200 for teaching five days and two nights a week for 51 weeks of the year. The fact that his night-school students were tired after working all day spurred him on. "One gentleman old enough to be my father would sit in the front row and sleep the first five minutes of every class. I figured if he had come to learn from this young squirt, I had better knock myself out to get something across. He always woke up after five minutes."

Through those years, his heart remained at Notre Dame. In 1949, he gladly accepted a job teaching English at the University; three years later he helped found the General Program of Liberal Studies with a curriculum built around the Great Books. He is proud to be the only charter member of the group that founded the General Program who's still teaching in it.

Cronin maintains a lively correspondence with several generations of grateful students. Although he won the Father Charles Sheedy Award for Excellence in Teaching in 1977 and Sorin Hall's Paul Fenlon Teaching Award in 1982, he considers letters from former students his greatest honors. Paul Radde '62 recalls, "Sometimes we'd talk into the wee hours of the morning, and he would deliberately turn the clock around so he couldn't tell how late it was getting. He figured if he knew what time he went to bed, he'd just feel more tired in the morning." Radde also has fond memories of the whole class being invited to the Cronin home on a Friday evening. Over cheese toastwiches and a tub of beer, Cronin shared his ideas and family life, with children occasionally wandering in to sit on his lap. . . .

Reading is still his first love. He regularly brings home shopping bags full of treasures from the Saint Vincent de Paul Thrift Store. "I can spend the day teaching books," he says, "and when I come home I relax by reading the same kind of stuff I'm teaching. Not many accountants can say that."

—JILL A. BOUGHTON[4]
(PROFESSOR CRONIN PASSED AWAY IN 2005)

A TEACHER MUST accept responsibility not only for what a student learns, but for what he or she becomes. Our best teachers know that true education means teaching things that are worth being in love with.

—PROFESSOR EDWARD FISCHER

GOOD TEACHING IS a sort of sacramental action, a communication of spirit.

—REV. JOHN W. CAVANAUGH, C.S.C.

GIVEN SUCH A large and seemingly inevitable movement in education toward the "benign neglect" of religious faith, or even outright hostility toward it . . . , our own University must be considered something of an anomaly. To confess Our Lady and Our Lord in an educational climate dominated by the agnosticism of the secular state, indeed, to profess any faith in any supernatural reality as the ground and justification for learning seems anachronistic. . . . The very fact that here we are able to contemplate and speak of "faith," or "spirit," or even the *possibility* of realizing a "Christian community" of scholars, and to contemplate and speak such words seriously, witnesses to the continuing durability of those words. Their very *presence* is significant. Writes Emerson: "Now the words 'God,' 'Grace,' 'Prayer,' 'Heaven,' 'Hell,' are . . . sacred words, to which we must still return, whenever we would speak an ecstatic and universal sense. There are objections to them, no doubt, for academical use, but when the professor's gown is taken off, Man will come back to them." That we consider and act on these "sacred words" and "come back to them" in an academic setting is striking and good. . . . For all its flaws and imperfections—which are, after all, the flaws of our own condition—there seem to me few more committed yet complex places through which to journey, and few more potentially and actually Christian universities in which to consider the truth and continue the questioning, than this one.

—PROFESSOR THOMAS WERGE[5]

THERE AREN'T MANY places where faculty feel that a life devoted to the University and what it stands for is a life well spent. Many faculty feel that way about Notre Dame.

—ROGER A. SCHMITZ, VICE PRESIDENT, NOTRE DAME

THE BEST COLLEGE talk is high minded, in the midnight hours, searching, groping, for goals and God.

—PROFESSOR THOMAS STRITCH

USE YOUR FOUR years at Notre Dame as a period for exploration, dreaming, and vocational discovery!

I about had a heart attack in my Core class last Thursday when I found out that many of my students felt that their four years here were being spent training to get a job rather than to discover a "calling." While I understand that the more than $130,000 it costs to get an ND education is an investment in the future, part of me still thinks that we—students, faculty, and administrators—must find a way to make vocational discernment a more central part of our curriculum. Maybe four years isn't long enough to think, explore, pray, and dream. Perhaps collegiate education should be extended by a year—I don't know. What I feel fairly certain of is that if Notre Dame is to remain a vital center of Catholic learning throughout the third millennium, we must create an undergraduate environment that encourages and rewards original thinking, experimentation, conversation, the unfettered engagement of great texts and ideas, open-ended exploration, and unabashed dreaming.

So, my last words to you are work purposefully, live a balanced and whole life, discover your passion—your calling; open your heart to your neighbors; explore tirelessly; dream unabashedly; discover what really matters to you—embrace it, yield to it, let it transform you; and at the end of your sojourn at Notre Dame, this place of dreams, go forth with courage to offer your ideas, your skills, and your love to the world as a gift.

—Rev. Hugh R. Page Jr., Walter Associate Professor of
Theology and Dean of First Year of Studies[6]

ON THE SECOND day of the events described in Plato's *Symposium*, Alcibiades crashes the party and is led to deliver a speech in praise of Socrates as a teacher. Alcibiades warns his audience not to listen to anything Socrates has to say because he will cast a spell that will shame those who hear him away from lives of happy enjoyment and into the austerities recommended by philosophy. He insists that he means to describe much more than what one might find in a great orator. Indeed, his claim is an ascription of a mysterious power that greatly exceeds mere excellence of address.

For several decades, until 1974, there was a teacher at Notre Dame named Frank O'Malley whose powers were beyond the legendary. To many of us who were his students, O'Malley's classes on Modern Catholic Writers and Philosophy in Literature bordered on the miraculous. Some years later, I can remember sharing wonderment with a fellow graduate student, Jim Conerty, as to the strange and amazing power of O'Malley's which had gripped and changed us both so deeply. It did not seem to us to be a matter simply of the depth and seriousness of his ideas. After all, great truths were the substance of education and available in many classes at the University. On the contrary, there was something about the quality of apprehension attainable through the lectures of O'Malley's that made the experience rare and exceptional, that made it an experience of profound revelation.

Our attempts to explain this effect were short-lived and unfruitful. However, I do remember that we facetiously suggested that perhaps O'Malley's power lay in the mere sound of his voice. I was actually struck by that suggestion, although I did not admit to it at the time.

Looking back, it seems to me that O'Malley's arrival was the occasion for a wave of awe to pass through the classroom. To me, the awe reached the level of shock. Having attained my senior year, I knew well enough that the University had many good teachers, but this man was doing something quite different. O'Malley was not just a good teacher, teaching an interesting course. He was prophetic. He was a witness to the truth, the truth being something that most were quite blind to, even within the hallowed precincts of Notre Dame.

Not that O'Malley engaged in the denigration of his colleagues and their efforts. Rather, he revealed to us an understanding of things, made available through faith and thought, which was different from and infinitely more profound than the mix of parochial school religion and complacent middle-class values that was the norm everywhere in American Catholic culture. Claiming to much prefer "the ravings of Kierkegaard" to "the comfortable bromides of Benjamin Franklin," O'Malley made us realize that all was *not* well in Christendom. On the contrary, there was a great misunderstanding abroad which failed to see the "fear and trembling" promised by St. Paul and which seemed to offer a false "promised land" of spiritual comfort and material prosperity as the reward of the Faithful. All the while, we were in danger of falling victim to a desperately misguided spiritual complacency that gave no heed to Christ's warnings regarding mammonism and mediocrity. The need for love and heroism, for the extremes of passion, was revealed to many of us for the first time. Indeed, even the misery of heart of the wretched sinner was preferable to lukewarm spiritual complacency and self-satisfaction.

O'Malley read aloud the poetry of Gerard Manley Hopkins; he quoted Thomas Aquinas, Søren Kierkegaard, Romano Guardini, and Jacques Maritain; he analyzed the thoughts of Georges Bernanos, François Mauriac, Graham Greene, T. S. Eliot, Evelyn Waugh, and others, all with the purpose of providing insight into the truth of things, that we should see the world for what it really is and that we should understand those "deep down things" which our faith would allow our honest intelligence to see. In other words, he revealed to us an existence of a wisdom, at once Christian and Humanistic, which tore aside the veil of banal interests and gave us a view of meaning and importance that changed everything, even though outward appearances changed very little. Christ was placed in the center of life, as someone whose suffering and love we all shared and as the measure of all value and all meaning.

O'Malley's power to move his students to see could be explained by his use of such great authors and thinkers, but it is only partially so. There *was* something about his actually giving voice to their visions that captured us, that made the truth of the insights irresistible. It became as though, suddenly, a fire was enkindled deep in the soul and we hung on every word O'Malley uttered.

There were royal moments. I know of no other way to describe them. O'Malley's class instantly transformed me and continued to sustain me for the remainder of the year. I felt that if I had done nothing else in my four years at Notre Dame than hear Frank O'Malley, the experience had been an absolute and total success. I was, by the way, only an auditor.

I returned to Notre Dame four years later with a graduate degree from another university in hand and a year's curatorial experience in an art museum. I did so in order to take up further graduate studies, this time in philosophy. I had received an appointment to teach art history at Saint Mary's College. Naturally, it occurred to me to renew my acquaintance with O'Malley and to sit in on one or two of his lectures just for memory's sake and perhaps to see if now, grown-up and sophisticated fellow that I had become, I would still find him to be so impressive. Sometime in midyear I did, and it was still a shock. Just as before, his words were charged with insight, windows to the truth. O'Malley's was a voice quite beyond mere scholarly learning. . . .

To his students, the idea that O'Malley gained their admiration through flattery was ridiculous, since dishonesty of any sort in Frank O'Malley was unthinkable. It is true that his estimate of the potential of the student, an estimate which was as keenly considered and deeply felt as every other serious observation to cross his mind, led him to the conclusion that "judging the potential of the student by measuring the actual is illogical" and, moreover, that the potential of any human person is "unfathomable."

I heard him make this observation in a summer graduate seminar on "Teaching the Humanities," which he co-taught with Professor Robert Caponigri from the Philosophy Department. O'Malley subtitled his part of the presentation "How to avoid acts of aggression against students" and gave us rules for doing so, the spirit of which is, I believe, well represented in the passage below, one of the few notes on the subject of "the teacher's attitude" that I have not lost.

"Teaching involves a selfless dedicated concern for the unique working out [to adulthood] of each soul, a delicate sense of the peculiar needs and aspirations of each, for the peculiar way with knowledge, that is each one. This sympathy, this capacity to appreciate the requirements of another's fulfillment . . . seems a function of prudence, perhaps an extension of the prudence of the father. The teacher must respect the delicate sacred interiority of each student, he must encourage the timid efforts as genuine utterance and integration."

But, again, having the right attitude toward the student will not suffice for an explanation of O'Malley's greatness. Even though it may have been an indispensable part of his character as a teacher, I believe that those of us, his former students who went on to teach with exactly that right attitude toward the student, will confirm that it did not provide us with such authority and power as O'Malley's seemed overwhelmingly to possess. There did, indeed, seem to be a strange power in the very sound of his voice, halting and almost inaudible as it often was, much as there may sometimes be in the mere sound of the voice of a great singer or poet or dramatic actor, to move the soul.

The ancients had no rational answer to account for the superhuman excellence of great art and developed the theory of inspiration by the muses. Christian philosophers have no difficulty believing that the Holy Spirit is at work in such ways. In his famous debates with Siger de Brabant on the teachings of Aristotle, St. Thomas Aquinas informs us that whatever proposition is true is true by the power of the Holy Spirit, no matter who asserts it, pagan or Christian. And the Gift of the Holy Spirit which is called The Gift of Words, which renders the truth lucid to its hearers, is directed precisely at the empowering of utterance, at the spoken word.

During O'Malley's time, advanced degrees among the faculty members were essential to academic respectability for a university and therefore prerequisites for tenure and promotion. Scholarship and publication, which offered the prospect of national reputation to the individual as well as the university, were honored and encouraged. Teaching ability did not generally carry sure importance, although, to its credit, Notre Dame made exceptions in the cases of O'Malley and a few others.

Today, at least at the undergraduate level, the importance and the authority of the teacher is further undermined because of the two new influences. We live in an era when much is made in higher education of something called "student-centeredness," which is the natural child of changes brought about by the 1960s regarding freedom and authority. More and more often, students are encouraged to pursue whatever interests them, without regard for any particular tradition of knowledge and culture. For many, there is no body of knowledge the attainment of which constitutes an education and there is no wisdom to be gained by the study of the thoughts of particular minds. The traditional liberal arts curriculum has been virtually abandoned in many institutions, replaced by courses and programs of practical and professional purpose. Lacking authority, the teacher has been reduced to the position of facilitator in the learning process rather than leader or guide. Further worsening this situation, great hope is now being placed in the promise of computer technology, as though there is no longer any need for the living presence of a teacher.

In opposition to this stands the example of Frank O'Malley. He represented and proclaimed an understanding of existence that was held to be wisdom. And his physical presence in the classroom materially and dramatically affected his communication of that wisdom to his students. For those concerned with such things, it would seem well to remember that his influence on generations of Notre Dame students was so profound and so vast in its consequences that it may find no parallel in the history of the University, if not the history of American higher education.

—GEORGE McCLANCY B.A. '52, M.A. '60 [7]

MY LAST CLASS at Notre Dame was Frank's class on Monday, May 7, 1973. Exactly one year later, May 7, 1974, Frank O'Malley passed away. And although I could not foresee his death, Frank could feel its closeness. Somehow, something compelled me to jot down those final words he spoke to us:

> I appreciate the presence, hope, and beauty of your lives.
> These are the last words you'll hear from me—for the time
> being anyway. I don't know what's in store for me in the
> near future or far-off future. And I hope you'll remember
> these words. I have a wish and hope for you. I hope that
> time will never trap you, and that the world will have time
> for you. I hope that you will be happy forever, and that you
> recollect the happiness of human existence which is some-
> times sorrow and suffering, and sometimes love. My love to
> you! Peace and thanks!
>
> —GARY J. CARUSO '73

THE CATHOLIC COLLEGE must be characterized by inwardness, an intellectual largeness and intensity, a descent to sources from which the universe of thought and love proceeds, a meeting of the mind, of man, with the mystery of things. Its concern with realities must begin with intuition (the primal, immediate contacts of intelligence and sensibility with the inner secret of these realities) and, proceeding through exposition, analysis, criticism, etc., return to the total insight, to a keener, more fully released knowledge in which the conclusion is seen in the principle, the developed work in the formative fire of the germinal idea. The rational elaboration of thought, the prudential ordering of life and action, the artistic qualification of the material are meaningful only in terms of origin and termination at the experience of existence, which is the act of acts, the form of forms. When the rational elaboration of thought is not a sign but a screen, a separate enclosed system, a sort of autonomous mental art-work; or when the acquisition of virtue and the development of insti-tutions and organizations and techniques are pursued without the sense for that which alone quickens discipline, the pull of the deter-mining good; or when art seeks beauty in design, when the splendor of meaningful form is forgot in the gratuitous refinements of integrity and proportion: then there is dry death. For Christian thought, as well as Christian love and Christian making, must open onto exis-tence, the act of the real tasted with the mind and thought with the fingers. . . .

These realizations ought to be more firmly and powerfully yours because you have come here to this place of Notre Dame, this great and dominant Catholic university of the United States, a place con-cerned through all the years with integrating a true faith and a true philosophy with the life of culture. In your time here, you must have become better aware of the composition of life, of the nature of true primacy. You must have considered here and found here the answer to "the old question which traverses the sky of the soul perpetually, the vast, the general question, what is the meaning of life?" If you are convinced of your answer, you will not be deluded by the lies and phrases; you will be able to resist the pressure of the age. Possessed as you should be of a true spiritual culture, you will not be too much disconcerted or ravaged by contemporary civilization; you will not feel yourselves prisoners of life, scratching on the walls of your cells; you will not succumb to the sorrows of the savage world. Instead, you will save yourselves and save all those who encounter you in your var-ious works and ways and vocations.

—PROFESSOR FRANK O'MALLEY[8]

SURELY A PERSONAL remembrance ought to begin with a reveal-ing anecdote or sparkling instance. But since John T. Frederick retired from Notre Dame's faculty as chairman of the English

Department in 1962, time has worked its effects. Generations of students and many faculty members now know him, if at all, only by name, and have no notion of his many diverse yet somehow related accomplishments. So—to begin with—a few bare biographical facts.

John Tower Frederick was born near Corning, Iowa, on February 1, 1893. He died in Iowa City one day before his 82nd birthday, in 1975. Almost sixty years of his life were spent in teaching, at the University of Iowa, at Moorhead Teachers' College in Minnesota, at Pittsburgh and Northwestern, and at Notre Dame.

In 1922, at Iowa, he taught what was probably the first college course ever given anywhere in contemporary American fiction. An observer wrote of him at the time: "Many of his students had an admiration for him that stopped just this side of idolatry." Earlier on, in 1915, while still an undergraduate at that same university, he founded one of this country's most distinguished literary magazines, *The Midland*, which his own fierce effort, money, and sacrifice kept alive until it perished in the Depression in 1933.

During some of the later Depression years John served as director of the Federal Writers' Project in Chicago. Between 1937 and 1944 his radio program, *Of Men and Books*, was broadcast weekly out of Chicago over CBS. From the start its audience was wide, grateful, and enthusiastic.

John published two novels, quite a few short stories, a great lot of articles, both popular and scholarly, and a few rare poems. He collaborated on a couple of exceptionally good textbooks on writing and wrote a little manual on the short story which is the best thing I've ever read on the subject. He was coeditor of a massive two-volume anthology of American literature, edited a pair of admirable anthologies of stories, and when the *Chicago Sun* was born in 1941 he did a weekly book column for its Sunday pages. Later he took over the monthly book review section of *The Rotarian*.

But all that is pretty much catalog detail. The story I know best began in the late 1920s, when a young Holy Cross priest, Father Leo

L. Ward, began sending stories to *The Midland*. John liked those stories, wrote to the author, published the work, and then—characteristically—came to Notre Dame to visit this bright new talent. The visits were repeated, and on one of them Father Ward brought his friend and editor to a meeting of The Scribblers, a club of undergraduate would-be writers. It was there, in the winter of 1928–29, that I first met Mr. John T. Frederick.

He was then, as he stayed through the 40-some years of our growing friendship, a tall thin man who did not so much stoop as lean forward a little when speaking or listening. His mustache, which grayed through the years, was always so closely trimmed that you wondered sometimes if it had been there the last time you saw him. Behind his glasses his eyes were thoughtful. He had an old-fashioned courtesy and a quiet modesty of manner; there was no affectation or show in him. He had the direct simplicity of a man absolutely honest, informed, and wise.

By the fall of 1930 Father Ward had persuaded him to come to Notre Dame to teach part-time. Thursday was his day. Living in Chicago, still teaching at Northwestern, he'd arrive here on the South Shore (which in those days provided hourly service to and from Chicago) late on Wednesday, teach classes from 8 in the morning until noon, eat hurriedly in the caf, and teach again from one to four.

Later on, when he was teaching only at Notre Dame, he still would commute here each semester for three intensive periods of a few weeks each. Only in the final eight or 10 years was he in permanent residence.

I don't think he ever realized what a killing schedule he followed for so many years. Once he told me that he'd been plagued by insomnia. I asked him how he handled it. "Oh, I just lie there," he said, "and I plan the next day. Or"—he had a way of tilting his head slightly when he smiled—"maybe the next three or four days."

I marveled then (as I do now) at his constant calmness, his capacity for work, his unwearied energy. He had a built-in sense of order—not the fussy clock-watching or neat-desk kind, but an interior serenity the like of which I've never known in another person. I never once saw him hurry, yet he was never late, never missed a train or appointment; and he always acted as if whatever he was doing was the sole business on his mind.

Before I came to Notre Dame in considerable trepidation in 1936, to begin my own teaching, he asked me to meet him at his office at the Chicago campus of Northwestern. He spent hours that summer afternoon telling me what I might expect in what was for me an absolutely new life, and what I ought to be careful about. He gave me invaluable counsel and reassurance; but he did it with so much grace, such warm friendliness, that I thought at the time we were simply having an extraordinarily good talk.

Mind you, he had no obligation to quiet my mind at that time. I'm sure he never thought of his act as one of great kindness. It was simply the sort of thing his nature impelled him to do.

I learned later that it was the sort of thing he did a thousand times to a thousand assorted people all through his long life. I became that day, and many times afterward, one of his countless beneficiaries.

A few years after I came back to Notre Dame Father Ward, now head of the English department, suggested that John and I team-teach a class devoted to the writing of short fiction. Graduating in the spring of 1930, I had of course never been formally a student under John, though I had already learned so much from him. But sharing that writing class, and later sharing other classes in contemporary fiction, I turned into a constant learner. And I realized, too, that when he taught it was not merely the subject matter that came through: there was also an attitude, a sense of reverence for life itself, a humanity rich and alive with vision and wonder. All those radiated from his every word.

"Sharing" was one of his favorite words. He used it in many contexts. A story had to share its matter with its readers, so they could share the experience treated. All good novels were thus examples of sharing. The classroom was a place for and the private conference an occasion for sharing. The word expressed some inner necessity for John, a necessity that found its finest expression in his everyday life.

He spoke beautifully, in a slow, grave voice. You could almost feel his sentences taking shape in his mind just before he uttered them. When he read poetry aloud the voice fell, not to a whisper but to a softness that put a hush over a crowded room.

Except in the writing class, in which there was always spontaneous give-and-take, his method was lecture. But unlike many other excellent lecturers, he supplemented his class periods with constant private conferences with students.

I learned this approach from him. But while for me it was always easier to teach for three hours than to confer for one—conferences drained me, and I kept them up only because I knew from his practice that the method was right—for John these private sessions, one student after another for hours on end, seemed absolute joy. They refreshed him and stimulated him; he felt rewarded by those endless "visits" in which he shared with students his sympathy, experience, and sense.

Perhaps his attitude toward students and his regard for teaching come through most clearly in his own words, spoken to the Department of English just before he left it: "I feel more keenly than ever just how much they deserve of us. They deserve, simply, our best; and even that best is not going to be good enough. . . . We all know that, however always laborious and often thwarted, ours is a high calling, of high rewards."

When he retired from Notre Dame 18 years ago at age 69, he moved to a farm owned by his second wife, Lucy, just outside Iowa City. For the next six or seven years he taught as a visiting professor at Iowa. In those years he published more poems and articles and a book on W. H. Hudson, a favorite writer. His desk and his mind were full of further projects, some already in work, when his final illness came upon him.

Memories of a man like John Frederick are not subject to dimming. When I think of the immeasurable influence he has had upon my own life—an influence so unobtrusive that often I become aware of it only in retrospect—I think of the innumerable other persons whose lives he subtly made richer and fuller and better everywhere he went, for so many good and generous years.

—RICHARD SULLIVAN '30 TAUGHT AT NOTRE DAME FOR PARTS OF FIVE DECADES, INSTRUCTING GENERATIONS IN THE WRITER'S CRAFT AND PRACTICING IT LIBERALLY HIMSELF.[9]

ONE OF THE things I swallowed often was we would have players not admitted to Notre Dame, but they were accepted to other schools we competed against. When this particular recruit would excel at another school, we would get letters saying what a bum job we did in recruiting, how we didn't recruit this guy, how could we miss him, and so forth. We swallowed hard because we did not want to hurt any kid by saying he couldn't get admitted. Just because he was not academically qualified didn't mean he couldn't be a great citizen and achieve great things. A lot of marginal students have done exceptionally well.

—ARA PARSEGHIAN[10]

I'D HAVE TO say hiring Ara [Parseghian] was one of the smartest things we did. . . . But Ned's [Joyce] and my ideal of athletics' place in the academic model had never wavered. People might have just thought it did. We always believed athletics was subsidiary to academics.

—REV. THEODORE M. HESBURGH, C.S.C.

OUR CULTURE FORGES a tight link between success and identity—your accomplishments give you worth. But Our Lord and his church teach just the opposite. . . . All of us, those who are driven and those who are relaxed, those at the top of the class and those who have struggled, those who today relish the future and those who are gripped with fear—all of us derive our tremendous worth because God in Christ calls us sons and daughters. . . . One goal of Christian education is to instill in students a passion to ground their identity in that love and acceptance—the priceless treasure before which all of their achievements will pale.

—NATHAN HATCH, PROVOST AND ANDREW V. TACKES III
CHAIR OF HISTORY, NOTRE DAME[11]

MY NOTRE DAME experience changed my life. It's not just the victories, it's the perspective on life you receive there. For example, the first thing we did after winning the National Championship was to have Mass—before we celebrated, before we met with our friends and family. Lou Holtz himself delivered the homily. That showed all of us there are more important things in life.

—REGGIE HO IS BEST REMEMBERED AS THE 5'5", 125-POUND EXTRA-
POINT AND SHORT-FIELD-GOAL KICKER WHO KICKED FOUR FIELD GOALS
IN A 19–17 WIN OVER MICHIGAN TO OPEN THE 1988 FOOTBALL
SEASON, WHICH CULMINATED IN A NATIONAL CHAMPIONSHIP. HE
TURNED DOWN A FIFTH YEAR OF ELIGIBILITY TO ATTEND MEDICAL
SCHOOL AND IS NOW A CARDIOLOGIST WHO SAVES LIVES.[12]

A NOTRE DAME legend, Emil T. Hofman is at once feared and revered. Feared for his famous chemistry quizzes meant to test the mettle of aspiring doctors and engineers, revered for his devotion to students in and out of the classroom.

Having entered the University in 1950 as a graduate student and teaching assistant in chemistry, Hofman received his master's degree in chemistry in 1953 and was appointed to the chemistry department's faculty. Nine years later he received his Ph.D., also from Notre Dame, and a year later was selected the first recipient of the

Thomas P. Madden Award for excellence in teaching freshmen. At one time as many as 1,000 freshmen a year took his course in general chemistry, and it is estimated that during his teaching career he taught more than 32,000 students, including thousands who are now physicians, engineers, and scientists.

The number of quizzes he administered is equally impressive: Every Friday for thirty Fridays a year for forty years, Emil quizzed his students. Presiding over his class like a drill instructor, he would begin by booming "Okay!" and then recite the Lord's Prayer in the voice reminiscent of the radio announcer he once trained to become. Twenty minutes after distributing the quiz, he would order the students to stop and would then begin the day's lesson.

But behind the stern facade always has been a sense of humor and a desire to see his students succeed. When asked why he worked so hard to create and grade so many quizzes, Hofman explained that he used to run into his freshmen wherever he went in South Bend, so he decided the only way he could get an evening to himself would be to give his students a weekly quiz that required them to study hard the night before. His plan worked: Eager chemistry students developed a Thursday-night ritual of gathering in the library to prepare for the dreaded Friday quiz, which meant Thursday night was Emil's. So determined were his students, he recounts with a smile, that during the blizzard of '67 "I slipped on some ice on the way to class and thought I was paralyzed. I lay there on the sidewalk in pain, and the students just stepped right over me. They didn't know what had happened to me, but they knew there would be a quiz that morning."

Emil's trademark quizzes were part of his bigger lesson that commitment and responsibility are keys to success in life. "This is a course without obstacles," he was fond of telling his students. "If you make the effort and learn the material, you will succeed. The help is available. And I'm very disappointed when a student fails." Though legend has it that legions failed, in reality less than 5 percent did not make the cut each year. And even they remember Hofman as a dedicated and caring role model.

Because of his success with first-year students, in 1971 Emil was appointed dean of Freshman Year of Studies. He oversaw a major revision of the first-year curriculum and organized a counseling program that has reduced total attrition in the freshman year to less than one percent. But more important, he got to know more than 600 of his students and freshmen each year, many of whom he tutored, counseled in his office, shared lunch with in local restaurants, and took on field trips to Chicago.

One such student was Lena Jefferson. When she arrived at Notre Dame in 1986, she was in search of a community with a strong sense of spirituality and commitment to helping students get the most out of their education. Having been raised until the age of thirteen by her single mother, who at that time was diagnosed with bipolar disorder, and then by her grandmother, Lena sought mentors and support. She found both in Emil. When Lena was in danger of failing not only his chemistry class but out of school, Hofman dedicated himself to helping her through. By her sophomore year, Lena, an African-American, started calling Emil "Dad," a title he happily accepted. In 1990, Jefferson received her bachelor's degree in psychology. But her goal was to become a psychiatrist, so she stayed on an extra four years at Notre Dame, taking the science classes she needed to pass the Medical College Admission Test and apply to medical school. With a strong letter of recommendation from Emil, she was accepted into Indiana University and the University of Cincinnati. She picked the latter, and when she became engaged to nurse James Wilson in 2002, she did not hesitate to ask Hofman to walk her down the aisle. He was delighted to do so.

Since retiring in 1990 with many awards and honors to his credit, Dr. Emil T. Hofman has been a staple at the University. Occupying a bench in front of the Administration Building in good weather and a couch in LaFortune Student Center on rainy and snowy days, both of which he refers to as his field office, he is always a popular conversation partner for students who remember his quizzes and for those who only know the stories. His image is now permanently depicted on the "Wall of Honor" in the Main Building, which depicts the exceptional men and women whose contributions to Notre Dame are "lasting, pervasive, and profound."

—JEREMY LANGFORD

AN ANCIENT PROVERB in the Palestinian rabbinical schools of Christ's time divided all students into four classes. The first pair of these classes might be called the all-or-none groups. There was, first of all, the Sponges, who absorbed everything imparted in the lectures without any exceptions, the details, the illustrations, as well as the principles. The second group was called the Funnels. For the Funnels information and instruction passed through minds without obstruction, and with no retention, in one ear and out the other. The second pair of groups might be called the discriminating students. The first of these two groups was known as the Strainers, students who let the good wine of the lectures run through, keeping only the dregs, that is, retaining only what was of secondary importance. And the last group was the Sifters, those students who kept everything important, passing over only what was negligible, the chaff.

We cannot but speculate as to the future of you who have sifted well and successfully during your stay here at the University. As in the old proverb, we may classify our graduates into types based upon the attitudes which they adopt on two important matters: the University from which they have received the degree, and, secondly, the education therein received.

In their attitude toward this University graduates fall into four classes, similar in some ways, but also quite different, to those we have just mentioned. For the first group, called the Optimists, the University can do or has done no wrong. Like the Sponges, they accept everything. Faculty, campus, student body, all these leave nothing to be improved upon. The Optimists support the University in a general way, are proud to be graduates therefrom, but they cannot get enthusiastic about any of the University's projects, because the University is adequate enough as it is.

The second of these classes might be entitled the Indifferent. The Indifferent are something like the Funnels: by no gesture, word, or action would the Indifferent ever admit that they have committed the indiscretion, it seems, of having graduated from the University of Notre Dame; they retain nothing from it. The University attracts them to its functions no more than it would draw other persons in the community. They are present at the University when its teams are topflight, when its concert artists are world-renowned, and when its lecturers are spectacular, famous, or fashionable. Alumni news, University announcements, college publications, are consistently stored in that circular file, commonly known as a wastepaper basket. Alma mater means no more to them than an assembly line means to the automobile which rolls off it.

Corresponding to the Strainers, we have the Critics or the Panners.

For the Panners, nothing is right at the University. They pan all decisions, criticize all policies; they predict a doleful future to all ventures; they paralyze all initiative. It seems as though they have retained from their experience with the University only the negative, the faulty, the defective—in a word, the dregs. They grasp nothing of its promise, its vision, its value, and its worth.

The last class of students who adopt an attitude toward the University from which they have graduated are the Realists. Like the Optimists, the Realists are anxious to send worthy students here. Like the Critics, they diagnose needs in the University but they are anxious and willing to help remedy these deficiencies. They recognize that if the University is to have an ever-increasing influence upon the minds and characters of its students, and through them upon the community, it must have the support, both financial and moral, of friends, and above all, of its alumni. They acknowledge that the social, academic, and even economic value of their degrees depends upon the prestige of the University that confers it. As the University of Notre Dame extends its reputation and enhances its glory, so do its degrees become increasingly valuable. These Realists then isolate and emphasize that which is valuable in the University; they are the Sifters. Today we hope that you graduates will become Realists to the fullest degree.

But the University would be derelict of her duty, were she not concerned about the attitude which her graduates take toward their education. For some students, a college education is a terminal process, something finished once and for all, a dead-end street which leads no farther. Or it might be considered, in their eyes, as the top of a mountain, scaled with difficulty, with nothing beyond to conquer. For such graduates, too often a college education, even that aimed at an advanced degree, is a necessary evil, or a social necessity to achieve status and acceptance in certain circles, or an economic wedge by which one can obtain a job, a better position, or more salary. Now that it is completed some graduates settle down to a state of intellectual and academic stagnation. They become educational vegetables, passively existing wherever God puts them.

But there is another class of college graduates for whom a college education is a transitional process, a stage in life but not its conclusion. For them, education is like a primer of a pump, something that gets the flow of mental activity started, a mental activity that will never cease until death does soul and body part. They recognize that college education is more like a freeway than a dead-end street, that it is a time in which one can travel with the greatest speed, with the fewest obstructions, and a minimum of signs and traffic lights. But one does not stay on a freeway indefinitely, but must turn onto other streets where the travel is more difficult, but nonetheless necessary and valuable, and life is lived.

A university can only hope to impart a smattering of the inheritance of the ages, the wisdom of the entire race—the facts, the information, the concepts, and the principles men have discovered and lived by. A Catholic university can only give the rudiments of that broad vision of life and living that makes up our Faith; it can only take an education that is catholic—small c—in the general scope of its interests and concerns, and make it also Catholic—large C—in its attitude and values.

Skillful expression; habits of thinking, judging, and evaluating attitudes and views of self, God, and the world about us: these the University can inaugurate, but they need to be strengthened and deepened, if we are to become truly educated men and women. The reading of books and magazines, the participation in study clubs, discussion and action groups, the enrolling at University courses, the cultivation of stimulating friends—these are some of the ways to continue our lifelong process that we call education.

It is our hope, today, that you realize this ideal in your lives, that you may not only make a living, you may live, and live, as Christ wishes, ever more abundantly.

—Rev. William A. Botzum, C.S.C., then associate dean of the
Notre Dame Graduate School, speaking to the graduates of
Summer Session 1970[13]

THE LIFE OF a Notre Dame alumnus should typify commitment. A person who does not seek to grow spiritually is not a Notre Dame alumnus. A person who does not seek to act morally is not a Notre Dame alumnus. A man who is afraid to confront old problems with new ideas, who is afraid to confront himself, has wasted four years at Notre Dame.

—Excerpt from speech delivered by Guy DeSapio, ND student,
at a luncheon of the ND Alumni Board and Senate, 1970

NOTRE DAME IS a magical place that successfully combines the atmosphere of a residential liberal arts college with the dynamic qualities of a research university. The integration of teaching and scholarship is superb at Notre Dame, but our distinctive spirit and enduring competitive advantage reside in our Catholicism, which reinforces both learning and scholarship.

As part of its Catholic identity, Notre Dame seeks to address the whole person, to educate spiritually as well as intellectually. Notre Dame's holistic model of learning has motivated its graduates to become among the most loyal and supportive in the world. The Italian philosopher Giambattista Vico has argued that for an institution to flourish, its members must also align themselves with it emotionally. Notre Dame invites this kind of identification. More important, the way our students and graduates identify with Notre Dame and its values contributes to the continuing formation of their individual identities.

At Notre Dame, the moral and spiritual formation of students is purposely fostered. Prayer and liturgy belong to our students' college experience. Spiritual questions arise in all our disciplines. Students at Notre Dame pursue theology, for example, not as the disinterested science of religious phenomena but as faith seeking understanding. They study the classics and history in order to learn not simply about the past but also from the past. Students employ the quantitative tools of the social sciences not simply as a formal exercise but in order to develop sophisticated responses to pressing social issues. They cultivate the aesthetic imagination not only to experience creativity but also to partake of the transcendental value of beauty. The generous commitment of the Holy Cross religious to our campus and the ways in which they serve as role models reinforce this integration of learning and character, of college and community, of faith and life.

Notre Dame's Catholicism, which motivates our elevation of both faith and reason as well as our distinctive focus on the wisdom of the Christian tradition, also enriches the research university. Christianity developed the concept of universal human rights, with its emphasis on the dignity of every person and the value of the common good. This concept and its concomitant obligations toward other persons, especially the needy and the suffering, is the inspiration behind Notre Dame's scholarly focus on social justice issues, including, for example, poverty and development. While these issues are pursued most visibly in the humanities and the social sciences, an emphasis on social justice animates all our pursuits. The Mendoza College of Business, for example, seeks to educate knowledgeable professionals whose work is informed by moral principles, a goal that is distinctive in business education. The College of Engineering views its research as the utilization and development of the earth's resources in order to help humanity and thereby serve as an agent for God's work, not a common, contemporary view of the purposes of engineering. And the School of Architecture views its mission as involving not only artistic self-expression but also service to the community. By excelling in scholarship, Notre Dame has gained a national platform as a distinctively Catholic institution that addresses issues of broader consequence, including the moral challenges of the twenty-first century.

Another defining aspect of Notre Dame's Catholicism is its emphasis on community and love. Catholicism elevates to an unusual degree the embeddedness of the individual within a collective identity. Not surprisingly, our students are extraordinary in their attachment to their residential communities and to Notre Dame generally, as well as very devoted to community service. Approximately 85 percent of Notre Dame undergraduates participate in some kind of community service during their undergraduate years. These activities range from programs available to all students through the Center for Social Concerns to those that require disciplinary knowledge, such as the Notre Dame Legal Aid Clinic or Engineering Projects in Community Service. Each year more than 10 percent of graduating seniors dedicate themselves full-time to community service, in many cases beyond American borders. The Catholic Church, in its universalism, encourages internationalism.

In contrast to a modern, secular world characterized by the

proliferation of, and splintering into, ever more discrete subsystems of values and discrete disciplines of inquiry, without any recourse to the unity of knowledge, the Catholic tradition cultivates meaningful and integrative thought across the disciplines. Notre Dame's strong sense of community enhances this search for organic knowledge. We entrust ourselves to one another in our faith and engage one another in searching dialogue. The spirit of community and love on our campus is directed to one another as well as toward truth and toward God.

—MARK W. ROCHE, DEAN OF THE COLLEGE OF ARTS AND LETTERS

OUR MISSION IS to be a law school that is concerned with moral values. It's a place of mixing faith and reason. The values of the Catholic intellectual tradition are our guidepost. We are a national leader not in spite of our Catholic nature but because of it.

—DAVID LINK, WHO EARNED HIS B.A. IN 1958 AND HIS J.D. IN 1961,
SERVED AS DEAN OF THE LAW SCHOOL FROM 1975 UNTIL 1999,
DURING WHICH TIME HE TOOK THE NATION'S OLDEST CATHOLIC LAW
SCHOOL FROM A SMALL MIDWEST INSTITUTION TO ONE OF THE TOP 25
LAW PROGRAMS IN THE COUNTRY.

BODY

All my teaching career I've been running into unlikely
bespectacled students playing evening basketball in the Rock,
noon handball in the old Fieldhouse, and baseball everywhere.
They'll organize into teams and leagues between dribbles.
I know this is true to some extent of all youth, but I believe it
more true of Notre Dame than anywhere else.

—LONGTIME PROFESSOR TOM STRITCH IN HIS MEMOIR
My Notre Dame

NO INSTITUTION EVOKES as much pride, passion, or loyalty as Notre Dame and its sports teams. Of course, Notre Dame football is legendary: eleven national titles; seven Heisman Trophy winners; Rockne and Leahy; Ara, Devine, and Lou; the Gipper and Four Horsemen; Rudy and O'Neill; and countless heroes who have gone on to play in the National Football League. But Notre Dame's prowess in sports is not just about brawn and is certainly not limited to football. The school's academic standards and graduation rate for student-athletes are perennially at or near the top of all colleges and universities, and its storied sports history includes excellence in men's and women's basketball, tennis, fencing, swimming, soccer, track and field, cross country, lacrosse, as well as men's hockey and women's volleyball, softball, and rowing. Coaches in these sports face stringent transfer and redshirting policies and must ensure that student-athletes' classroom work takes precedence over practice and games. In fact, from 1925 until 1970 Irish athletes were not allowed to play in postseason games because it would interfere with their educational pursuits.

In addition to varsity athletics, Notre Dame hosts club sports as well as interhall and campuswide competitions in everything from hockey and tennis to boxing and football. The annual Bookstore Basketball Tournament has reached epic proportions, with hundreds of students participating and many more, including local residents from the area, cheering from the stands. Since 1931, the Bengal Bouts has tested the skills and strategies of student boxers who compete for themselves, but more important for the Holy Cross missions in Bengal, now Bangladesh. Interhall football, which hosts the championship game in the Notre Dame Stadium every year, showcases the talents of many students who were high school superstars or solid athletes who count among their dreams looking up from the stadium turf to see Touchdown Jesus looming over a crowd of fans.

From National Championships to pickup games, Notre Dame has emphasized sports as being part of a well-rounded education. Besides the obvious physical benefits, sports teach teamwork, endurance, strategy, and healthy competition. Sports also provide some of the greatest stories of inspiration, as players individually and together have overcome tremendous odds, risen to new human heights, and electrified fans.

KNUTE ROCKNE

He was the greatest coach in the history of college football, and his name will be remembered as long as the game is played.

His players—including the legendary George Gipp and the most colorful cavalry to ever charge across a gridiron, the Four Horsemen of Notre Dame—rank among the finest and the most famous to ever earn the distinction of All-American.

His words have inspired generations of Americans to overcome impossible odds and "win just one for the Gipper."

The name of his team ranks among the six most exciting words in sports.

The Fighting Irish of Notre Dame.

His own name ranks among the most revered.

There is no argument that the most cherished symbol of the University of Notre Dame is a gleaming, golden dome crowned by a nineteen-foot statue of the Blessed Virgin Mary. It is only fitting; the University was named to honor her.

The second most cherished symbol of Notre Dame is Knute Rockne. . . .

The Notre Dame football tradition is rich with heroic myths and affectionate apocrypha, conjuring images of gold-and-blue champions on the field of play while little blue nuns listen intently to their radios on an autumn afternoon, praying on Rosary beads for a Notre Dame victory. Indeed, the everyday lexicon of Notre Dame is a fascinating blend of words and phrases drawn from the school's three most easily identifiable traditions: Catholic, Irish, and football. On crisp, clear autumn afternoons, even a first-time visitor to Notre Dame may easily explore the campus just by asking for directions to such well-known landmarks as the statue of the aforementioned Fair-Catch Corby, The Huddle, Number One Moses, and the 132-foot-high stone mosaic known as Touchdown Jesus.

The spirit, idealism, and success of Notre Dame's Fighting Irish rank among America's greatest and most beloved success stories. But the greatest Notre Dame legend of them all is Knute Rockne, the celebrated coach who led the Fighting Irish to 105 victories in 13 seasons while establishing a shining tradition and an incredible winning percentage that may never be surpassed.

When Knute Rockne first arrived at Notre Dame as a student in 1910, Notre Dame Avenue was still unpaved. But certain elements of the famous "spirit of Notre Dame" were in place. The Notre Dame Victory March had already been composed—the song had first been performed at Washington's Birthday exercises held at the school on February 22, 1909—and would appear to have had an immediate impact. According to the record books, the Notre Dame football team won seven and tied one later that same year.

Rockne's impact on Notre Dame was remarkable by any measure. During his 13-year head coaching tenure, which began in 1918 and ended in 1930, the Fighting Irish won six National Championships and put together five undefeated and untied seasons. His teams produced 20 first-team All-Americans. His lifetime winning percentage of .881 (105 wins, 12 loses, 5 ties) still ranks at the top of the list for both college and professional football.

And, he won every one of the last 19 games he coached.

Rockne was the most innovative coach of his era. He was the first football coach to initiate intersectional rivalries and build a national schedule, setting a pattern that Notre Dame follows to this day. Rockne took his team, traveling by train, all over the country— from the Polo Grounds to Soldier Field to the Coliseum. Millions of Americans adopted the team as their own, calling themselves Notre Dame Subway Alumni and sharing in the joy of being Irish—if only for an autumn afternoon.

As the football crowds grew to 50,000 per game, Notre Dame's star ascended. The Rockne era brought dramatic change to Notre Dame. In 1920, for example, the school's 67-member faculty taught 1,207 who paid tuition, room, and board of about $574 per year. During the next decade, while the Fighting Irish football team won national prominence for the University, Notre Dame's faculty would increase and its enrollment would nearly triple—to 3,227 in 1930–31.

Through the years, Knute Rockne's legend has grown as his life story has been retold in one medium after another. In 1940, Warner Bros. released a motion picture, *Knute Rockne—All American*, in which actor Pat O'Brien gave a memorable performance as the Notre Dame coach. In the 1950s, on television, The Prudential Insurance Company of America (in a tribute from one great "Rock" to another) sponsored a documentary, *Rockne of Notre Dame*, as part of a CBS News series, *The Twentieth Century*, which was hosted and narrated by Walter Cronkite. Today, on video-tape, images of Rockne live on in an Emmy Award–winning documentary produced by NFL Films, *Wake Up the Echoes: The History of Notre Dame Football*.

There have been many other tributes to Rockne's memory. Perhaps no greater measure of his celebrity was that the Studebaker Motor Company once named an automobile after him—the Rockne. Each year, the Notre Dame Club of Chicago sponsors the Knute Rockne Awards Dinner to raise scholarship funds for deserving young men and women who attend Notre Dame. On the Notre Dame campus, "the Rock"—the Knute Rockne Memorial Building, an athletic facility built in 1937—remains a popular place where college students and university presidents alike can play, of all things, basketball. In March 1988, the United States Postal Service [issued] a Knute Rockne commemorative stamp to mark the centennial of his birth. The stamp [was] unveiled by no less than the President of the United States.

Rockne was at the height of his profession during that last football season in 1930. His team had marched to victory 10 straight times—extending a winning streak to 19 games. The Fighting Irish outscored their opponents 265 to 74 and finished the season with a 27–0 victory over the University of Southern California.

A few months later, Knute Rockne would be dead at the age of 43. There would be no more victories, no more cheering, and the voice of one of the most popular men in America would be silenced forever.

The great American humorist Will Rogers said at the news of Rockne's death, "It takes a big calamity to shock this country all at once, but Knute, you did it. You died one of our national heroes. Notre Dame was your address, but every gridiron in America was your home."

—ROBERT QUAKENBUSH '76 AND MIKE BYNUM[1]

THE STADIUM WAS jammed and not very inviting for Notre Dame. It was cold and clammy and kind of scary. Rockne let the boys go out on the field to warm up prior to the game. They were out there about fifteen minutes and then he pulled them in and he told 'em to all lay down on the floor. He had 'em lay down on these olive-drab blankets, instead of on that oily, clammy floor that the Yankee ball-club once used. For a while, silence prevailed.

Finally, he recalled standing beside the deathbed of George Gipp and told of reaching out his hand and listening to the dying athlete say, "Coach, when the going gets rough, especially against Army, win one for me." And he went on to emphasize not only how important winning was to themselves, but likewise to answer the prayer of the Gipper, who converted to Catholicism on his deathbed. So you see there was a touch of spiritual motivation about it all. And I'll tell you, there wasn't a dry eye in the house.

—ED HEALY, LINE COACH OF THE 1928 NOTRE DAME TEAM,
DESCRIBING THE GIPPER SPEECH BEFORE THE ARMY GAME, WHICH
UNDERDOG NOTRE DAME WON, 12–6

OUTLINED AGAINST A blue-gray October sky, the Four Horse-men rode again.

In dramatic lore they are known as Famine, Pestilence, Destruction, and Death. Those are only aliases. Their real names are Stuhldreher, Miller, Crowley, and Layden. They formed the crest of the South Bend cyclone before which another fighting Army team was swept over the precipice at the Polo Grounds yesterday afternoon, as 55,000 spectators peered down on the bewildering panorama spread out on the green plain below.

A cyclone can't be snared. It may be surrounded, but somewhere it breaks through to keep going. When the cyclone starts from South Bend, where the candle lights still gleam through the Indiana sycamores, those in the way must take to the storm cellars at top speed. Yesterday the cyclone struck again, as Notre Dame beat Army, 13–7, with a set of backfield stars that ripped and rushed through a strong Army defense with more speed and power than the warring cadets could meet.

Notre Dame won its eighth game in 11 starts [over Army] through the driving power of one of the greatest backfields that ever churned up the turf of any gridiron in any football age. Brilliant backfields may come and go, but in Stuhldreher, Miller, Crowley, and Layden, covered by a fast and charging line, Notre Dame can take its place in front of the field.

—*NEW YORK HERALD TRIBUNE* SPORTSWRITER GRANTLAND RICE'S
FAMOUS ACCOUNT OF THE 1924 NOTRE DAME–ARMY GAME. THE 1924
IRISH WENT ON TO A 9–0 SEASON AND THE NATIONAL CHAMPIONSHIP.

ONE OF THE coach's tricks was to ignore his team completely during halftime. He would sit sullenly in a corner, then finally get up and say disgustedly, "All right, girls, let's go." On another occasion, when Notre Dame had played a poor first half, Rockne merely opened the door to the dressing room, peeked in, and said: "I beg your pardon. I thought this was the Notre Dame team."

Jim Crowley, one of the Four Horsemen, remembers:

We were playing Georgia Tech in 1922, and they had been undefeated on their home field for years. Rockne came into the dressing room carrying a telegram. "I have a wire here, boys, and it probably doesn't mean much to you but it means a great deal to me. It's from my poor, sick little boy Billy, who's critically ill in the hospital in South Bend." And then he read the wire, with teary eyes, a lump in his throat and quivering lips. "I want Daddy's team to win." So we knocked him down, went through a pole at the door, and got on the field about ten minutes before game time. We took a hell of a pounding from this great Georgia Tech team because they had been out to beat us for years, but we won the game for little Billy, 13–3.

Well, when we got back to South Bend, there must have been about 20,000 people to greet us. And as we stepped down off the train racked in pain, the first face we saw was Rockne's kid. He was in the front line. There was "poor, sick little Billy looking like an ad for Pet Milk."[2]

LEAHY AND HIS LADS

Frank Leahy (1908–1973) was, after Rockne, the greatest coach in Notre Dame history. A tackle on Rockne's 1929 National Championship team, Leahy dreamed of one day coaching the Fighting Irish. With his former mentor's help, he secured an assistant's job at Georgetown and later coached at Michigan State, Fordham, and Boston College, where he was head coach and had a 20–2 record with an 11–0 season in 1940. Then, in 1941, his dream came true: he became Notre Dame's head coach. From 1941 to 1953, with two seasons off for military service in World War II, Leahy coached the Irish to four undisputed National Championships, a record of 87 victories, 11 losses and nine ties, unbeaten squads in six of his 11 seasons, and a Notre Dame record of going undefeated in 39 straight games. He was named Coach of the Year five times for good reason: four of his players won the Heisman Trophy, 36 were named All-Americans, two won the Outland Trophy, 11 are in the College Football Hall of Fame, and numerous graduates of his program played at the professional level.

A formal, almost enigmatic man, Leahy was a perfectionist; for him "practice makes perfect" was more than a cliché. He and his assistants drilled and drove the players in practice with repetitions that allowed little room for chance on Saturdays. Leahy's teams were fast, well conditioned, trained to follow Leahy's strategy in every game. He was a master not only of offensive use of the T formation, but of defense as well. His 1946 team allowed a total of 24 points in nine games! Like some military genius, Leahy prepared for every detail, orchestrated every maneuver.

But his almost obsessive quest for perfection took a toll on his health. He was 45 years old when he coached his last game for Notre

Dame. His players remember him with respect and awe to this day. Jack Connor's book, *Leahy's Lads,* records the incredible bond that still exists among his former players as evidenced in their annual reunions held since 1971, and the memories they have of the master. "Leahy was the greatest football coach in the history of the game," says All-American Jerry Groom. Heisman Trophy winner John Lujack adds, "Frank Leahy helped us in a lot of the things that are important in life. He taught you dedication. He taught you sacrifice so that you must be willing to pay the price for success . . . the real character of a person is measured by the ability to come back after a disappointment. These are things that he taught us." Adds Heisman winner Leon Hart, "Frank Leahy influenced my life more than any other man who ever lived—including my father."

Though unable to attend the first reunion, Leahy summed up his feelings in a telegram:

Words cannot adequately express the depth of my sadness over not being with you during the most unique gathering in athletic history.

Four National Championship teams together after 28 years, which proves conclusively your love for each other and for Notre Dame. Never lose contact with that famous Lady who reigns so serenely over our beautiful campus. Give Her a chance not to forget you by seeking assistance when necessary. She stands ready and willing to reciprocate for your unsurpassed representation during and since graduation.

A privilege of attending Notre Dame has given you an enviable mark of distinction. People everywhere expect more from you because you are a Notre Dame man, because you were a Notre Dame team, and at all times you have and will continue to measure up . . .

You are men endowed with qualities that forged our

nation to greatness. Notre Dame leadership is more important now than ever before . . . you have learned many
invaluable lessons at Notre Dame, especially the realization
that games can never be won, character developed, that
nothing of lasting value can be achieved without desire,
hard work, loyalty, self-discipline and depravation . . .[3]

Leahy died of leukemia less than two years later, on June 21,
1973. His nuggets of wisdom endure:
"Discipline is indispensable in the education of a gentleman."
"Pay the price in sweat, effort, and sacrifice and strive for per-
fection in each day's drill."
"Egotism is the anesthetic that deadens the pain of stupidity."
"Remember this, lads, never, never, never give up."

ARA'S ERA

When Terry Brennan and Joe Kuharich were unable to return the
Irish to the stature of the Leahy years, and Hugh Devore, as temporary coach, suffered a 2–7 season in 1963, Notre Dame was in trouble.
But not for long: That same year Ara Parseghian, whose Northwestern teams had defeated Notre Dame four years in a row (1959–
1962), contacted Father Ned Joyce, the legendary Executive Vice
President who served with Father Hesburgh. Ara did not think he
had much of a chance of getting the coveted coaching job; if hired,
he would be the first non-Catholic, non-graduate since Rockne to
coach the Irish. Father Joyce explained to Parseghian that Notre
Dame has people of all faiths on faculty and campus, and that while
it was always nice to hire Catholics, decisions have always been
based on a candidate's capabilities. And so, in 1963, Notre Dame
hired Ara Parseghian as its twenty-second head coach.
    Immediately Ara made a positive impression on players and fans.
He had a presence about him that comes from being a man of char-

acter and inner strength. He stressed unity, loyalty, and sacrifice, wasted no time moving players to new positions, instilled confidence in an unknown quarterback named John Huarte. And he won. In his first season, the Irish took a 9–0 record into the final game only to fall to Southern California, 20–17. Tom Pagna describes what happened when the team returned to South Bend from that devastating loss:

> When we landed that night we were asked to remain on the plane for a few minutes. We had no way of knowing what was planned, but the short delay made final arrangements possible. The route of the buses that would take us to campus had been publicized, and all along the way people had their porch lights on and were standing out applauding us in nine-degree temperatures. We expected to go to the main entrance of the campus as usual, but instead the buses headed for the old Fieldhouse.
>
> Assembled there was a larger crowd than for any rally. The overflow was forced to stand outside in the snow. As soon as the fans spotted us they erupted. We were escorted to our normal place in the balcony with the cheers still building. This lasted for at least 20 minutes. There were no speeches planned, but Ara made an attempt at one. He fought to get the words out as he considered the tribute these people were paying us. "We wanted to bring you back the National Championship . . . ," he stammered. "You did, you did, you did . . . ," they roared. He couldn't continue.
>
> That had to be the most stirring event any of us ever lived through. I looked around at the team and the other coaches. None of us, including Ara, could hold back the tears. We were all that touched and hurt that we couldn't have pulled it off. The band played the Victory March and the Alma Mater, and the gathering broke up.[4]

Two years later, in 1966, Parseghian led the Irish to their first National Championship in fifteen years. In 1973, his undefeated Irish, led by quarterback Tom Clements, beat Alabama 24–23 in the Sugar Bowl for another National Championship. Bob Thomas kicked the winning field goal, a wobbly 33-yarder.

When Ara asked him why the kick had barely made it, Thomas said that if it had been perfect and beautiful, nobody would remember it. "This way," he said, "they'll be talking about it for years."

After one more season and a 13–11 Orange Bowl victory over Alabama, denying them the National Championship, Ara stepped down. His 11 seasons at the helm had restored Notre Dame to glory, carried them with class through very tough times of student unrest, and amassed a record of 95–17–4. He has devoted much of his post-coaching life to raising money for medical research to find a cure for Niemann-Pick disease.

THE FIRST TIME I drove up Notre Dame Avenue after being named head football coach, an enormous sense of responsibility overwhelmed me. The Notre Dame football program had been in a period of decline. It is hard to believe, but Notre Dame had had several losing seasons in the previous years. Yet all of the elements for success were there. The great Notre Dame Tradition of Rockne and Gipp, Leahy and Lujack was still alive, despite the eclipse. There were talented athletes ready and anxious to win. The primary task at hand was to restore confidence and belief in the Notre Dame spirit, in the winning attitude that had prevailed here for so many years.

I didn't realize the magnitude of Notre Dame until I actually came to the campus and began to be exposed to all it is and represents. There is a Notre Dame mystique that defies definition or description. It is something special in its combination of religion, education, and athletics. It is not only national but international in scope. And there is a real tradition of achieving excellence whatever the odds.

It was that tradition that we wanted to restore on the football field.

I had the good fortune of assembling a fine group of associate coaches. A team is no stronger than its weakest player on the field or the weakest coach on its staff. The coaches, like the team, need to work together, to channel energy in one direction, toward one goal. We did not necessarily look for coaches who had the deepest technical knowledge of football. What we wanted was quality people of integrity, people who could contribute knowledge and enthusiasm to our joint effort. We found them and they joined us.

Our first season was successful because the players and coaches wanted to win and believed that we could. People couldn't wait to come to practice. Their confidence and enthusiasm carried us to nine straight wins before a tough loss in our last game. It was an exciting beginning. Once begun, spirit, dedication, and character have a way of building their own momentum. You could sense it in the way our people played and in the manner in which they conducted themselves, win or lose.

During eleven years at Notre Dame we regarded each and every game as a "big" game and we were able to win a large share of them. But the very success that requires and comes from intense and focused energy can also bring impossible expectations. Some writers seemed to think that the only "big" games we ever played were the ones we lost. Looking back now I have to say that the game that stands out most in my mind is the 1973 Sugar Bowl game against Alabama. Despite their great football traditions, Notre Dame and Alabama had never played each other before. It was a clash between two undefeated teams with the National Championship on the line. It was a potentially explosive situation with its North-South and religious undertones. What happened was not fights or violence by players or fans. Instead, two class teams met in an intense contest. After the game there was an enormous respect for each other, and another great series in college football had begun.

My decision to leave coaching when I did was well thought out, and I have never had reason to second-guess it. I can say in all honesty that the Notre Dame years were the greatest period in my life and my family's life. Our loyalty to and respect for Notre Dame will always be a part of us.

—ARA PARSEGHIAN[5]

NINETEEN-SIXTY-SIX IRISH CAPTAIN Jim Lynch summed up the feelings of countless Domers when he said: "Being part of Notre Dame is being part of a tradition much bigger than any one man, one team, or one season. But Ara embodies that quality which will always describe Notre Dame—class. Under him I learned how to win and how to lose. Ara is, very simply, the finest man I have ever been associated with."[6]

DAN DEVINE

Though Ara and many fans had hoped that Tom Pagna would be named as his successor, the University turned the reins over to former Arizona State, Missouri, and Green Bay Packer coach Dan Devine. In his six seasons at the helm, Devine led the Irish to a record of 53–16–1; three bowl wins—over Penn State, Texas, and Houston; and a National Championship in 1977.

A complex, shy, and sensitive man, Devine never completely captured the hearts of the fans the way Ara had and Holtz would. Still, he recruited and coached some of the best athletes ever to play for Notre Dame. After 8–3 and 9–3 records in 1975 and 1976, and an early season upset in 1977 at the hands of Mississippi, the Irish ran the table, including the green jerseyed 49–19 thumping of Southern Cal, and headed to the Cotton Bowl to face number one Texas, led by Earl Campbell. While it might have appeared that the odds were not in Notre Dame's favor, these were the Irish of Browner and Fry, McAfee and Golic, Bradley, Hughes, Ferguson and Heavens, and Joe Montana. The Irish won, 38–10, and once again were crowned National Champions. After an 8–3 season in 1978, the Irish returned to the Cotton Bowl and Joe Montana's miracle comeback win over Houston, 35–34. Father Hesburgh was there, and he congratulated Devine and the Irish, saying, "This is a real Notre Dame victory." After a 7–4 record in 1979, Devine's last year produced a 9–1–1 regular-season record and a near upset of Georgia in the Sugar Bowl. Devine described his tenure this way:

THE BEST WAY I can think of to describe my six seasons at Notre Dame is that they were anything but boring.

Those years turned out their share of victories that don't seem to stick in my mind for any particular reason. They also produced some losses that I hope won't stick in my mind for too long.

But most of my fondest memories about Notre Dame involve those games that somehow ended up in the win column after just about everyone was resigned to losing. I'm still not sure exactly how or why some of those amazing rallies came about. I'm sure there was a little luck involved at least a few times. I guess, above all, those games taught me a little bit about that Notre Dame spirit described in the Victory March. The odds might have been great or small, but some of those comebacks made it seem like they simply had been destined to be that way. I didn't have the fortune of attending Notre Dame, but I certainly became a believer in a few short weeks!

It seems that everywhere it's said that people are what make Notre Dame such a great place. I couldn't agree more. From Fathers Hesburgh and Joyce down through the faculty and athletic administration to the students themselves, Notre Dame people are special in their own way. I also was blessed with superb groups of assistant coaches, not to mention an awfully impressive list of young men who wore

Notre Dame football uniforms in my years. The university always has emphasized the term student-athlete, and that's probably part of the reason I so enjoyed getting to know those young men as individuals as much as I enjoyed watching their successes on the field.

I'll always remember some of the obvious highlights of the years 1975 through 1980.

That first game in '75 against Boston College on national television was my baptism as far as Notre Dame was concerned. I found out a little bit more about subway alumni that Monday night—and I also came to realize that you can go anywhere on the globe and find Notre Dame fans.

The next year we managed to defeat Bear Bryant and Alabama— and then finished the year by beating a good Penn State team in the Gator Bowl.

The '77 season turned out to be a once-in-a-lifetime experience for all of us connected with that team. That was the year that Southern Cal came back to town armed with a three-year winning streak and hungry to make it four. But we were hungrier. The Trojans were met by a Fighting Irish football team wearing green, not blue, and playing with the intensity and the drive characteristic of a championship team. It was a week of electricity, a day of glory, and a victory that was among the sweetest.

Winning football games and bowl games is a thrilling experience. But when they add together to equal a National Championship title, well, that has to be one of the most amazing experiences in which I have ever been involved.

I don't think any of us will forget the scene in the locker room at the Cotton Bowl after we had beaten undefeated Texas. That was a feeling that would be tough to match, anytime, anywhere. Yet, once you are handed that National Champion designation, you become something special for the next year. The reception we received, no matter who was connected with that team, wherever we went over the next year, proved to all of us that there are an awfully large number of people in this country who enjoy college football.

We enjoyed our third straight bowl victory in '78 by defeating Houston in the final seconds of the Cotton Bowl—and we closed out the '79 campaign by traveling to Tokyo, where we played Miami in the Mirage Bowl. I'll never forget the reception Vagas Ferguson received in Japan and the way he was treated like some sort of folk hero. The name Notre Dame seemed to stand for something special even to those people who had never seen the Golden Dome.

As far as buildup for a single football game, one that impressed me a great deal was our match with Alabama in 1980. We knew months ahead of time that the Alabama people had been waiting years for that game. They tried to let us know what was in store for us in Birmingham, so much so that we felt like Daniel in the lion's den for a few seconds. But I would be the first to credit the Alabama fans—they were some of the greatest fans of college football that I've ever run into. And our young men, to their credit, came up with one of the grittiest efforts I've seen for sixty minutes on a football field.

The loss to USC in Los Angeles in 1978 and our defeat in the Sugar Bowl against Georgia are a couple of games that I'll probably wonder about for a long while. On both those afternoons, it seemed like we somehow should have ended up winning the football game—but it just didn't happen that way.

Despite all those moments, what really stands out most in my mind are some of those come-from-behind wins.

I'll always remember Joe Montana coming off the bench two weeks in a row as a sophomore to help us rally to beat North Carolina and Air Force on the road. He did nearly the same thing two years later against Purdue in West Lafayette in the '77 season—and he even finished his Notre Dame career by doing it against Houston in the Cotton Bowl. That was the day he helped make chicken soup famous. The effort by the whole team that day, under those weather conditions, deserved more than just a pat on the back. Even if the sun had been out and the dial read 70 degrees, it would have been an astounding performance.

Rusty Lisch caught that same bug the next year with a last-minute drive against South Carolina—and even Harry Oliver and Blair Kiel picked it up to beat Michigan in 1980. I guess those are the kinds of games that keep the fans coming back every Saturday. They almost made me wish I could sit up in section 26, eat a hot dog or two, and yell, too!

People like Rockne, Leahy, Brennan, and Parseghian took part in plenty of those extra special Saturday afternoons during their stays at Notre Dame—and Gerry Faust and others will be a part of their share of extraordinary moments in the future.

In between there, I hope I was able to do a little something to help make Notre Dame the unique place that it is today. An awful lot of Notre Dame rubbed off on me in six years—and I know I've left a little bit of my heart behind, too.

—DAN DEVINE[7]

WE'VE GOT SOMETHING to be proud of here. So, when the student cheering section stands up and says, "We are ND," let's truly be ND—everything it stands for. I'm proud to be a part of it.

—DAN DEVINE

SOMETIMES I THINK you can appreciate Notre Dame more if you haven't gone to school here. Notre Dame is different. There are a lot of things that add up: the Grotto, the church, the pregame Mass, the band marching across the field and through campus after their practice, the students coming out on the field, the roar when we came out in those green jerseys . . .

—DAN DEVINE[8]

LOU HOLTZ

It was in December 1985 when Lou Holtz exercised an escape clause in his contract with the University of Minnesota and came to South Bend to rescue a program in disarray, one that had bottomed out in Jerry Faust's last game, a 58–7 thrashing by Miami on November 30, 1985.

"Look at me," he said when he landed the Notre Dame job in 1985. "I'm five-foot-ten, I weigh 150 pounds, I talk with a lisp, I look like I have scurvy, I'm not very smart, I was a terrible football player, and I graduated 234th in a high-school class of 278. What do you think it feels like to be named head coach at Notre Dame?"

Though the Irish went 5–6 in his first year, it was clear that things had changed; an 8–4 record in 1987 added to the impetus, even though a 35–10 thrashing at the hands of Texas A&M was ample proof that there was still a long way to go.

From 1986 to '96, Holtz's Fighting Irish won 100, lost 30, and tied 3. They finished the season ranked sixth or better five times and won five of the nine bowls they played. Holtz coached a Heisman winner (Tim Brown) and Heisman runner-up (Raghib Ismail) and numerous consensus All-Americans, including linebacker Michael Stonebreaker, offensive tackle Andy Heck, cornerback Todd Lyght, defensive tackle Chris Zorich, offensive lineman Aaron Taylor, and cornerbacks Jeff Burris and Bobby Taylor.

Of many great seasons, Holtz's third was sensational. Using discipline, commitment, motivation, and confidence as his tools, he molded a 1988 team that would win a special place in Notre Dame history. From a 19–17 opening win over Michigan to the 34–21 whipping of West Virginia in the Fiesta Bowl, the National Champion Irish went 12–0 and in the process defeated four teams that finished in the top ten in the nation. But it was the Miami game that remains as one of the greatest wins ever.

Notre Dame was ranked fourth when top-ranked Miami came to town. This was the matchup Irish fans had dreamed of and waited for ever since the 58–7 drubbing Miami had inflicted on Notre Dame in

Gerry Faust's last game as head coach. The intensity was undeniable; it was on T-shirts, in the stands, during warm-ups; it was everywhere. The two teams engaged in a scuffle in the tunnel as they headed toward the dressing rooms for final instructions. There was no love lost here. As in the 1966 battle with MSU, the field was studded with stars. Holtz knew he didn't need to fire up his men. He simply tried to coax them to relax. As the call came to take the field, he looked at his team and said with passion, "Save Jimmy Johnson's ass for me." It wasn't exactly a Rockne speech, but it worked. Tied 21 all at the half, the game rocked back and forth, great defense against great defense. Late in the fourth quarter, Reggie Ho kicked a field goal to give Notre Dame a 31–24 lead. The final two minutes were manic, hyperbolic, almost surreal. Each team fumbled. With 51 seconds to go, Miami scored a touchdown. The crowd was stunned. Johnson elected to go for two points and the win. Steve Walsh, who had already thrown for a record 424 yards, lofted a pass into the corner of the end zone. Notre Dame's Pat Terrell was there and knocked it down. Anthony Johnson recovered the onside kick, and Notre Dame had won perhaps one of the most storied games in its history. Chris Zorich remarked: "It came down to the final seconds, and I wasn't scared. I was confident. Coach had all of us confident. I came to Notre Dame for games like that—for pressure like that." Said Holtz, "It was a win by the spirit of a group of guys who just refused to fold, and who believed." Navy, Rice, Penn State, and Southern California all fell before the Irish, and a 34–21 win over West Virginia in the Fiesta Bowl earned the Irish the National Championship. Holtz summed it up: "We did it as a team. We are a real family. And as long as I live, I'll always remember this team."

IT WAS LIKE we could feel all those Irish legends out there. I kept hearing those lines from our fight song about shaking down the thunder and waking up the echoes.

—CHRIS ZORICH

"WE ARE ND." Notre Dame is no average school. Notre Dame is not comprised of average people. Notre Dame wants to be outstanding in all fields of endeavor . . . Notre Dame is the easiest place in the world to win, because of the discipline and the love and the family atmosphere and the intelligence and the commitment to excellence. . . .

—LOU HOLTZ

FOLLOWING THE STUNNING victory over Miami, the Irish ran the table against Air Force, Navy, Rice, Penn State, and Southern California. The final game was the Fiesta Bowl matchup with third-ranked and undefeated West Virginia. The heralded Mountaineers offense was stopped by the rugged Irish defense, and the game was more lopsided than the 34–21 score indicated. In the locker room after the game, Lou told his team:

> You've joined the Notre Dame greats now. You've won more games than any team in history at Notre Dame. You beat the number two, three, and four teams. If it weren't for you, Miami, West Virginia, and USC all would be unbeaten. We were only the fourth team in the history of the NCAA, and the first one in 45 years, to win the National Championship and defeat four teams that finished in the top 10 in the final poll. To the seniors, juniors, sophomores, and freshmen, I say thank you. You'll find the trip to the top has been great. Staying there is a whole different matter, but we'll talk about that later. We'll be all right if you believe in the Notre Dame spirit. Take the lessons we have learned this year and apply them in your future endeavors and make certain you are a positive force in our society.[9]

Later, at the press conference, Holtz added:

I think Knute Rockne would be proud of this team because it exemplifies what the Notre Dame spirit is all about. They subjugated their personal welfare for the welfare of the team and they played together. They cared about each other, and I can't say anything that would compliment this group more than that. There may be more talented teams and there may be better-coached teams, but there can't be a team that typifies the Notre Dame spirit better than this one.[10]

When the team visited the President at the White House, President Reagan added his accolades:

My life has been full of rich and wonderful experiences. Standing near the top of the list is my long and honored association with the University of Notre Dame and its legendary hero, Knute Rockne. . . . You young fellows here today are living proof of the truth of Rockne's ideals. All of you, coaches and players, have made sacrifices and borne many a burden. And you did it all for one goal—to be the very best.

GROWING UP IN the Middle West as I did in the Rockne years and loving football as I did, long before I played in high school and college, I was one of that great, nationwide unofficial Notre Dame cheering section.

There always seemed to be a spirit that lifted the Fighting Irish when things seemed to be going against them. During my sports announcing years, there was the team that dedicated the game with Ohio State to the Notre Dame captain who died in an accident. With two minutes to play, Notre Dame trailed, 13 to 0. In those two minutes, Notre Dame scored three touchdowns to win, 18 to 13.

I had the feeling I saw that same Notre Dame spirit with Coach Lou Holtz and his National Championship team.

—RONALD REAGAN

THERE'S A MYSTIQUE about Notre Dame that needs to be experienced over a period of time. It cannot be expressed in words. The school means excellence to many Americans—excellence not only in sports, but in attitude, spirit, character, academic achievement, and the arts. It is that quality of striving for greatness that has won Notre Dame an affectionate place in the hearts of most Americans.

—GERRY FAUST, WHO COACHED FROM 1981 TO 1985
AND AMASSED A 30–26–1 RECORD

"BOB DAVIE HAS brought good students and good people to Notre Dame," said Athletic Director Kevin White at the press conference announcing that Bob Davie would not be retained as head coach. "He has supported and has taken an active interest in the academic progress of the players. He has encouraged good citizenship. . . . Davie has always praised the academic accomplishments of his football teams. Last year, the football grade point average reached its two highest semester averages, and Notre Dame won the AFCA Academic Achievement Award for graduating 100 percent of its players, the first time the Irish reached the 100 percent mark since 1988. However, we also expect and intend to excel on the field, and there, unfortunately, our results and progress have been disappointing."

"I've talked to our football team every single day, and it's not the bad things that happen to you that's important, it's how you handle them," said coach Bob Davie of his dismissal after a 35–25 record in five seasons at Notre Dame.

TYRONE WILLINGHAM

When Notre Dame decided not to renew coach Tyrone Willingham's contract (2002–2004 with a win-loss record of 21–15), the players and everyone who had come into contact with him agreed on one simple truth: He is a man of extraordinary character, goodness, and integrity. I saw it firsthand. It was in the summer of his first season as Notre Dame coach. I was hosting a dozen ten-year-olds from the projects in Chicago for the weekend and took them on a walking tour of campus. After seeing the Dome, lakes, Grotto, and Basilica, then dorms and classroom buildings, I was frustrated to find the stadium locked and the Joyce Athletic and Convocation Center (JACC) unavailable because it had been rented out for a car show, and I started taking the children back to where our van was parked. Then I saw coach Willingham's car pull into his JACC space. I told the children to wait by the Moose Krause sculpture while I talked to Coach. He must have thought, "Here comes another alumnus or fan. . . ." But he listened attentively as I introduced myself and asked whether he would come over to speak to the children. He didn't hesitate. I suspect that most of the children did not know much about Notre Dame football. What they saw and heard was a strong, passionate, African-American man telling them that they need to study now, to resist peer pressure and drugs, and to make decisions that would bring them to a place like this for an education. I am sure that a number of prominent coaches would not have had the willingness or taken the time to do what coach Willingham did. Or the experience to relate to the children the way he did. I do know this: Those children will remember the camp and campus. Most of all, they will remember that man who spoke to them with such power. I could not wish for them to take home a better memory than that.

—JIM LANGFORD

CHARLIE WEIS

As he returned to Notre Dame, now as head football coach, his demeanor was less one of awe than of confidence. A 1978 ND graduate, Weis learned coaching under Bill Parcells and Bill Belichick. Offensive coordinator of the New England Patriots, Weis has three Super Bowl rings to support his contention that if the talent is fairly equal and it comes down to Xs and Os, the Irish will win most of the time. He gives you a strong sense that, once again, Notre Dame is coming back. At his first press conference after accepting the job, Weis told the crowd of reporters: "This is obviously a high-profile, big-time job, but it's one that I, a long, long time ago, thought—'Wouldn't that be something if you could ever be the head coach at University of Notre Dame.' You know, when we all grow up [we have] aspirations. I grew up in New Jersey. I was an avid sports fan, wasn't a very good athlete, mind you, but I was an avid sports fan. At one time I wanted to be a sports announcer, because I recognized at an early age, 'I don't think I'm going to play pro, so I'm going to be a sports announcer.' And then I went to Notre Dame and I said, 'Oh, maybe not a sports announcer. Maybe I'll get involved in some other way, I'm not really sure how.'

"So I was getting a degree in speech and drama, and communications as an emphasis. I also decided to get certified to teach just in case I wanted to go in that direction and be involved in the coaching. I remember my parents saying to me, 'You're going to Notre Dame to be a teacher?'

"Well, my father, God rest his soul, he's smiling in heaven today, because if he ever knew I would have been where I am today, he would be a very proud man."

—JIM LANGFORD

BEFORE EVERY FOOTBALL game, twenty-one student managers perform what has become a sacred rite at Notre Dame: They paint the Irish helmets. More than one hundred helmets are sanded down, treated with paint thinner, and smoothed. Then they are painted with two coats of gold spray paint before a final coat that contains actual gold dust is applied. Whether home or away, Notre Dame fans cheer proudly when they first see the Fighting Irish take the field in their shiny "Golden Domes."

—JEREMY LANGFORD

MR. NOTRE DAME

The litany of legendary athletes at Notre Dame is almost endless. But there is only one who has unanimous acclamation for the title "Mr. Notre Dame." That man is Edward "Moose" Krause (1913–1992). Recruited from DeLaSalle High School in Chicago, Krause came to Notre Dame in 1930. He went on to be a star defensive tackle for the Irish. His 6'3", 230-pound frame belied his finesse and agility. His real stardom was on the basketball court, where be became a two-time All-American. Jason Kelly, in his wonderful book *Mr. Notre Dame*,[11] tells of Krause's upbringing in the tough Back of the Yards neighborhood of South Chicago, the son of Lithuanian immigrants who ran a grocery store, and of his desire to go to Notre Dame. He was a standout football player, but even better at basketball. Kelly tells a story that illustrates Krause's ever-present sense of humor: In 1933, the Irish were trailing Butler by two points with only seconds remaining in the game. With time running out, Krause missed a shot that could have tied the game; there was a crush of bodies seeking the rebound. Krause landed on the floor. "There I was, stretched out on the hardwood," he recalled, "with players jumping on and off my head as fast as I could count." Then his own missed shot bounced right back into his arms. Lying on his back, he shot and hit the tying basket and the Irish went on to a 42–41 win in overtime.

Coach George Keogan kidded Krause, saying that he should shoot from the horizontal position more often. The next morning, Krause played it to the hilt. As the team left the hotel, a kid was on the sidewalk selling the Indianapolis Star: "*Morning Star,*" he chanted. "Good morning, young man," Krause said, patting him on the head. Later, in practice, Coach Keogan found his entire team flat on their backs, laughing as they rehearsed the Krause shot.

But not all was humor. During his senior year, his father was murdered by a man robbing the grocery store. Jason Kelly suggests that Krause let that horrible event arrange his priorities forever. Winning and losing were not on the same scale as integrity and sportsmanship.

After graduation, Krause coached at St. Mary's College in Winona, Minnesota, and then at Holy Cross College in Massachusetts. In 1941, Frank Leahy brought him back to Notre Dame as line coach. He was home now, with wife Elise and son Edward, and, but for his military service in World War II, he would be at Notre Dame for the rest of his life. In 1946, back as head coach of the basketball team and line coach of the football squad, Krause became a mainstay of Notre Dame's national presence. A lively and sought-after speaker, this gentle giant let humor, sincerity, and integrity become his trademarks. And he became the best ambassador Notre Dame athletics ever had. Named athletic director in 1949, he never stopped working to ensure the excellence and integrity of sports at Notre Dame. Nor did he ever stop his good humor. I remember my dad, Walter Langford, the tennis and fencing coach at Notre Dame, telling how he had asked Moose for at least a few scholarships that could draw stars to his teams. "How am I supposed to win if I can't bring in the best players?" With a smile and twinkle, Krause answered, "Great coaching, Walter, great coaching." Actually, the formula did work: Walter Langford's tennis and fencing teams won 249 times against only 66 losses!

Moose and Elise Krause were hosts to the famous and the unknown in their cozy house. Their three children would invite people, they would invite people, and people would invite people until the house was brimming with guests. Thus it was until that fateful day, January 21, 1967. Moose and Dr. Nicholas Johns were slowed by a snowstorm on their way back from a meeting in Gary, and Elise offered to represent him at a cocktail party hosted by some Notre Dame friends. She took a cab. Minutes into the trip, the cab was broadsided and pushed into a telephone pole by a car whose driver had run through a stop sign. Elise suffered broken bones and severe head injuries. She was in intensive care for several months, lost one-third of her weight, and suffered great pain. Worse than all of that, brain damage caused an enormous change in Elise's personality; she became verbally violent, aggressive, unpredictable. Eventually, after various medical procedures failed to improve her condition, and against medical advice, Moose took Elise home. He bore the brunt of her rage, the demands that required constant attention, and never did he lose his calmness or his hope. The toll on Moose was incalculable, and he turned increasingly to scotch for solace. Meanwhile, he continued to oversee the Athletic Department, now with the help of Colonel Jack Stephens as assistant athletic director. Colonel Stephens commanded a regiment in the South Pacific during World War II and most recently had been in charge of the ROTC at Notre Dame. Moose and the Colonel were a Mutt-and-Jeff pair, different in style and demeanor, but devoted to the deep friendship that evolved. The Colonel kept the ship afloat while Moose fell deeper into the throes of alcoholism. Friends like Ara, the Colonel, and others joined the Krause children, Phil, Ed, and Mary, in a concerted effort to stop his downward spiral. Two heart attacks made their warnings even more urgent.

Not only did Moose agree to join Alcoholics Anonymous, he went public with his illness and advised friends, colleagues, and even strangers who contacted him for help.

For the last eight years of her life, Moose spoon-fed his wife twice a day at a nursing home and, in the last months before her death in 1990, he would go back to sing her to sleep. He had called the aftermath of her accident a "veritable crucifixion." But his devotion and courage and calmness made it somehow redemptive. Father Hesburgh once said that if anyone deserved the title "Mr. Notre Dame," it was Moose Krause. And he added that if he himself had known anyone at Notre Dame who was a saint, it was Moose.

Krause stepped down as athletic director in 1980 after thirty-one years at the helm. He continued to be a presence at Notre Dame functions over the next dozen years, always greeted everywhere he went. When he died in his sleep on December 11, 1992, at the age of seventy-nine, people in all fifty states mourned his passing. A billboard went up in downtown South Bend with a picture of the Dome in one corner and one word, MOOSE, in the other corner. On December 15, throngs crowded Sacred Heart Basilica on campus to say good-bye to this gentle man. From stellar athletes to humble custodians, all of Notre Dame's tradition was there to bid farewell. Even then there was humor. Ara Parseghian, riding in the limousine with the other pallbearers, got off the quip of the day when he said to his fellow pallbearers, "Who recruited this group of pallbearers? It's the worst recruiting job I've ever seen. I forgot my cane, George Connor has trouble walking, Lou Holtz has a hernia, George Kelly can't breathe, Dick Rosenthal has two balloons for knees, and Colonel Stephens is so short his feet don't touch the ground. Moose in the casket is in better shape than any of us."

Jason Kelly describes the scene at the graveside:

At Cedar Grove Cemetery along Notre Dame Avenue at the edge of the campus, Krause was laid to rest beside his wife. With collars turned up against the cold, the mourners remained in silence for an awkward moment after the ceremony ended, unable to let go of this piece of their past. As if out of the mist, a song began. Father Hesburgh sang the opening words slowly and softly—so softly that only those standing near him could identify him as the source—and soon everyone joined in the impromptu farewell serenade [of the alma mater].

—Jim Langford

The Legend Behind the Microphone

Anyone who followed Notre Dame in the postwar forties and early fifties must remember the rich baritone voice and the classic style of the man who was one of the greatest sportscasters ever and who became synonymous with the Fighting Irish on the air. Until his untimely death at the age of fifty-five in February 1960, Joe Boland brought thrills to the nation on the radio network he built to cover Notre Dame football. His heart was Blue and Gold, but he covered games fairly, factually, and with controlled excitement. Having played under Rockne, Boland knew football. More important, he was a man of genuine character and integrity.

As accolades poured in following news of his death, it became clear that Joe embodied the spirit of Notre Dame. Jim Butz said, "I can't think of a single time that Joe ever said an unkind word about another human being," while Warren Brown explained, "Joe Boland was, I think, more things to more people in furthering the cause of Notre Dame, or certainly of Notre Dame's spirit and Notre Dame's men, than anyone I can readily remember."

Joe Pertritz, former sports information director at Notre Dame, put it well: "Joe Boland didn't make a million dollars, but he lived his own principles in both his public and private life. He altered the patterns of radio and television reporting for the better, and he made more than a million friends."

—Jim Langford

BENGAL BOUTS

Legend has it that, before he came to Notre Dame as a student, Knute Rockne earned money for college as a boxer who toured with a carnival. It was his job to take on local challengers and defeat them. Rockne was a tough fighter and he seldom had trouble winning. But one day, in Abilene, Kansas, he met his match. After battling to a draw, the two fighters sat down for a while. The challenger asked Rockne how long he planned to earn a living by fighting. "Oh, I'm just doing this to earn money so I can go to Notre Dame. My name's Knute Rockne." "Nice to meet you. I'm headed for West Point. I'm Dwight Eisenhower."

The Holy Cross Brothers, under Brother Alan McNeil, C.S.C., organized a Notre Dame boxing tournament in 1920 to support the Bengal Missions. Knute Rockne helped develop the program as a way of keeping his football players in shape, but it was not until 1931 that a tournament was set up and the proceeds from admissions set aside for the Holy Cross missions in Bengal (now Bangladesh). Within a few years, the annual tournament came under the wing of Dominic "Nappy" Napolitano, a man whose goodness marks him as a Notre Dame legend. Nappy coined the motto of the Bouts: "Strong bodies fight that weak ones can be nourished." He loved boxing, but he was even more dedicated to seeing that the proceeds went to the poor of Bengal. When Nappy suffered a stroke in 1971, several former boxers volunteered to shepherd the program. Tom Suddes and Terry Johnson donate their time every year, coming from Dublin, Ohio, and Chicago, respectively, to ensure the continued success of the program. Locals like Professor Charlie Rice, Pat Farrell, Jack Zimmerman, and, until last year, Jack Mooney all work to prepare the 125 or so Notre Dame students for the bouts. Attendance has soared to the point where the bouts have raised and contributed $400,000 to the missions in just the past six years.

Having boxed a little in high school, I thought about training for the Bouts as a freshman in 1956. The tennis coach, Charlie Samson, had called and invited me to be a walk-on with his team, and I thought that maybe boxing would be a good way to stay in shape over the winter. But the memory of how much it hurts to take a solid shot to the head steered me to fencing instead. Now, thirty-four years later, my son Josh announced that he would be a Bengal Bouter. He lived in Morrissey Manor, the same dorm my dad had lived in back in 1929. I kidded him that the two months of training were just another way to avoid the books; though bright, *his idea of work/life balance left the life side of the equation squarely on the ground.*

And so it was that I joined the large and loud crowd attending the opening rounds of the Bouts. Josh "The Janitor" emerged from the shadows and climbed into the ring. His fans were there with mops signifying that he would clean up on his opponent. It is almost surreal to see your son, flesh and blood, in a robe entering a ring. The fights last only three rounds, but you cringe with every blow landed on your offspring. I had to do more than cringe. Josh's style was straight up and straight ahead—a sort of Rocky Balboa approach. He would land a few jabs and march ahead through a barrage of punches, looking for a chance to explode with a right.

It was when he started to bleed that I began to understand the psyche of wrestling fans who want to join their hero in the ring. Something in me wanted desperately to climb through the ropes to protect my boy from a beating he seemed unwilling to back away from. He lost the match. As Jeremy kidded him, the headlines would read: "The Janitor gets swept; Opponent cleans up." But all was not lost, not by a long shot. Not only was Josh in the best physical shape of his life from the intense training, he had earned the respect of many. Referee Tom Suddes told me later that he admired Josh's courage; he had never seen anyone plow ahead with such dogged-ness, as if trying to hit a homer in the bottom of the ninth. As a teacher, my mind calculated differently: courage, A+; strategy, D-. But here is how things work in the Notre Dame network: That same

Tom Suddes hired Josh after graduation, taught him the ropes in the business world, and helped him move into a career that has propelled him to a vice presidency at the age of thirty-one!

Many of the "strong bodies" who fight so that weaker bodies may be nourished explain that the experience of Bengal Bouts encouraged them to continue fighting for those in need as they graduated and developed successful careers. Josh, for one, has been involved in charitable giving since he graduated. Thankfully, he has hung up his boxing gloves.

—JIM LANGFORD

DOMINICK J. NAPOLITANO (1908–1986)

Nappy was smiling at me. I was in the boxing room of the old fieldhouse, anxiously looking for my name in the schedule of elimination matches. So many students had signed up for Bengal Bouts my freshman year that some had to be weeded out before the tournament started.

"You don't see your name up there, do you?" Nappy said in that dry flute of a voice. "That means you're pretty good."

I hadn't been much of a success at high school sports, and my interest in boxing had been met with skepticism among family and friends. Nappy's compliment made me feel pretty good.

In the year I graduated, columnist Jack Griffin of the *Chicago Sun-Times* said of Nappy, "In all the college campuses I have ever worked, I have never met a man who had such a grip on the young people he worked with." It was true, and still is. . . .

For 50 years Nappy showed young men like me the way around the ropes. He had come to Notre Dame as a student in 1928, and the first person he met was Knute Rockne, who gave him directions because he looked lost. He came here to box, but in that year the University scrapped the varsity program. In 1931 Rev. Vincent Mooney, C.S.C., came up with the idea of a student boxing tournament to raise money for the Holy Cross Missions in what is now Bangladesh. He asked Nappy to help out with the coaching, and the Bengal Bouts were born. . . .

Nappy had no children of his own, but he loved his boys. "He said time and again that we were his family," says Mike DeCicco, fencing coach since 1961 and one of Nappy's closest friends. "When he passed away, alumni from all over the country called to express their condolences. One guy wasn't even a boxer. He had Nappy as a phys ed teacher one semester, and he couldn't stop telling me how much he liked him. . . ."

Two things surprised me most about the Bengal Bouts: the rigor of the workouts and Nappy's soft-spoken manner. The two qualities are not at odds; they are, in fact, common among men with extensive backgrounds in boxing. Nappy had been a successful amateur boxer around his hometown of Pleasantville, New York. "I was more of a fancy Dan than a hitter," he once told Bill Gleason of the *Chicago Sun-Times*. But when you remember his compact shoulders, thick neck, and a head that came up like the cap of a welding tank, you wonder.

Tom Suddes, a Bengal Bouts coach and referee [since 1970], might question Nappy's fancy Dan status, too. "One day, Nappy picked me for a demonstration, because we were about the same size. 'How are your nerves today?' he asked. He told me to throw a jab and then said, 'Now watch this opening' and landed a good solid punch right in my breadbasket. The other guys got such a kick out of it that he used me all the time."

—JAMES LOVERDE '68, WINNER OF THE RUPERT MILLS AWARD FOR
BEST FRESHMAN BOXER IN THE 1965 BOUTS[12]

BOOKSTORE BASKETBALL

Outside of football games and graduation ceremonies, few events on campus bring people together at Notre Dame like the annual Bookstore Basketball Tournament (or just "Bookstore"). The event, which takes its name from the basketball courts found behind the old bookstore on South Quad, allows all students, faculty, and staff on campus to enjoy some friendly competition each spring.

Started in 1972 by Fritz Hoefer and Vince Meconi, Bookstore grew from a small part of the An Tostal Spring Festival into the 700-plus-team extravaganza it is today. It can safely be called the largest five-on-five, single-elimination basketball tournament in the world. I was privileged to be a commissioner for Bookstore in years nineteen through twenty-one. Since I was a terrible player, volunteering to help organize the event was a great way to be involved in this unique tradition. I loved being on the courts every day, signing people in, doing the coin toss, and watching some very good basketball.

Upon reflection, Bookstore taught me two things about Notre Dame: First, this school attracts a lot of very good athletes. And I don't just mean those on the many Division I teams the school fields. Whether the students or faculty I watched were chemical engineers or computer scientists, accountants or anthropologists, poets or priests, virtually all of them excelled at one sport or another, and it showed on the courts.

Second: The student body as a whole has a tremendous amount of creativity . . . particularly when it came to naming their teams. Below are some of my favorites:

Current-Event Related:
Bobby Knight and the Chair Throwers (1985)
Tylenol, Challenger, and three other deadly capsules (1986)
Tsudents for Tsongas (1992)

On-Campus Humor:
I'm in love with the Circus Lunch Clown (1990)
Escape from Badin-traz (1992)

Just Plain Silly:

Elvis is dead, and we don't feel so good ourselves (1991)

One guy, another guy, and three other guys (1989)

Moe, Larry, Digger, and two other Stooges (1990)[13]

Overall, Bookstore gave everyone on campus a chance for fifteen minutes of Fame. Whether your team was destined for a first-round pummeling or making it all the way to the Final Four, you could always count on your friends and some curious onlookers to be there to witness your moment in the spotlight.

—ANDREW CAVALLARI '92, CO-COMMISSIONER FOR
BOOKSTORE BASKETBALL 1990–92

I AM CONTINUALLY amazed with the power of this place. What strikes me daily is how Notre Dame people take care of their own. We clearly do that more genuinely than any other institution in this country, and it is really refreshing to see. It is certainly something that our older players can relate to after being Notre Dame men for a while. It is the ultimate team mentality!

—MIKE BREY, HEAD BASKETBALL COACH

NOTRE DAME IS: . . .

The 1966 slugfest between the Fighting Irish and Michigan State— two undefeated Leviathans, a match billed as the "Game of the Century." All-Americans were all over the field that day, on both sides. Irish star Nick Eddy was out with an injured shoulder. Terry Hanratty separated his shoulder in the first quarter. On came Coley O'Brien, diagnosed earlier in the season as a diabetic. Before halftime, O'Brien hit Bob Gladieux for a score and cut the MSU lead to 10–7. The teams battled back and forth, MSU's defense led by Bubba

Smith and George Webster, Notre Dame's by Alan Page, Mike McGill, Jim Lynch. The fourth quarter opened with Joe Azzaro's 28-yard field goal to tie the game at 10. By now, O'Brien is exhausted; Kevin Hardy's punts and Tom Schoen's two interceptions kept the Spartans at bay. With five minutes left, Azzaro missed a 42-yard field-goal attempt. MSU couldn't move the ball and had to punt. With one minute and twenty-four seconds to go, O'Brien gained a yard on fourth and one at his own 39. On the next play, Bubba Smith nailed O'Brien for a loss of seven, and Notre Dame let the clock run out.

Ara's logic has been questioned and defended, but no one can doubt his understanding of the courage of his team that day. Eddy, Hanratty, Goeddeke, Gladieux, and Bleier were injured, Lynch played with a bad charley horse and Gmitter was going on only one good knee. Ara told his team: "I'm proud of you. God knows I've never been prouder of any group of young men in my life . . ."

Maybe it was appropriate that the two best teams in the nation each went out undefeated and tied for the National Championship.

. . . ONE OF THE most celebrated comebacks in history . . . Notre Dame down by 13–0 at the start of the fourth quarter against the highly touted Ohio State Buckeyes, Notre Dame rallies for three touchdowns, two in the final two minutes, to claim an 18–13 victory. It was a win of mythic proportions, the kind of minor miracle that came to be expected of Notre Dame.

. . . MINOR MIRACLES. Trailing 27–26 against bitter rival Michigan in the second game of the 1980 season, Notre Dame had the ball on its own 20-yard line with 41 seconds remaining in the game. Coach Devine called on freshman Blair Kiel to orchestrate a miracle. After two pass completions, there were only four seconds left. On came left-footed, soccer-style kicker Harry Oliver to attempt a 51-yard field goal against the wind that had been blowing hard all day. Jeff Jeffers described what happened:

> The snap from Siewe is perfect, as is Koegel's hold. Oliver swings his leg, and the ball is airborne. It appears to pause, then turn over and gain speed. The descent is agonizingly slow, then another jolt of speed propels the ball earthward. Fans at the base of the southern goalpost peer upward as the ball falls through the uprights for the biggest field goal in Notre Dame history . . . Fighting to overcome tears in a tearful locker room, Devine recalled the kick: "I knew right away that it was true and that he kicked it good . . . I've never seen Oliver kick one that far, but it went through today, and that's all I care about."[14]

It is said that the wind quieted for the kick. Perhaps tackle Pat Kramer summed it up best: "This could only happen here."

. . . LOU HOLTZ SAYING, "The real pressure is when you have to win to keep your job. At Notre Dame you have to win often. It's not in the contract. It's in the tradition."

. . . A TRADITION OF excellence in intercollegiate fencing, including six National Championships, the most recent in 2003–4, and a lifetime record of 798–86–2. That is a winning percentage of .895.

. . . BASEBALL FROM THE days of Adrian "Cap" Anson, the decades of Coach Jake Cline, the return to glory under Pat Murphy and to the College World Series under Coach Paul Mainieri. Who will forget the scrappiness of Mainieri's Irish as they upset Mississippi State for the berth in Omaha?

IT IS MEN'S lacrosse coach Kevin Corrigan, 132–74 including a trip to the Final Four in 2001 at Notre Dame, pointing out that every lacrosse player since the sport achieved varsity status in 1981 has graduated.

THE ALWAYS-FORMIDABLE women's soccer team, National Champions in 1994 and again in 2004!

NOTRE DAME IS Terry Brennan's 93-yard kickoff return against Army in 1947, Tom Clement's clutch pass to Robin Weber in the 24–23 win over Alabama in the Sugar Bowl, a win that made ND the 1973 National Champions. Notre Dame is the Joe Montana miracle game in the 1978 Cotton Bowl; it is the thrill of watching Rocket Ismail and Tim Brown, Browner and Fry—the list is almost endless.

THE WOMEN'S NCAA basketball championship team, coached by Muffet McGraw and led by Ruth Riley, Niele Ivey, Alicia Ratay, Erika Haney, and Kelley Siemon. Notre Dame is also the incredible reception given the Champion Lady Irish in spite of a 20-degree temperature and the fact that it was nearing 3 A.M. As Mark Bradford describes the scene: "Then in the finest of Irish tradition, the band played the Notre Dame alma mater and 3,000 chilly fans and one brand-new championship team raised their No.1 fingers in unison as the song rose as one voice to its finale."[15]

TWO NCAA CHAMPION tennis teams, winning traditions in baseball, hockey, swimming, volleyball, diving, track and field, a first-rate
system of interhall sports competition, Bookstore Basketball, it is all
here, all geared toward healthy competition and development of the
whole person.

NOTRE DAME IS a storied tradition of basketball. Old-timers will
remember the thunderous atmosphere of the Fieldhouse, especially
when a top-ranked team from Kentucky, DePaul, Marquette, St.
Louis, or Indiana came to play. Four thousand fans, most of them
students, crammed into bleachers so close to the court that the noise
was deafening. Legendary Kentucky Coach Adolf Rupp declared that
it was "impossible" to win at Notre Dame, and his 0–6 record there
confirms that the Irish were always "psyched up" to play him, and his
team was always "psyched out" by the Notre Dame crowd. He could
bring his stars, Alex Groza, Ralph Beard, Bill Spivey, and so on, but
with the band placed strategically behind his bench, the screaming
students everywhere and rows of black-robed clerics seated directly
across from him, Rupp couldn't communicate with his players. With
the loss in 1950, he vowed never to play in "the pit" again.

WITH THE OPENING of the Joyce Athletic and Convocation Cen-
ter came a succession of great players and sometimes great teams.
Some names, when recited, bring graphic still shots from the mem-
ory. If you saw them, you can see them still: Krause, Klier, Bertrand,
Leslie, Barnhorst, O'Shea, Stephens, Hawkins, Arnzen, Whitmore,
Carr, Shumate, Dantley, Branning, Hanzlik, Tripuka, Brokaw, Clay,
Woolridge, Paxon, Paterno, Rivers, Ellis, Garrity, Murphy, Humphrey,
Thomas . . . Coaches like Keogan, Krause, Jordan, Dee, Phelps,
MacLeod, Doherty, Brey.

Remember Digger's gamesmanship, how he could rally the crowd, his mastery at pulling the upset of number ones . . . UCLA, Virginia, San Francisco, Kentucky, North Carolina, DePaul. Before the famous UCLA streak-ending game in 1974, Phelps had the players practice not only their shots but also cutting down the nets.

Today, Coach Mike Brey is waking up the echoes, loud and clear.

. . . NOTRE DAME IS people such as George Kelly, former linebacker coach and longtime associate athletic director. He was one of the most insightful and delightful Domers of all time. When he died on March 3, 2003, the flags at the Joyce Center flew at half-staff in memory of his achievements, which included developing stellar linebackers such as All-Americans Bob Crable, Bob Golic, and Steve Heimkreiter, and in overseeing development of a schedule that always ranked as one of the toughest in the nation. George Kelly went out of his way to be there for anyone who needed him. Colleague Brian Boulac said it best: "George was like the needle that pulled the thread that makes Notre Dame."

. . . THORLAKSON, TANCREDI, AND Buczkowski, not a law firm, but a trio of All-Americans who led Coach Randy Waldrum's Fighting Irish Women's soccer team to the 2004 National Championship.

NOTRE DAME DOES not lay claim to perfection; it does not promote a superiority complex. But neither does it offer any apology for seeking excellence, win or lose, on its playing fields.

—JIM LANGFORD

SPIRIT

*I don't know how they get it, but they get it like three minutes after
they get here—it's like a contagion for good in the air—and they
become bonded to the place immediately.*

—Rev. Theodore M. Hesburgh, C.S.C.,
on how students catch the spirit of Notre Dame[1]

SPIRIT IS HARD to define. It is a fire in the belly, a sense of purpose, a reason for getting up in the morning and doing your best all day, every day. It is at once invisible and obvious, deeply rooted and transcendent. However one defines spirit, all agree that Notre Dame has plenty of it. Rarely do people speak of the school without referencing its incredible spirit.

Where does it come from? Tradition certainly. One need only attend the band concert on the steps of Bond Hall before a home football game and follow the march through campus to get a sense that this still relatively small school is proud to take on all comers.

And it comes from an atmosphere that bespeaks a can-do attitude; the names on the buildings honor scientists and leaders and donors whose quest for excellence was nurtured here.

It both generates and reflects a bond, a commonality that really does result in care for one another. That carries over from the campus to the local community to alumni everywhere.

The Notre Dame spirit is an ongoing quest for excellence. Father Hesburgh says it well:

"People say to me, 'What makes this place special?' . . . If you really want to know, stand in the dark of night and look up at the golden figure on the Dome."[2]

THE SPIRIT OF NOTRE DAME IS REAL

How does one describe the spirit of Notre Dame? Is it a mind-set? Is it a concept? Or is it something else, maybe even a myth? Perhaps it is all of these and more.

Stand on the Main Quad and look up at Our Lady's statue atop the Main Building or the steeple rising high above the Basilica of the Sacred Heart. Or look toward the Founders' Monument near the Log Chapel. Let your mind wander back through more than 160 years of the University's history. When Father Sorin arrived in northern Indiana on that bleak wintry day in November 1842, and as he and the brothers with him began their work of building the University's foundation, the spirit was born and it is real.

His vision was to create a university where young people would be formed in faith and understanding. But he knew he could never accomplish this or anything else alone. The spirit that led him here—pioneering, entrepreneurial, thoroughly American despite his French upbringing—became the cornerstone of the University, and it was dedicated to a higher purpose than educational advancement. The Lady who sits on top of the Dome, as Sorin himself proclaimed, assures the world that the Notre Dame spirit is alive.

So it is not a myth. It's as real as the peaceful feeling one has at the Grotto, and as real as the laughter of friends. On campus or off, it's the greeting of a fellow Domer and the hug and the lift you receive in time of need. It feeds from the wellspring of Faith and it is fed by generations telling, living, and making the story of Notre Dame: of Father Sorin against heavy odds, of Rockne against a mighty Army team, of Peace Corps members in Chile and volunteers in service elsewhere, of men and women doing their duty for God, Country, and Notre Dame, of parents doing right by their children.

Yes, it's real, and this is Notre Dame.

—CHARLES F. LENNON, JR., '61, '62, MA, EXECUTIVE DIRECTOR OF
THE NOTRE DAME ALUMNI ASSOCIATION AND ASSOCIATE VICE
PRESIDENT FOR UNIVERSITY RELATIONS[3]

THE GREAT PARADOX of Notre Dame is that it requires no explanation, yet constantly needs to be explained. . . . The university is indeed a place of optimism and possibility, for its religious foundation encourages a concentration on the universal values of goodness, truth, and freedom. Norman Mailer says he likes Notre Dame because "you can say the word 'soul' there and no one snickers." Of course not, since "soul" is what Notre Dame is essentially about. Religion may be muted elsewhere in our increasingly secularized society, but at Notre Dame it's ringing loud and clear—chapels in every dormitory, a Basilica, a Lourdes-like Grotto, and the Mother of God bestowing her blessings from the Dome. There is also a running—and revealing—campus joke that goes something like this: The President of the United States visited the Pope and noticed a gold telephone with a direct line to God. The President phoned the Almighty for some advice, and the White House was billed $10,000 for the call. The next month, the President was visiting Notre Dame when he noticed that there was also a gold telephone on Father Malloy's desk. He again phoned the Almighty, but this time the charge was only twenty-five cents. The President contacted Father Malloy and asked how it could possibly be so much cheaper to telephone God from Notre Dame. "From Notre Dame," explained Father Malloy, "it's a *local* call."

Yes, everybody knows of Notre Dame and its reputation. The university occupies a singular place in American education and culture, and the paraphernalia, the football games, the jokes, and the stories are legion. But nobody seems to fully comprehend the university until they've actually shared in its rituals, witnessed its pervasive sense of spirit, and become part of the mystique themselves. Notre Dame has its own ethos, a unique combination of religious values, athletic tradition, academic achievement, and inspired loyalty and comradeship among undergraduates and alumni. Those elements are the essence of the mystique, and if any of them were to disappear, the university would not be the same. Like any vital culture, Notre Dame has its own defining legends and folklore, and its multitude of multilayered traditions are the means by which it keeps its identity through the changing times and generations. The only thing that explains Notre Dame—and its mystique—is Notre Dame.

—DAMAINE VONADA[4]

NOTRE DAME IS a university, a community, a place, an idea, a landscape, and a mood, among other things, and, as any of these things, it reflects the glories, squalors, foibles, splendors, and contradictions of the Church to which it belongs. That is what has fascinated me about it for the last quarter-century of my life. It is an intensely human phenomenon, like the Sacred Heart of Jesus which breaks, bleeds, and replenishes the campus, honored by a badly crafted statue at the center of the campus.

When I was a child, Notre Dame was a stop on the journey from Springfield, Illinois, to Sharon, Pennsylvania, where my father was born and my grandparents still lived. It was a green place with shining lakes, abundant ducks, and fascinatingly nonchalant squirrels, a place where there were old brick buildings with odd designs and figures carved into them and big steamy, noisy rooms in which hot chocolate and waffles were served and where there was a cavernous old church filled with the bones of holy people long dead and where there was a cave filled with candles where Mary seemed to live and, whether she lived there or not, where we all prayed to her and knew she heard us.

It was a place of which my father used to speak with particular fondness, a place where men he'd known when he was young had conversed sincerely and wisely about things that mattered deeply to him and, consequently, to me. It was a place I came back to in the most turbulent years of my own life and generation, astonished and grateful to find some of those same men, now joined by younger men and women, too. Frank O'Malley spoke of those whose "blood was in the bricks," and it has been my privilege to keep company with some of them.

The workplace environment here is bewildering, the Eucharist made available before business hours, at lunch, or on the way home. Colleagues pray for each other, yet not in some histrionic, cloying, and ostentatious way.

Those of us who quarrel and fume and grumble and whine about Notre Dame do so because Notre Dame can never be, for us, an "it," but must always be a "we." We are all pilgrims, to be sure, and we have no abiding city here. Nevertheless, this odd community on a wooded lakeside in northern Indiana is more than a place we pass through. It passes through us as well.

—MICHAEL GARVEY, ASSISTANT DIRECTOR, NEWS AND INFORMATION,
UNIVERSITY OF NOTRE DAME

DYING IS NO big deal. The least of us will manage that. Living is the trick.

—RED SMITH '27

MANY POINT TO Notre Dame's humble beginnings, its religious character and mission, and its success in football to explain the spirit of the place. I wouldn't disagree. But I think a key factor, often cited more as a weakness than a strength, is location. Father Sorin founded the university in near wilderness in November when the weather was turning cold. All these years later, anyone who has attended Notre Dame knows how weather and location force the community to rely on its own human relationships perhaps more than other colleges and universities closer to large urban areas, filled with distractions. I think it helps explain the intense relationships, friend to friend, and alum to campus. With its spiritual mission and storied history, Notre Dame would still not be what it is without that relative isolation (and the space on which a beautiful campus was built). So, asked to describe in one word what is the underlying basis for Notre Dame's spirit, one could do worse than respond, "February."

—Matthew Storin, Associate Vice President for News and Information and Concurrent Professor of American Studies

If the edifice stands, we will never regret the price and sweat that it has cost us.

—Rev. Edward Sorin

Rockne taught us the basics—things like honesty, courage, the will to win. With Rock, the starting point was 100 percent. He was always looking for more than that, and that's what we always tried to give him.

—Adam Walsh, All-American center, 1925

The biggest obstacle for Rockne playing football in the first place was his parents' disdain for the game. He was one of the smaller, though faster players. But he played in a time when size and strength always trumped speed.

One day when Rockne got pummeled in a sandlot game, his parents refused to allow him to ever play again. . . .

But baseball agreed with them. Young Rockne then devoted all his time and passion to that sport until he got into an argument one day. Rockne's crooked nose, which is readily apparent even in photos taken during his coaching days, was a result of that argument that day. He got hit in the face with a bat.

Instead of despair, Rockne reportedly ran home excited. "You think football is a rough game," he told his parents. "Look what I got from baseball."

His parents relented and let Rockne play football. . . .

—Eric Hansen[5]

The Legend of Rudy

Rudy spent the first twenty-seven years of his life preparing for twenty-seven seconds of college football glory. He has spent the rest of his life making sure that everyone hears his story.

Daniel "Rudy" Ruettiger had a familiar dream. Like many young men of his generation, Rudy imagined himself in a gold helmet running through the tunnel at Notre Dame Stadium as a member of the Fighting Irish. What separated Rudy from so many others was his fanatical devotion to this impossible dream. Rudy's work ethic far outstripped his talent. His high school grades were far from outstanding. As one of fourteen children, Rudy's family could not afford to send him to college.

Rudy's dreams lay dormant for several years. Rudy spent two years as a turbine operator for Commonwealth Edison. During the Vietnam War, his job was interrupted by two years in the Navy. When he returned to his factory job, Rudy shared his dreams with his best friend and coworker.

"I wanted something better," he said, "but I didn't know how to get it."

Tragedy brought Rudy the answer when his friend was killed in an accident at the power plant.

"He had told me how he regretted not going after his dreams. Then he got [sic] killed on me. That's when I realized I was going after Notre Dame and after my dream."

At the age of twenty-three, Rudy moved to South Bend and enrolled at Holy Cross College under the G.I. Bill. While attending

Holy Cross, Rudy would walk to Notre Dame to watch the 1973 championship team practice. When they left the field, he put himself through the same drills.

He also worked hard in the classroom. After failing his first four tests, he turned things around to finish with a solid 3.4 grade point average. He applied to Notre Dame after his first semester, but unfortunately his application was rejected. A semester later, Rudy was rejected again. In fact, it was not until he completed Holy Cross's two-year program with honors that he was accepted to Notre Dame.

After a considerable effort, Ruettiger managed to convince Notre Dame head coach Ara Parseghian to give him a spot on the Notre Dame team. As a member of the scout team, Ruettiger's job was to prepare the first team by being, essentially, a living tackling dummy. His chief value was that it didn't matter if he was injured. On his very first play, the 5'6", 185-pound Ruettiger squared off against 6'4", 255-pound Steve Neece, who knocked him right on his sitter. They told him to get up, and he did.

Rudy got up again and again as his minuscule frame was wantonly tossed about each day at practice. Indefatigable, Rudy refused to quit. Former teammate Willie Fry recalls, "Our attitude at first was 'Go away.' But he wouldn't go away. Basically, you had to like Rudy because you couldn't get rid of him."

Eventually, Ruettiger's bruised body had earned him the respect of teammates and the coaching staff. According to Parseghian, Rudy "had earned the right to be here."

But Rudy had not yet earned the right to wear the blue and gold. At the time, NCAA rules permitted only sixty players to dress for home games. Notre Dame had more than enough scholarship players to meet this limit. After his first season, Dan Devine took over for Ara Parseghian as head coach. Rudy had finally gained Parseghian's respect, and now he had to start all over again with Devine. He began his final year—his last chance at glory—with a clean slate.

Week after week, he checked the dress list but never found

"Ruettiger." This was disheartening for both Rudy and his teammates.

"All our players idolize this kid because he is a man. Rudy works hard every day and never misses a practice," said the lineback coach, George Kelly.

"Some seniors like Randy Payne, Bob Zanot, and Pat Sarb came to us and said they wanted Rudy to dress before them," added defensive line coach Joe Yonto.

"If there was a spot open, they wanted Rudy to have it."

Before the final game, against Georgia Tech, cheers rose from the ranks of the players as Devine announced that Rudy would dress for the final game. Rudy's dream came true on November 8, 1975, when he ran through the tunnel into a stadium of 59,075 screaming fans.

Although he had achieved his dream of running through the tunnel, Ruettiger's chances of taking the field remained bleak. With under a minute to play, Notre Dame's offense still held the ball.

"We almost had to use him as a split receiver," said Kelly.

"We were afraid time was going to run out before we got back on defense."

But then the offense scored, and Ruettiger took the field to defend the kickoff return. The ball sailed through the end zone for a touchback and Rudy looked to the sidelines for a replacement, but none came. Ruettiger stayed in the game for the final two plays as the left defensive end.

On the first play, Rudy burst through the blockers and nearly got to Georgia Tech's quarterback, ironically named Rudy Allen. On the next play, Ruettiger ended his Notre Dame football career with an exclamation mark, sacking Allen for the final play of the game. After the tackle, Rudy rose up from the ground and onto the shoulders of teammates Ron Cullins and Tom Parise, who carried him off the field and into the locker room. Rudy's dream continued. Sweat and tears streamed down his face as teammates chanted, "Rudy, Rudy."

"I've waited twenty-seven years for this," Rudy said.

"When you achieve one dream," Rudy said, "dream another."

—JOHN WALS, WITH ASSISTANCE FROM PUBLICATIONS WRITTEN BY
JOE TYBOR, KAREN SCHNEIDER, BONNIE BELL, JOHN FINERAN,
BILL MOOR, AND MILAN SIMONICH

ALTHOUGH A LOT of academics prefer not to admit it, it was Notre Dame's football team that first earned the University national fame. The team's first game against Army in 1913 was significant for two reasons—it marked the first outstanding use of the forward pass and the unveiling of Notre Dame on the national scene.

Turned down for admission to the Midwest's "Big Nine" conference, Notre Dame was forced to travel to the East and Far West for football games. In terms of both athletics and academics, the University remained relatively obscure outside of Catholic circles.

The forward pass had been used elsewhere, but the Eastern teams either hadn't noticed or chose to ignore it. Knute Rockne, a Notre Dame senior and team captain in 1913, had perfected the play on the beach at Cedar Point on Lake Erie during summer vacation. In the first three games before meeting Army, Notre Dame piled up a cumulative score of 69–7. All that was credited to the pass, a play that would revolutionize the sport and usher in the "Gold Age" of collegiate football in the 1920s.

But Notre Dame's 35–13 win over Army was nonetheless an upset. ND completed 14 of 17 passes as left end Rockne and quarterback Gus Dorais kept up a steady stream of aerials. Rockne scored two of the team's four touchdowns. The victory earned Notre Dame tremendous publicity in Eastern newspapers.

"Although we were not the first to use the forward pass, it can be truthfully said that we were one of the first to learn how it should be used," Rockne wrote later in his autobiography. "The press and the football public hailed this new game, and Notre Dame received credit as the originators of a style of play that we had simply systemized."

The 1913 season was significant for other reasons as well. For one, it was the first year that Notre Dame did not lose money on its athletic program; indeed, the team enjoyed such popularity that it suddenly was being sought after as an opponent. Football also helped provide the financial means for the University to expand its physical plant and academic programs. From $235 in 1919, the annual football season profits climbed to $529,420 in 1929.

The 1913 season also was important for Rockne personally; he was asked to stay on after graduating magna cum laude in pharmacy. He taught chemistry and served as assistant football coach under Jess Harper until 1918, when he moved up to head coach and athletic director.

For many Americans, Knute Rockne personified Notre Dame. His immigrant background, driving personality, and immense coaching talent made him a national celebrity—and arguably Notre Dame's most durable legend.[6]

Scholastic
SEPTEMBER 18, 1942
Dear BOB:
Instead of sending you the Log this week I'll try and answer your question, and if a few other people see this letter, I'm sure you won't mind.

I've told you about the navy here, but your question "What is the spirit of Notre Dame?" has me a bit stumped. But here is a try. . . .

Notre Dame is truly a way of life. To describe it is to challenge the power of descriptive words, at least mine. You see, Notre Dame is the mist rising from the lagoons at dawn as the spirit awakens and pushes the mists skyward. It's the whispering "amens" from the trees as the priests, young and old, say their morning prayers and give thanks for the things we're fighting to retain.

Or maybe Notre Dame is the nuns, who have dedicated themselves and their lives to a cause within our cause. Christianity is a democracy. It might be the shadows, as they drift lazily into the corners in rooms of men whose names are now legend. They're all gone now, but the shadows and fading rays of light are the sparks of time that keep their spirits aglow in the rooms they left long ago.

Or perhaps the spirit of Notre Dame is the grin on the face of the junior who delights in telling the navy why he joined the marines.

It might be the thrill of the Angelus at eventide, or the face of the statue in the grotto. Perhaps it's the kind, old Brother in Washington Hall. Whose eyes have a way of shaking hands when he says good morning. Maybe the spirit of Notre Dame is the ancient Irish gardener, who always has his wife awaken him when it rains at night so he can hear God's gift to his "children," the lawns and shrubs.

Some folks would say the spirit of Notre Dame embodies the unwritten words to the hymns the priest plays on the organ in the church on quiet summer afternoons, when the breeze is gone. You have a feeling it, too, stopped to listen. Maybe it's the majestic dignity of the painted windows as they wait patiently for the setting sun to get behind them, each in turn, so that they may daily tell their part in the story of the Creator of all things.

Those things belong to you and to me, Bob. You'll receive those gifts when you come here and carry them always under that spot on your tunic, reserved for medals. And you'll leave this school and this earth, knowing and believing that Notre is truly a way of life.

SINCERELY,
BUD

THE WAR WAS only a few weeks old when the names of Notre Dame's first casualties began coming in. Their names were placed on a plaque in the vestibule of the church and carried in the hearts of the priests who had taught and loved them. Father O'Donnell had a Mass said for them every day during the war. Three hundred and thirty-three alumni and students, according to the latest count, paid with their lives. This does not include the number of casualties sustained by members of the midshipman school or the navy trainees.

During the war, the University had conferred on Admiral Chester Nimitz an honorary degree. Not until after victory was the Admiral able to come to the campus to receive his honor. On May 15, 1946, there was a gala convocation in the Navy Drill Hall. Father O'Donnell addressed the body, presented the degree, and Admiral Nimitz replied.

"Father O'Donnell," he said in conclusion, "you sent forth to me, as to other naval commands on every ocean and continent, men who had become imbued with more than the mechanical knowledge of warfare. Somehow, in the crowded hours of their preparation for the grim business of war, they had absorbed not only Notre Dame's traditional fighting spirit, but the spiritual strength, too, that this University imparts to all, regardless of creed, who come under its influence."

—ARTHUR J. HOPE[7]

In the early twenties, the Ku Klux Klan waged a war against Catholics. When they picked a fight with Notre Dame as one of its main targets, they picked the wrong opponent. The students not only taught the Klan a lesson but were instrumental in helping bring about the group's demise.

KLAN PARADES, IN full regalia, were very much in vogue. A parade was planned for South Bend on May 17, 1924. The students of Notre Dame were itching for a chance to show their resentment to the Klan. The administration was deeply worried about the consequences of the student temper. On the preceding day, May 16th, which was a Friday, Father Hugh O'Donnell, who was Prefect of Discipline, had a conference with Larry Lane, the chief of police of South Bend. Lane assured Father O'Donnell that the parade would not come off, that permission had been refused. The Klan, of course, was resolved to parade anyhow, and Klansmen from the neighboring towns poured into the city on the morning of the 17th.

Father Walsh issued a bulletin that morning. In part, it read as follows:

> . . . Notre Dame is interested in the proposed meeting of the Klan, but not to the extent of wishing to interfere with whatever plans may have been made for a demonstration. Similar attempts of the Klan to flaunt its strength have resulted in riotous situations, sometimes in the loss of life.
>
> . . . There is only one duty that presents itself to Notre Dame men, under the circumstances, and that is to ignore whatever demonstration may take place today. This suggestion should be taken in all seriousness. . . . Let South Bend authorities take care of the situation. The place for Notre Dame men, this afternoon and tonight, is on the Notre Dame campus. . . .

Undoubtedly, some of the day students, coming to the University on the morning of the 17th, saw some disturbing scenes in South Bend. When they arrived on the campus, they told the resident students of great mobs of Klansmen pouring in by train, interurban, and auto, of hooded figures that stood on the corners directing traffic, or "fiery crosses" brandished from the Klan headquarters at Michigan and Wayne Streets. Bulletin or no bulletin, the students rushed to town. It was a very unwise thing to do, but who would ever accuse hot-blooded students of prudence and wisdom?

Every street-car, every bus, every interurban vomited forth its strangers, each carrying under his arm a suspicious bundle. The students of Notre Dame were the first to greet them. With a smile, they would touch the arm of a descending resident of Goshen or New Carlisle and ask, "Are you from the Klan? Have you come for the parade? This way, please!" Up an alley, down a side street, through a dark entrance, and a Klansman would emerge without his sheet, and sometimes with a black eye. For the students it was glorious adventure. They had the time of their lives. Forming a flying wedge, they would advance on a white-clad figure that was directing traffic, and then he was there no longer. . . .

It was pointed out to the chief of police that had he firmly met the situation on Saturday, he might have prevented this fresh outbreak on Monday. Instead of making any serious effort to prevent Saturday's disorders, the police had been conspicuous by their absence. Now, however, with time to reflect, they had made up their minds to show the people "who was running this town." For that purpose, the sheriff, a well-known Klan partisan, had deputized a number of Klansmen, under the old "Horse-Thief" law.

Thus it happened that when the students began their demonstrations they met a force they had not expected. Saturday, it had been so easy, and so thrilling! Now, the deputies laid about them with clubs and bottles and there was many a cracked skull, bleeding face, and bruised shin. In the midst of this furor, Father O'Donnell arrived and, with the chief of police, forced the students to listen to him. He enjoined them to cross the street and gather on the lawn of the Court House. Father Walsh was waiting for them, and he mounted the cannon and spoke to the students:

Whatever challenge may have been offered tonight to your patriotism, whatever insult may have been offered to your

religion, you can show your loyalty to Notre Dame and to
South Bend by ignoring all threats. The constituted authorities have only the desire to preserve order and peace and
protect everyone. That is their duty. Others can well leave
to their hands the maintenance of peace and the punishment of anything that is wrong. If tonight there have been
violations of the law, it is not the duty of you and your companions to search out the offenders.

I know that in the midst of excitement, you are swayed
by emotions that impel you to answer challenge with force.
As I said in the statement issued last Saturday, a single
injury to a Notre Dame student would be too great a price to
pay for any deed or any program that concerned itself with
antagonisms. I should dislike very much to be obliged to
make explanations to the parents of any student who might
be injured—even killed—in a disturbance that could arise
out of any demonstration such as has been started tonight.

There is no loyalty that is greater than the patriotism of
a Notre Dame student. There is no conception of duty
higher than that which a Notre Dame man holds for his
religion or his university. I know that if tonight any of the
property of the university or any of its privileges were
threatened, and I should call upon you, you would rise to a
man to protect it. It is with the same loyalty to Notre Dame
that I appeal to you to show your respect for South Bend
and the authority of the city by dispersing.

Father Walsh, pointing a finger at the building in which the Klan
had holed themselves up, said: "I know that if I told you boys to go
back there and show the Klansmen of what stuff you are made, you
would tear that building apart, leaving no stone upon a stone!" There
was almost an instinctive surge toward the building, a movement
which Father Walsh stopped in his next sentence. "But I know, too,

that you have confidence enough in me, so that if I tell you to go back to the college, you will obey me, and you will leave to my judgment what is best to be done. And so, I tell you: Go back to the college!" With a roar, the students formed ranks and in columns of four, marched back to Notre Dame.

. . . The crusade of hate finally exhausted itself. "Kluxer" became a term of opprobrium except in the most unenlightened circles. Almost everyone expressed indignation if it were suggested that he had been a member of the Klan. Without exception, former members blushed at their gullibility. Catholics, who had been waving the flag of tolerance for generations, learned the irony of their belief that "it can't happen here." If the action of the students that May day, 1924, did more, as was alleged, to bring upsurge in favor of the Klan, it must be admitted that the Klan's actions achieved a great success in welding the Catholic Church into a strong and striking unit. At Notre Dame, too, the students and faculty grew closer. The whole episode forced everyone to reflect on the treasures of friendship and faith fostered on campus.

—ARTHUR J. HOPE[8]

THE GLISTENING DOME in the light of the orb of day presents a most brilliant spectacle to the travelers on our railroads as they draw near to South Bend, and to the observer elsewhere for miles around.

—AUGUST 14, 1886, SCHOLASTIC

I HAVE ALWAYS said that coming back to Notre Dame—getting into the spirit of things on campus, visiting the Grotto—brings back pleasant memories for me. When I hear the Notre Dame Victory March, I still get goose bumps—I can't recall a time when I didn't. I call coming back a retreat because it cleanses your soul.

—HEISMAN TROPHY WINNER JOHNNY LUJACK IN 1998

THE NEXT TIME you're staring up at the Basilica and the Dome, . . . and you marvel at how immense and magnificent these buildings are, . . . consider that Sorin built them when Notre Dame had just a few hundred students on campus—and half of them were in prep and elementary school programs. Some of them paid their tuition in chickens or grain.

—CAPPY GAGNON '66, LONGTIME MANAGER OF
SECURITY/POLICE DEPARTMENT AND COORDINATOR OF
STADIUM PERSONNEL[9]

WINNING, OF COURSE, is the goal of every coach and team, and the will to win is surely an important part of the Notre Dame spirit, but there's a great deal more than that at stake in the special spirit of Notre Dame. Here athletic programs have always been, clearly and very deliberately, part of a larger educational effort. In their day and in their own ways, Rockne, Leahy, and Parseghian were among the preeminent "professors" on the campus. Rockne taught more than the game of football: He taught a philosophy, a way of looking at life and living its opportunities, misfortunes, and challenges. He had once taught science, and although he chose to give up the science, he never gave up being a teacher. He wanted to be a builder of men and of character.

—ED "MOOSE" KRAUSE

WHEN PEOPLE COME to the University of Notre Dame, whether for the first time as strangers or "subway alumni," as people on bus tours or fans of an opposing team on a football weekend in the fall, or even as proud graduates with their families in tow, there are so many places that are so filled with meaning that they become essential destinations. All of them offer photo opportunities, but so often so much more than that is at stake.

There is the Golden Dome, of course, with Mary under the title of the Immaculate Conception, patroness of our country, of our local diocese, and of the University as well.

There is Touchdown Jesus, barely visible after the addition of many more feet in the expansion of the Notre Dame Stadium almost a decade ago. Most of these visitors remember how Touchdown Jesus loomed over the original stadium's wall, seemingly supporting improbable Notre Dame touchdowns and last-minute Notre Dame field goals. A number of people attribute a slight decline in football fortunes at the University in recent years to the new bowl of the expanded stadium which hides the mural's view of what is taking place on the field of "the house that Rockne built." Some suggest, with appropriate gravity, that the wall behind the north goal should be lowered for this reason, which springs as much from tradition as it does from a yearning for simpler gridiron days.

There are the two beautiful lakes, named after the mother of Jesus, Mary, and her faithful protector-spouse, Joseph.

And no list would be complete without the Grotto of Our Lady of Lourdes. Built by priests and brothers of Holy Cross with the assistance of people from the surrounding area. It is a smaller replica of the Grotto in Lourdes, France, where Mary appeared to a simple girl, despite claims one occasionally hears that there is a similar grotto in France. At the request of the beautiful lady, Bernadette scratched the earth's surface. The waters have been a healing source for many. Some have been literally cured from physical illness and disease. Many, many more have come to the knowledge and appreciated the miracle of knowing how much their family and friends love them through their solicitous care for them despite the continuation of their suffering and limitations. When Bernadette asked the beautiful lady who she was, Mary responded, "I am the Immaculate Conception."

The Catholic Church has a long-standing tradition of "faith seeking understanding." While revelation was over with the death of the last apostle, the last living witness to the facts and truths of the life, death, and resurrection of Jesus, facets of what was present at that moment can be understood in the context of tradition—what is passed on to believers over the centuries—and a deeper understanding of inspired Scripture.

For many years, faithful believers understood and accepted the fact of the Immaculate Conception; Mary was the Mother of Jesus, and as such, it was not such a stretch to accept that she was therefore granted the special grace of always being a sinless virgin, spared uniquely from the stain of humanity's original sin.

Yet it was not until 1854, barely 150 years ago, that the multi-millennial Catholic Church solemnly declared the doctrine of the Immaculate Conception as part of the deposit of faith.

Perhaps one of the least frequently visited spots on the Notre Dame campus provides an essentially critical insight into what Notre Dame is really all about. A few dozen feet from the shores of St. Mary's Lake, in front of the statue of St. Joseph which commemorates the founders of Notre Dame, and just a few feet to the east of Old College, the first permanent building on campus, there is a bronze image of a letter Father Edward Sorin, C.S.C., Notre Dame's founder, wrote to Servant of God Father Basil Moreau, C.S.C., the founder of the Congregation of Holy Cross. Father Moreau had sent his most talented "recruit," the then-twenty-eight-year-old Edward Sorin, to the United States to establish a Holy Cross foundation. The letter, written just months after Father Sorin's arrival on the 300 wooded acres the Bishop of Vincennes had given to him to found a school in 1842, ignored the obvious hardships of life on the wild frontier for a member of France's landed gentry.

The winter's beautiful blanket of white snow, Father Sorin wrote, reminded him of the purity of the Virgin Mary, a reference surely to a doctrine that would only be declared twelve years later, but that was so much a part of the popular devotion to Mary and love for her role in the life of Jesus. Father Sorin went on to write that, as he and the brothers returned to their simple quarters after clearing woods, the sight of the sanctuary light in their chapel, indicating the presence of the Blessed Sacrament in their tabernacle, was a welcome sight.

This place is *the* essential spot to visit to understand the enduring spirit of Notre Dame.

The tribute to Mary on the Golden Dome, under the title of the Immaculate Conception, was meant "to let all future generations know why we have been successful here." Just seven years after Father Sorin's death, the Grotto was dedicated to Mary, also under the title of the Immaculate Conception. The sinless virgin's protection and patronage would prove to be powerful indeed.

And all succeeding generations of Holy Cross priests and brothers, spearheaded by John Cardinal O'Hara, C.S.C., took the next logical step and made Notre Dame "The City of the Eucharist." This is why there are over forty active chapels on campus today where Mass is celebrated. To make it easy for those who live on campus and those who visit to have the opportunity to receive the Body and Blood of Jesus, the Son of the sinless virgin, is and always will be recognized as Notre Dame's greatest legacy.

A freshman came to speak to me one Tuesday night in the fall, after our 11:00 P.M. residence hall Mass, to tell me about what he thought was a strange conversation he just had with his parents. He called them at 11:30 P.M. and was asked by them why he was calling them so late. Was he already in trouble after just a few weeks on campus?

"No," he replied. "I just came from Mass."

"Mass on Tuesday night," they said. "Have you already skipped Sunday Mass after just a few weeks away from home?"

"No," he replied. "I went to Mass Sunday, but I go to Mass during the week as well. I have discovered a part of me I never knew existed."

And, if Notre Dame worked its magic, I am sure he also discovered the depth of Mary's loving presence in his life on campus, as he glanced at the Dome, as he prayed at the Grotto, and forever afterward.

—RICHARD V. WARNER, C.S.C., DIRECTOR, CAMPUS MINISTRY,
UNIVERSITY OF NOTRE DAME

WE SHALL ALWAYS want Notre Dame men to play to win so long as there is a Notre Dame . . . to win cleanly according to the rules . . . because Notre Dame men are reared here on campus in this spirit and because they exemplify this spirit all over the world, they are the envy of the nation.

—REV. JOHN J. CAVANAUGH, C.S.C., 1949

I CHOSE NOTRE Dame because it has special qualities: a heart and a soul.

—FRANK J. PASQUERILLA, AFTER DONATING $7 MILLION FOR THE
CONSTRUCTION OF RESIDENCE HALLS

WIN OR LOSE, exemplifying the "Notre Dame Spirit" has become a Notre Dame tradition and a philosophy worth living up to, passed on in the Notre Dame family throughout the generations. One day at the University Archives I heard someone shout, "Stop everything! A nursing home is calling. They need the words to the 'Notre Dame Victory March.' A 100-year-old Notre Dame alumnus is dying and he wants them to sing it to him." The words were faxed to the nursing home by the Archives, and his last request was granted. He passed away on St. Patrick's Day. It is stories like this one that have created a mystique about the University of Notre Dame, its alumni, and its campus, unequaled anywhere else.

The "Spirit of Notre Dame" has become synonymous with these words penned by Rudy Ruettiger: "This uncanny ability Sorin had to triumph in the end was very like what has been attributed to an atmosphere on campus: a certain force—an energy allowed each person to perform on a level higher than usual. It came to be called the God loop. It provided good luck when least expected."

—DOROTHY CORSON,
UNOFFICIAL HISTORIAN OF NOTRE DAME[10]

THE WALL OF Honor in the ground floor hallway of the Main Building celebrates such people as Father Sorin, Father Hesburgh, Knute Rockne. And now it honors the building's former janitor.

Earlier this year, the names and likenesses of three more individuals were added to the wall: legendary band director Joseph Casasanta '23, who wrote the alma mater and "Hike Notre Dame" and other football songs; Helen H. Hosinski, secretary to Hesburgh from 1943 to 1990; and Curry Montague, principal custodian of the Main Building from 1970 to 2000.

Montague, the only one still living, "provided the Notre Dame community and its guests a congenial, memorable, and inspiring example of how hard work, devoted service and charity transform duty into joy," a news release said of his selection.

A letter sent to all faculty and staff last November invited nominations for additions to the Wall of Honor. The responses, which totaled more than 300, were reviewed by a committee appointed by President Malloy. The committee then submitted recommendations to the University's officer group for its approval.

Created in 1999 at the re-opening of the Main Building following renovation, the Wall of Honor is intended to recognize "exceptional men and women whose contributions to Notre Dame are lasting, pervasive, and profound," according to an official description. The additions of Casasanta, Hosinski, and Montague bring the total of honorees to 25.[11]

COMPLETE LIST OF HONOREES ON THE
WALL OF HONOR

Rev. Edward F. Sorin, C.S.C.—the University's founder

Rev. Stephen Badin—the first priest ordained in the United States. He donated to the Diocese of Vincennes the land that is today the heart of campus.

Mother Mary Angela Gillespie, C.S.C.—founder of Saint Mary's College

Rev. John A. Zahm, C.S.C.—scholar, teacher, and administrator

Rev. Julius Nieuwland, C.S.C.—discovered the formulae for synthetic rubber

Knute Rockne—legendary football coach

John Cardinal O'Hara, C.S.C.—the University's 12th president

Brother Borromeo Malley, C.S.C.—supervised and expanded the power plant and founded the Notre Dame fire department

Frank O'Malley—legendary English professor

Waldemar Gurian—political scientist and "refugee scholar"

Rev. Theodore M. Hesburgh, C.S.C.—president of Notre Dame from 1952 to 1987

L. A. O'Shaughnessy—benefactor

George Shuster—a Laetare Medalist and longtime president of Hunter College who returned to Notre Dame, his alma mater, to help develop graduate studies and research programs

Ivan Mestrovic—sculptor

Edmund Stephan—first chair of the Board of Trustees

Emil Hofman—chemistry professor

Julian Samora—sociologist

George Craig—biologist

Sister John Miriam Jones, S.C.—director of the University's transition to coeducation

Donald Keough—benefactor and former board chair

Rev. Edmund P. Joyce, C.S.C.—executive vice president from 1952 to 1987, national leader in intercollegiate athletics

James E. Armstrong—alumni secretary from 1926 to 1967, laid foundation for international Notre Dame family

Helen H. Hosinski—long-serving and indispensable secretary to Father Theodore Hesburgh, C.S.C.

Curry L. Montague—principal custodian of the Main Building from 1970 until his retirement in 2000

Joseph Casasanta—director of the Notre Dame Band from 1923 to 1942[12]

IN THE FALL of 1999, Notre Dame embraced another in a long line of firsts: its first African-American leprechaun. Then a junior, Michael Brown not only outperformed eight other applicants for the job but in many ways redefined the role of the University's famed mascot. Brown, a former tailback and quarterback for St. Vincent High School in Milwaukee, was so rabid about Notre Dame football that his freshman roommates and fellow fans in the student corner of the stadium encouraged him to try out to be the leprechaun. Even before he went before the judges two years later, he had already caught the eye of Jo Minton, ND's cheerleading coach, when she saw Michael perform with the First Class Steppers at halftime of a women's basketball game. After a Stomp-like dance, he grabbed the microphone and got the crowd really fired up. As the twenty-second student to portray the leprechaun since the folklore hero became Notre Dame's official mascot in the mid-1960s, Brown fired up countless adults and children alike at games and at nursing homes, hospitals, and other venues as the university's ambassador of cheer. When asked to reflect on being the leprechaun, Brown told the *Observer,* "It's a humbling experience. . . . The thing about it is that you touch so many people's lives."

WITH MORE THAN three hundred members, the Band of the Fighting Irish is the pulse of football weekends. A proud tradition, it was created in 1845—making it the oldest university band in continuous existence—and has played at every home game since football started in 1887. Among the first to include pageantry, precision drills, and formations, the marching band is famous for rousing fans at the pep rally the night before home games and on its famous pregame march from the steps of Bond Hall through campus en route to the stadium. Performances throughout games and during the halftime show keep fans excited, and win or lose, the band finishes each game by playing the fight song while players salute the student section with raised helmets and by playing the Alma Mater as fans lock arms, sway, and sing.

FOUNDED IN 1949 by then-director H. Lee Hope in an effort to add color to the band, the Irish Guard is an impressive and imposing force. Used to clear a path for the band, the ten members of the Guard have to be at least 6'2", able to stand and scowl for long periods of time, and skilled in step maneuvers and formations that have become a highlight of pregame shows. After fifty-one years, the Irish Guard, who wear a traditional plaid kilt and black bearskin shako, finally gained a member who knew how to wear a skirt. Then-senior Molly Kinder became the first woman member of the Irish Guard when she went up against twenty-seven men competing for six open spots on the squad. At 6'3", Kinder played on a state champion basketball team her senior year at Holy Angels Academy in Buffalo, New York, and was a member of the rowing team her first year and a half at Notre Dame.

THE UNIVERSITY OF Notre Dame has been a part of my life for a span of almost forty years, as a student, staff member, faculty member, and as an Officer, Trustee, and Fellow of the University. A long time ago, and after much frustration, I abandoned any attempt to describe the legendary "Spirit of Notre Dame." I concluded that to understand this elusive "thing" required what the philosopher Michael Polanyi once described as tacit knowing. Understanding the Notre Dame Spirit seemed to be much more intuitive than anything else. IT just WAS!

Perhaps it is age, time away in Portland, or the acquisition of a bit of wisdom, but I have a different take on the Notre Dame Spirit at this point in my life. It is certainly indomitable. However, it is rooted in a profound way in the people, things, and events that preceded the establishment of the University almost 163 years ago. The metaphors of community and family, the "liturgy" of football weekends, the academic rigor and reputation, the development and outreach programs, and the official rhetoric of mission are the results, perhaps, of this Notre Dame Spirit but not the core. These things are really transitory descriptors of this enduring indomitable spirit.

When the Holy Cross religious arrived on the frozen plains of northern Indiana on that November day in 1842, they came with a mission forged by two visionaries of very different worldviews and temperaments. The mission was to proclaim the Gospel and the coming of the Kingdom of God. While the mission was simple, the task of fulfilling the mission in the creation of the University was immense. Their grit, that indomitable spirit, was rooted in their Faith in the Lord, and their Hope was rooted in the many crosses that they would bear because they knew it all would lead to the fulfillment of the mission as well as their salvation.

With the growth of the University and the circumstances of its history, the indomitable spirit of many became the Spirit of Notre Dame. All of the attempts to describe it as this, or as that, are fine with me, as long as we remember where that spirit is really rooted. The Lady on the Dome that we claim as our own feeds that indomitable Notre Dame Spirit each day as her golden presence reminds us that she bore to us the ONE who is the source of our Faith and the bearer of our Cross of Hope.

"And Our Hearts Forever Praise Thee Notre Dame."

—REV. DAVID TYSON, C.S.C., PROVINCIAL FOR THE CONGREGATION OF
HOLY CROSS AND RESPONSIBLE FOR THE LARGEST AREA IN HIS ORDER,
INCLUDING CHILE, KENYA, UGANDA, AND TANZANIA

AFTERWORD:
NOTRE DAME, OUR MOTHER

⌒

BY REV. JOHN I. JENKINS, C.S.C.

IT'S A PLEASURE to participate in this book's contemplations about the spirit of Notre Dame. The subject is obviously important to me, primarily as one who has been privileged to share in that spirit as an undergraduate and graduate student at Notre Dame in the 1970s, as a faculty member since 1990, as religious superior of the Holy Cross priests and brothers at Notre Dame from 1997 to 2000, and as vice president and associate provost in the current decade. As the seventeenth president of the University, taking office July 1, 2005, I'll have the important duty of helping to sustain and strengthen the spirit of Notre Dame, as well as communicate it with clarity and conviction to many audiences who may or may not share the spirit, or even know about it.

I personally hope that my presidency will be a time when the spirit of Notre Dame will become better understood by more people around the world and will be more fully shared by everyone in our campus community and in the extended Notre Dame family every-where. I want to help offer this uplifting, uniting, empowering spirit to people who may be hungry for it during times of confusion, division, and vulnerability.

More than a few times, I've sung a Victory March that calls upon us children of Notre Dame to "sing her glory and sound her fame," to "cheer with voices true," to "shake down the thunder from the sky" so as to properly praise and promote the spirit of Notre Dame. We who sing this song wouldn't do so with such zeal if it were just about winning football games, although winning football games is a great way to reflect and replenish that zeal. We sing another song to remind us that, ultimately, we're spreading the word because of love and loyalty—love of what's important, of *who's* important, and loyalty to what's excellent, beautiful, and real.

We sing this latter love song to "Notre Dame, Our Mother/Tender, strong, and true." That invocation of Mary makes the first and foremost of many connections between the spirit of Notre Dame and people. It's not a spirit of a place, although many places on this campus seem to symbolize and transmit the spirit. It's a spirit of people, heavenly and earthly, from the past, present, and future, from all sorts of backgrounds, who share something special by dint of what is in their minds and hearts.

We Christians would trace this remarkable, transcendent commonality to the Holy Spirit, which is truly the driving force behind Notre Dame's spirit. We Catholics would go even further, finding another connecting point in Our Lady. Notre Dame was named after her, and its shield honors her as our "life, sweetness, and hope—*vita, dulcedo et spes.*" Our theology teaches that Mary had (and has) a special bond with the Holy Spirit, one of receptivity to all that the Spirit has to offer, and that this openness to God is not weakness but great strength; not passive servitude but happy freedom.

Thus, in a sense, the contemplation of Notre Dame's spirit might start at the beautiful Grotto that is one of our campus highlights.

People instinctively gather here for prayer that springs from love, and they sense that Mary returns their love and is as ready to say "yes" to them as she was to the Angel Gabriel.

Mary spoke of her own spirit when she visited her cousin Elizabeth: "My spirit finds its joy in God my savior," she said. Mary's presence as a cornerstone of Notre Dame's spirit helps to explain why there is a contagious joy here. Nothing but the sheer joy that arises from love, loyalty, faith, hope, and gratitude could explain the feelings that so many students, faculty, staff, returning alumni, and first-time visitors express—captivation, curiosity, excitement, nostalgia, generosity; a sense of abundance, of beauty, of being cared for, of being welcomed into a community, of wanting to welcome others and join with them in both work and play.

No wonder there is an element of pilgrimage in the hoopla of a football weekend. While the Super Bowl may be one of the few "liturgies" that our whole secular society still embraces, a Notre Dame football game shares its spotlight with the sacred; large numbers of those attending the game will also attend a Mass while they're on campus, or they'll visit the Grotto, or they'll simply meditate before a pretty scene or provocative sculpture. All of this goes together at Notre Dame. This sense of everything being possible, provided it works together for the good, is very liberating. It may be the original meaning of liberty, and of academic freedom.

Our Catholic identity and values—our desire to embrace, understand, and sanctify everything, rather than to compartmentalize, question, and label everything—are not the enemies of this liberating Notre Dame spirit. They make the spirit possible, or at least they enhance it and elevate it to a transcendent experience for those so inclined. The spirit brings out the wonder-filled, carefree child in us, which is good because Jesus tells us we must be like little children in order to enter the kingdom of heaven. A campus filled with young and young-again fans, ready to experience both a heightened dignity and a bowed-down humility and to have fun either way, reminds me of the comment by G. K. Chesterton: "Catholic doctrine and discipline may be walls, but they are the walls of a playground."

Like children in a playground, trusting in the providence of good parents who are watching nearby, and trusting in each other because we believe truth exists and can be learned and can be wonderful, we in the Notre Dame family build the spirit of this place by sharing stories. We become part of each other's stories. Our community of C.S.C. priests is tremendously enriched by being part of the lives of students in the residence halls, the lives of the scholars in our faculty, and the lives of staff members and neighbors in their day-to-day ups and downs. Our students report forming friendships that last lifetimes, and they're impressed that everyone on campus seems to want to help them on their path of learning. This momentum overflows beyond campus, inspiring service projects and compassionate outreach across town and across the world. We all get involved with each other at meaningful levels, compiling a record of respect that makes it easier to address the next day's challenges or the next wave of divisiveness sweeping onto campus from the popular culture.

Certainly, the building of mutual respect doesn't mean that we'll always agree with each other, but it does make it more likely that we'll communicate with each other. Sometimes, the open and plentiful exchange of our disagreements makes us look like we don't have our act together. That's true: With God's help, we're still writing the script and rehearsing our parts, so don't expect perfection. More important: I think Notre Dame can be proud of the dynamic marketplace of ideas that exists on campus and of the outpouring of interest that we generate throughout the American public when a controversy erupts here. There is a sense that what we do here matters because we are exercising judgment, pursuing virtue, and discerning truth. Colleges and other institutions that haven't built up that reservoir of respect by sharing each other's stories in a context of self-giving attentiveness find their communication channels breaking down, civility disappearing, and facts being set aside in order to soothe feelings or to allow flawed, half-true stories to stand unchallenged.

And so I return to the idea of sharing Notre Dame's spirit more avidly with those who do not know it. I have learned in my philosophical studies that something which makes a good means should not be turned into an end in itself. The spirit of Notre Dame must not exist solely for the sake of having enjoyable times and pleasant memories. Nor should it exist solely for the sake of preserving and promoting this wonderful institution, although it goes without saying that one cannot thrive without the other.

This spirit is bigger than the institution and is rooted in what Notre Dame represents and believes. We have chosen the spirit we want to pursue, and God has granted that many people and forces should converge over time in South Bend, Indiana, to give us a distinct, widely known and respected spirit whose difference from shallower, secular spirits and from the counterfeit spirit of self-gratification becomes clearer every day. We need to pray to discern how God would have us spread the gift of the Notre Dame spirit wherever and whenever it is needed, guided by these words from the First Epistle to the Corinthians: "We have not received the spirit of the world, but the Spirit that is from God, so that we may understand the things freely given us by God. And we speak about them not with words taught by human wisdom, but with words taught by the Spirit, describing spiritual realities in spiritual terms." Paul goes on to warn us that many people will dismiss our spirit as foolishness.

We cannot and shall not try to force anything on anybody. But we need to shine our light of invitation as brightly as possible, aiming it squarely into the darkest recesses of ignorance or hopelessness. We need to cultivate the gifts that this spirit of Notre Dame gives us, and we need to treasure and celebrate the fruits. And then we need to do what Notre Dame does best—go out and share stories about the relationships, the lessons, the places, and the legacies that still call out to pilgrims like us. By our fruits shall we be known and judged.

This book contains beautiful renditions of the fruits borne in many people's lives, recalling simple human joys even as they "wake up the echoes" of the momentous "yes" of Our Lady. I thank all the people who contributed to this book and thus advanced the story-sharing work I want to encourage.

As we close this book, let's pray to the Lord for guidance and assistance in spreading the spirit of Notre Dame. May we first receive His help as stewards of this spirit, as contributors to it and beneficiaries of it. Let's give thanks for the gifts and fruits, and let's ask forgiveness for the times when we don't adequately tend this garden. Finally, please join me in a commitment to His will and to His ineffable way of working wonders with frail earthen vessels. If I may slightly change the emphasis in a line our Lord spoke, I would say this with confidence about Notre Dame: Even if the flesh is weak, the spirit is willing.

—REV. JOHN I. JENKINS, C.S.C.,
PRESIDENT, UNIVERSITY OF NOTRE DAME[1]

Afterword: The Spirit of Notre Dame Is . . .

BY REV. THEODORE M. HESBURGH, C.S.C.

THERE IS NO one word or phrase that can sum up the soul of this place and its history, its present and its future. Those of us who have been blessed with the opportunity to work here, or to be trusted with its care, know that the spirit of Notre Dame stems from and is sustained by something more than natural causes. We can describe it better than define it. And there are words that spring to mind in forming that description:

FAITH. From the moment Father Sorin and his small band of brethren set foot here and dedicated the land and all efforts to the service of God under the patronage of Our Lady, somehow that contract was mutually binding. The Blessed Mother has taken it seriously. And so have we. The spirit of Notre Dame is, in its essence, belief in and commitment to the truths of the Christian faith, truths that need always to be pondered and lived.

FIDELITY. Faithfulness to its roots and its mission requires that this be a place where the Church does its thinking, where there is constant effort to understand and teach what it means to be a Christian in the contemporary world. Fidelity is not a hurdle to creativity; instead, it is a touchstone; it helps ground us in what we stand for and what we won't stand for.

VISION. Father Sorin could not have foreseen what Notre Dame would become. Perhaps in another 160 years someone will say the same of us. What we have is a vision of becoming the greatest Catholic university in the history of the world. That vision requires great leadership, hitherto unimagined financial support, tireless perseverance in the pursuit of excellence, and, above all, ceaseless dedication to the Lady on the Dome.

ZEAL. The spirit of Notre Dame requires the zeal that, fed by grace, allows us to do more than we ever thought possible, to acknowledge mistakes and correct them, to never rest in the comfort of human accomplishments, to seek always to bring the peace and love of Christ to a world sorely in need of those gifts. There will never be peace until there is justice. The spirit of Notre Dame needs always to place it in the front line of those institutions and people who struggle for justice as a prelude to peace.

—REV. THEODORE M. HESBURGH, C.S.C.[1]

ACKNOWLEDGMENTS

WE ARE GRATEFUL to Trace Murphy, Doubleday's editor, whose invitation to do this book gave us the unique opportunity to work together while exploring the roots of a place that means a lot to each of us and to our family. Throughout the research and writing process, our appreciation for the Notre Dame family grew deeper as faculty, staff, students, and alums shared their stories and pointed us in the right direction. We are grateful to Regis Philbin for writing the foreword, and to Kevin Cawley, Notre Dame's Archivist and Curator of Manuscripts, and Dorothy Corson, in our opinion, the unofficial historian of the University, for many leads and details we might otherwise have missed. Kerry Temple, Ed Cohen, Carol Schaal, and the talented staff of *Notre Dame Magazine* not only wrote many of the articles we relied on but graciously gave us access to their archives, which include *Alumnus, Notre Dame Magazine,* and many other historically significant publications. Father Edward Malloy graciously met with us for a lengthy conversation, wrote the introduction to the book, and allowed us to use his final presidential address as an interlude. Father John Jenkins took time out of his busy schedule as Notre Dame's new president to write the afterword. And Father Ted Hesburgh, Notre Dame's second founder, shared his blessing on the book and his wisdom in its pages because, as always, he believes the University's stories say something good about faith, intellectual inquiry, and service.

Chuck Lennon and Sean O'Brien of the alumni office wrote reflections for the book and, with their colleagues, helped us find stories. We could not have completed this project without the help of Caitlin Rackish '05, who combed archival issues of the *Scholastic* for inspiring stories, and Bethany Amber Long, a 2004 Loyola University of Chicago graduate, who says she has come to admire Notre Dame through her work editing the manuscript and hunting down references. Tom Sklafani provided invaluable ideas as well.

We thank Dan Reagan of the Development Office and Kathy McGowan of the Hammes Notre Dame Bookstore for their enthusiasm and encouragement.

And, of course, we thank our families for their love and support. Though a Creighton University graduate from the class of 1992, Jeremy's wife, Elizabeth Collier, embraced this project by helping to prepare parts of the manuscript and juggling her own writing and teaching schedule to make sure he had time to finish. Even if she can't yet imagine their one-and-a-half-year-old son Tyler attending Notre Dame, as the newest members of the Subway Alumni Association, her parents, Bill and Mary, are already helping the cause with bookstore paraphernalia and a piggy bank earmarked for tuition. Liz's sisters Lindy and Erin always asked how it was going, and Lindy's husband, Paul, even laid off the Michigan jokes.

NOTES

FOREWORD: WHAT IS THE SPIRIT OF NOTRE DAME?

1. Regis Francis Xavier Philbin, born August 25, 1933, was named after his father's alma mater, a Manhattan Jesuit high school, and grew up in the South Bronx. He graduated from Notre Dame in 1953, served in the Navy, and eventually went into radio and television. As one of the best-known television personalities, on August 20, 2004, he set a Guinness World Record for logging 15,188 hours on television with such shows as *Live with Regis and Kathie Lee, Live with Regis and Kelly,* and *Who Wants to Be a Millionaire?* Always generous with his time and money, Regis donated $2.75 million to create the Regis Philbin Studio Theater in the Marie P. DeBartolo Center for the Performing Arts at Notre Dame. He received an honorary doctor of laws degree from Notre Dame in 1999 in recognition of his previous gifts to Notre Dame in support of scholarships, along with his service as host of an annual fund-raising broadcast on behalf of the Center for the Homeless in South Bend. He and his wife, Joy, are the parents of two daughters, Jennifer and Joanna, both of whom have Notre Dame degrees.

PREFACE: LOVE THEE, NOTRE DAME

1. William Strode, *Notre Dame: A Sense of Place* (Notre Dame, IN: University of Notre Dame Press in cooperation with Harmony House Publishers, 1988), 15.

2. Damaine Vonada, *Notre Dame: The Official Campus Guide* (Notre Dame, IN: University of Notre Dame Press, 1998), 8.

INTRODUCTION: THE SPIRIT OF NOTRE DAME

1. In 2004, Rev. Edward A. Malloy, C.S.C., completed his eighteenth and final year as president of the University of Notre Dame. A native of Washington, D.C., he was born May 3, 1941, and earned his bachelor's and master's degrees in English from Notre Dame, where he also played on the basketball team. Earning a second master's degree in theology while studying for the priesthood, he was ordained in the Basilica of the Sacred Heart on the Notre Dame campus in 1970 and in 1975 earned his doctorate in Christian ethics from Vanderbilt University, which in 1998 established a chair in Catholic studies in his name. The University's sixteenth president, Father Malloy was elected by the Board of Trustees in 1986 after having served five years as vice president and associate provost. He led Notre Dame at a time of rapid growth in its reputation, faculty, and resources, which included growing the endowment to over $2.5 billion and constructing an unprecedented number of buildings to ensure that the campus meets the needs of students today. A member of the Notre Dame faculty since 1974, he is a full professor in the Department of Theology and not only continued to teach throughout his presidency but also maintained his residence in Sorin Hall, where he will continue to live. An avid reader and writer, Father Malloy published his fifth book, *Monk's Travels: People, Places, and Events,* in 2004 and will continue to write, teach, and serve Notre Dame in his post-presidency.

FAITH OF OUR FOUNDER: REV. EDWARD FREDERICK SORIN

1. Arthur Hope, *Notre Dame: One Hundred Years* (Notre Dame, IN: University of Notre Dame Press, 1948), 16.

2. Ibid., 36–37.

3. Kerry Temple, "A River Runs Through It," *Notre Dame Magazine* 20, no. 2 (Summer 1991): 16–21.

4. Arthur Hope, *Notre Dame: One Hundred Years* (Notre Dame, IN: University of Notre Dame Press, 1948), 183–86.

5. Robert Schmuhl, *The University of Notre Dame: A Contemporary Portrait* (Notre Dame, IN: University of Notre Dame Press, 1986), 1.

6. Thomas J. Schlereth, "A Man of Many Parts," *Notre Dame Magazine* 14, no. 1 (Spring 1985): 32.

7. Arthur Hope, "Father Edward F. Sorin, Founder," *Scholastic* 7, no. 4 (Winter 1954): 6–7.

FAITH

1. Dorothy V. Corson, *The Spirit of Notre Dame: Its History, Legends, and Lore* (2001), http://www.nd.edu/~wcawley/corson.htm.

2. Arthur Hope, *Notre Dame: One Hundred Years* (Notre Dame, IN: University of Notre Dame Press, 1948), 128–29.

3. Edward Fischer, *Notre Dame Remembered* (Notre Dame, IN: University of Notre Dame Press, 1987), 164–65.

4. Eric Hansen, *Stadium Stories: Notre Dame Fighting Irish* (Guilford, CT: The Globe Pequot Press, 2004), 118.

5. Mary Pat Dowling, *Grotto Stories: From the Heart of Notre Dame* (Notre Dame, IN: MarySunshine Books in cooperation with the University of Notre Dame Alumni Association, 1996), foreword.

6. Rev. John E. Fitzgerald, *Scholastic*, May 2, 1950.

7. Op. cit., Dowling.

8. Rev. Robert Griffin, C.S.C., *In The Kingdom of the Lonely God* (Lanham, MD: Rowman & Littlefield/A Sheed & Ward Book, 2003), 5, 75–76.

9. Rev. Nicholas Ayo, C.S.C., *Signs of Grace* (Lanham, MD: Rowman & Littlefield, 2001), 19–20.

10. Jack Egan, "Good-bye and Amen," *Notre Dame Magazine* 12, no. 3 (July 1983): 8.

11. Op. cit., Hope, 426.

HOPE

1. Charles M. Carey, "Why the 'Fighting Irish'?," *The Spirit of Notre Dame: Notre Dame Legends and Lore* (2001), http://www.nd.edu/~wcawley/corson/whyfightingirish.htm.

2. Dorothy V. Corson, "Frederick Snite, 'The Man in the Iron Lung,' a Legend at Notre Dame," *The Spirit of Notre Dame: Notre Dame Legends and Lore* (2001), http://www.nd.edu/~wcawley/corson/fsnite.htm.

3. A native of Colombia, South America, Montoya was sent to live with his aunt and uncle in San Diego when he was four years old because his parents knew his medical and educational opportunities would be greater in the United States. He now directs the membership sales for the San Diego Hispanic Chamber of Commerce. He also works with Always Positive, Inc., a California-based company, in delivering motivational presentations across the country, and is working on a book. Alex's diverse career has included bit parts in two Steven Spielberg movies and ushering at San Diego Padres and Chargers games. In his free time he maintains a humorous online discussion group about Notre Dame athletics.

LOVE

1. Carol Schaal, "The Little Princes Feared Their Irish Principal . . . And Loved Her: Sister M. Aloysius (1845–1916)," *Notre Dame Magazine* 20, no. 2 (Summer 1991): 12–13.

2. Arthur Hope, *Notre Dame: One Hundred Years* (Notre Dame, IN: University of Notre Dame Press, 1948), 420.

3. Rev. Nicholas Ayo, C.S.C., *Signs of Grace* (Lanham, MD: Rowman & Littlefield, 2001), 22.

4. Margaret Fosmoe, "A Course on Life," *South Bend Tribune* (February 26, 1999): cover story.

5. Kevin Coyne, *Domers: A Year at Notre Dame* (New York: Viking Adult, 1995), 127.

6. Ken Bradford, "We Can't All Be Heroes, But Let's Always Remember Those Who Are," *South Bend Tribune*, March 23, 2004.

INTERLUDE: NOTRE DAME'S SECOND FOUNDER: REV. THEODORE M. HESBURGH, C.S.C.

1. James Langford and Leroy S. Rouner, eds., *Walking with God in a Fragile World* (Lanham, MD: Rowman & Littlefield, 2003), 36.

2. Ibid., 35.

COMMUNITY

1. William Strode, *Notre Dame: A Sense of Place* (Notre Dame, IN: University of Notre Dame Press in cooperation with Harmony House Publishers, 1988), 15.

2. Ibid., 19–20.

3. Margaret Fosmoe, "Turning Points," *Notre Dame Magazine* 20, no. 2 (Summer 1991): 4.

4. Edward Fischer, *Notre Dame Remembered: An Autobiography* (Notre Dame, IN: University of Notre Dame Press, 1987), 124.

5. Ibid., 4–6.

6. Luis Gamez, "Robert Griffin, C.S.C.: 1925–1999," *Notre Dame Magazine,* Winter 1999–2000, online supplement, http://www.nd.edu/~ndmag/griffw99.htm.

7. Arthur Hope, *Notre Dame: One Hundred Years* (Notre Dame, IN: University of Notre Dame Press, 1948), 427.

HUMOR

1. Jack Connor, *Leahy's Lads* (South Bend, IN: Diamond Communications, 1997), 70–71.

2. Ibid., 198–99.

3. Ed Cohen, "All Things to 250 People," *Notre Dame Magazine* 25, no. 4 (Winter 1996–97): http://www.nd.edu/~ndmag/rectrw96.html.

4. Lauren Beck, "Greetings from Father Sorin," *South Bend Tribune* (June 7, 2003).

5. Edward Fischer, *Notre Dame Remembered: An Autobiography* (Notre Dame, IN: University of Notre Dame Press, 1987), 143.

6. Kristy Katzmann, "May I have your attention, please . . .," *Notre Dame Magazine* 29, no. 3 (Autumn 2000): 13.

7. Ed Cohen, "Rude, Crude and As Popular As Ever," *Notre Dame Magazine* 31, no. 1 (Spring 2002): 2–3.

8. Jason Kelly, *Mr. Notre Dame: The Life and Legend of Edward "Moose" Krause* (Lanham, MD: Diamond Communications, 2002), 118–19.

9. Edward Krause, "Reminiscing," in *Out of Bounds: An Anecdotal History of Notre Dame Football,* eds. Michael Bonifer and L.G. Weaver (Blue Earth, MN: Piper Publishing, 1978), 8.

MIND

1. John Powers, "The Time Between the Wars," *Notre Dame Magazine* 20, no. 2 (Summer 1991): 22–25.

2. Barbara Mangione, *For the Love of Teaching*, ed. George Howard (Notre Dame, IN: Academic Publishing: 2004), 186.

3. Dennis Jacobs, *For the Love of Teaching*, ed. George Howard (Notre Dame, IN: Academic Publishing: 2004), 115.

4. Jill A. Boughton, "No One Can Make Me Feel Old," *Notre Dame Magazine* 20, no. 1 (Spring 1991): 11–13.

5. Thomas Werge, *Notre Dame Magazine* 1, no. 2 (April 1972).

6. Hugh Page, *For the Love of Teaching*, ed. George Howard (Notre Dame, IN: Academic Publishing: 2004), 163.

7. George McClancy, "The Inspired Teacher: Frank O'Malley," *Notre Dame Magazine* (16 Oct. 2002), http://www.nd.edu/~ndmag/reflect/mcclancy.html.

8. John W. Meaney, *O'Malley of Notre Dame* (Notre Dame, IN: University of Notre Dame Press, 1991), 147, 198–99.

9. Richard Sullivan, "A Sense of Reverence," *Notre Dame Magazine* 9, no. 4 (October 1980): 36–37.

10. Tim Prister, ed., *What It Means to Be Fighting Irish* (Chicago: Triumph Books, 2004), viii.

11. Nathan Hatch, *For the Love of Teaching*, ed. George Howard (Notre Dame, IN: Academic Publishing: 2004), 78.

12. Eric Hansen, *Stadium Stories: Notre Dame Fighting Irish* (Guilford, CT: The Globe Pequot Press, 2004), 11.

13. William A. Botzum, "Sifting the Sands of Education," *Alumnus* (September 1970): 12–15.

BODY

1. Robert Quakenbush and Mike Bynum, eds., "Knute Rockne: An Introduction," *Knute Rockne: His Life and Legend* (October Football Corp., 1988), 1–5.

2. Ken Rappoport, *Wake Up the Echoes: Notre Dame Football* (Huntsville, AL: Strode Publishers, 1975).

3. Jack Connor, *Leahy's Lads* (South Bend, IN: Diamond Communications, 1997), 298.

4. Tom Pagna and Bob Best, *Notre Dame's Era of Ara* (South Bend, IN: Diamond Communications, 1994), 76.

5. Dave Condon, Chet Grant, and Bob Best, *Notre Dame Football: The Golden Tradition* (South Bend, IN: Icarus Press, 1982), 100–101.

6. Tom Pagna and Bob Best, *Notre Dame's Era of Ara* (South Bend, IN: Diamond Communications, 1994), 258.

7. Dave Condon, Chet Grant, and Bob Best, *Notre Dame Football: The Golden Tradition* (South Bend, IN: Icarus Press, 1982), 132–33.

8. John Monczunski, "Dan Devine: Setting Sun or Rising Star?," *Notre Dame Magazine* 7, no. 4 (October 1978): 11–15.

9. Lou Holtz, *The Fighting Spirit* (New York: Pocket Books, 1989), 350.

10. Ibid., 353.

11. Jason Kelly, *Mr. Notre Dame: The Life and Legend of Edward "Moose" Krause* (South Bend, IN: Diamond Communications, 2002).

12. James Loverde "God Bless You, Nappy," *Notre Dame Magazine* 15, no. 2 (Summer 1986): 9.

13. Mary Beth Sterling, *Look Out for the Manhole Cover* (Chicago: Wagner/Mark Publishing, 1993).

14. Jeff Jeffers, *Rally: The 12 Greatest Notre Dame Football Comebacks* (South Bend, IN: Icarus Press, 1981).

15. Mark Bradford and Muffet McGraw, *Nice Girls Finish First: The Remarkable Story of Notre Dame's Rise to the Top of Women's College Basketball* (South Bend, IN: Diamond Communications, 2002), 187.

SPIRIT

1. Kevin Coyne, *Domers: A Year at Notre Dame* (New York: Viking Adult, 1995), 214.

2. Ibid.

3. Under Charles F. Lennon's leadership, the Alumni Association has earned a national reputation for innovation in programming. It was the first to

offer interactive continuing education seminars via satellite and has initiated community service programs that have been emulated throughout American higher education. Yale and Stanford Universities are among those with community service programs modeled on Notre Dame's. The Alumni Association currently has more than 104,000 members, most of them affiliated with one of more than 211 alumni clubs nationwide and in 22 foreign countries.

4. Damaine Vonada, *Notre Dame: The Official Campus Guide* (Notre Dame, IN: University of Notre Dame Press, 1998), 8–9.

5. Eric Hansen, *Stadium Stories: Notre Dame Fighting Irish* (Guilford, CT: The Globe Pequot Press, 2004), 24–25.

6. "Cheer, Cheer," *Notre Dame Magazine* 20, no. 2 (Summer 1991): 8.

7. Arthur J. Hope, *Notre Dame: 100 Years* (Notre Dame, IN: University of Notre Dame Press, 1948), 468–69. The entire story is well told by Todd Tucker in *Notre Dame vs. the Klan: How the Fighting Irish Defeated the Ku Klux Klan* (Chicago: Loyola Press, 2004).

8. Ibid., 373–78.

9. Cappy Gagnon, "Providence has been good to us," *Observer* 33, no. 30 (October 4, 1999).

10. Dorothy V. Corson, *Notre Dame Magazine* 27, no. 3 (Autumn 1998).

11. Ed Cohen, "Custodian Joins University's Immortals," *Notre Dame Magazine* 33, no. 3 (Autumn 2004): 11.

12. Ed Cohen, "Complete List of Honorees on the Wall of Honor," *Notre Dame Magazine* 33, no. 3 (Autumn 2004): http://www.nd.edu/~ndmag/au2004/famewall.html.

AFTERWORD: NOTRE DAME, OUR MOTHER

1. The Board of Trustees of the University of Notre Dame elected Rev. John I. Jenkins, C.S.C., as the University's seventeenth president after Rev. Edward A. Malloy, C.S.C., announced that he was stepping down. A vice president and associate provost at Notre Dame since July 2000, Father Jenkins was elected to a five-year term. He is an associate professor of philosophy and has been a member of the Notre Dame faculty since 1990.

Prior to his election as vice president and associate provost, Father Jenkins had been religious superior of the Holy Cross priests and brothers at Notre Dame for three years. As religious superior, he was a Fellow and Trustee of the University, but he relinquished those posts to assume his duties in the provost's office.

Father Jenkins specializes in ancient philosophy, medieval philosophy, and the philosophy of religion. He is the author of *Knowledge and Faith in Thomas Aquinas,* published by Cambridge University Press in 1997, and has had scholarly articles published in *The Journal of Philosophy, Medieval Philosophy and*

Theology, and *The Journal of Religious Ethics.* He delivered the annual Aquinas Lecture at the University of Dallas in January 2000 and was the recipient of a Lilly Teaching Fellowship in 1991–92.

Father Jenkins earned two degrees in philosophy from Oxford University, in 1987 and 1989. While at Oxford, he taught in Notre Dame's London Program. He earned his master of divinity degree and licentiate in sacred theology from the Jesuit School of Theology at Berkeley, California, in 1988. Prior to joining the Congregation of Holy Cross, he earned bachelor's and master's degrees in philosophy from Notre Dame in 1976 and 1978, respectively.

Father Jenkins was ordained a priest in Notre Dame's Basilica of the Sacred Heart in 1983. He served as director of the Old College program for Notre Dame undergraduate candidates for the Congregation of Holy Cross from 1991 to 1993.

A native of Omaha, Nebraska, Father Jenkins was born on December 17, 1953.

AFTERWORD: THE SPIRIT OF NOTRE DAME IS . . .

1. Rev. Theodore M. Hesburgh, C.S.C., was born in Syracuse, New York, on May 25, 1917. He was educated at Notre Dame and the Gregorian University in Rome, from which he received a bachelor of philosophy degree in 1939. He was ordained a priest of the Congregation of Holy Cross in Sacred Heart Church on the Notre Dame campus June 24, 1943, by Bishop John F. Noll of Fort Wayne. Following his ordination, Father Hesburgh continued his study of sacred theology at the Catholic University of America, Washington, D.C., receiving his doctorate (S.T.D.) in 1945. He joined the Notre Dame faculty the same year and served as chaplain to World War II veterans on campus in addition to his teaching duties in the Religion Department. He was appointed the head of that department in 1948 and the following year was appointed executive vice president in the administration of Rev. John J. Cavanaugh, C.S.C., University president. At the age of thirty-five in June 1952, he was named the fifteenth president of Notre Dame. When he stepped down on June 1, 1987, he ended the longest tenure among active presidents of American institutions of higher learning.

During his tenure, Notre Dame's annual operating budget went from $9.7 million to $176.6 million, the endowment from $9 million to $350 million, and research funding from $735,000 to $15 million. Enrollment increased from 4,979 to 9,600, faculty from 389 to 950, and degrees awarded from 1,212 to 2,500. The two major changes during the Hesburgh era were the transfer of governance from the founding religious community, the Congregation of Holy Cross, to a predominantly lay Board of Trustees in 1967 and the admission of women to the undergraduate program in 1972.

Father Hesburgh has served four popes and held fifteen presidential appointments over the years—most recently to the U.S.—related to civil rights, peaceful uses of atomic energy, campus unrest, treatment of Vietnam offenders, Third World development, and immigration reform, to name only a few. At the same time, he has remained a national leader in the field of education, serving on many commissions and study groups examining matters ranging from public funding of independent colleges and universities to the role of foreign languages and international studies in higher education. As chairman of the International Federation of Catholic Universities from 1963 to 1970, he led a movement to redefine the nature and mission of the contemporary Catholic university. He was the first Catholic priest to serve as director of the Chase Manhattan Bank and a trustee (later, chairman) of the Rockefeller Foundation; in a formal diplomatic role for the United States government as ambassador to the 1979 U.N. Conference on Science and Technology for Development; and as an overseer at Harvard University.

His stature as an elder statesman in American higher education is reflected in his 150 honorary degrees, the most ever awarded to an American. Highlighting a lengthy list of awards to Father Hesburgh is the Medal of Freedom, the nation's highest civilian honor, bestowed on him by President Lyndon Johnson in 1964. He has received numerous awards from education groups, among them the prestigious Meiklejohn Award of the American Association of University Professors in 1970. This award, which honors those who uphold academic freedom, recognized Father Hesburgh's crucial role in blunting the attempt of the Nixon Administration in 1969 to use federal troops to quell campus disturbances. His recent honors include the Franklin D. Roosevelt Four Freedoms Medal for worship, the Distinguished Peace Leader Award, the Elizabeth Ann Seton Award from the National Catholic Education Association, and the National Service Lifetime Achievement Award.

The author of *God, Country, Notre Dame*—his nationally best-selling autobiography published in November 1990 by Doubleday—and *Travels with Ted and Ned*, and editor of *The Challenge and Promise of a Catholic University*, Father Hesburgh remains very active in his retirement. His major retirement role is developing several Notre Dame institutes and centers he was instrumental in founding, principally the Kroc Institute for International Peace Studies and the Kellogg Institute for International Studies. The three other academic entities in which he continues to play a part are the Center for Civil and Human Rights; Notre Dame's Hank Environmental Research Center near Land O' Lakes, Wisconsin; and the University's Ecumenical Institute in Jerusalem. Among his more recent and visible off-campus activities has been as cochairman of the nationally influential Knight Commission on Intercollegiate Athletics. About 90 percent of the commission's reform agenda has been adopted by the NCAA.

Father Hesburgh's days are a blend of domestic and foreign travel, much of it as a member of international organizations; correspondence and phone calls; articles and speeches; guest appearances lecturing in Notre Dame classrooms and presiding over liturgies in University residence halls, and a quiet but important role advancing the interests of several Notre Dame academic institutes.